Telling Our Storie

INTERNATIONAL PERFOR
BY AND ABOUT WOMEN

Telling Our Stories of Home

INTERNATIONAL PERFORMANCE PIECES BY AND ABOUT WOMEN

The House

Happy

The Blue of the Island

Nine Lives

Leaving, but Can't Let Go

Questions of Home

On the Last Day of Spring

Letting Go and Moving On

Antimemories of an Interrupted Trip

So Goes We

Those Who Live Here, Those Who Live There

Edited and introduced by

KATHY A. PERKINS

To: Lauren Wimbush –
Enjoy the plays!

Love,
Kathy A. Perkins
3/7/2022
Durham, N.C.

methuen | drama

LONDON • NEW YORK • OXFORD • NEW DELHI • SYDNEY

METHUEN DRAMA
Bloomsbury Publishing Plc
50 Bedford Square, London, WC1B 3DP, UK
1385 Broadway, New York, NY 10018, USA
29 Earlsfort Terrace, Dublin 2, Ireland

BLOOMSBURY, METHUEN DRAMA and the Methuen Drama logo are trademarks of Bloomsbury Publishing Plc

First published in Great Britain 2022

Cover design: Rebecca Heselton
Map © iStock

A catalogue record for this book is available from the British Library.

A catalog record for this book is available from the Library of Congress.

ISBN: HB: 978-1-3502-5979-9
PB: 978-1-3502-5978-2
ePDF: 978-1-3502-5980-5
eBook: 978-1-3502-5981-2

Typeset by RefineCatch Limited, Bungay, Suffolk
Printed and bound in Great Britain

To find out more about our authors and books visit www.bloomsbury.com and sign up for our newsletters.

This anthology is dedicated to Channakeshava G.,
whom we lost before he was able to see the invaluable
contributions he made to this work.
This anthology is also dedicated to the many souls who have
departed this earthly home due to Covid-19.

The ache for home lives in all of us. The safe place where we can go as we are and not be questioned.

– Maya Angelou

Contents

Acknowledgments

I am grateful for the support and assistance of the following individuals: Nehanda Loiseau Julot, Shelia Bland, Sandra L. Richards, Bernard Tabaire, Annette Bühler-Dietrich, Velma Pollard, Francesca Talenti, Karishma Bhagani, Alexandra Aron, Viviane Juguero, Lynette Goddard, Samer Al-Saber, Anna Jayne Kimmel, Sonia Berah, Tanya L. Shields, and Cheryl Adams Odeleye.

Introduction

What is home? For much of my life, the answer seemed obvious: home meant a loving and protected environment – not only in my parents' home but also in my community at large. Even though I grew up in Mobile, Alabama during the turbulent Civil Rights Movement of the 1960s, home was always a safe place. It was where we held family gatherings, went to church, participated in school activities, and spent time with childhood friends who are still very much a part of my life. And, since Mobile is the original birthplace of America's Mardi Gras Carnival, it was where we celebrated tradition, life, and community. Home was a place of great memories to which I was, and still am, always excited to return.

Over the decades I have realized that the universal experience of home is far more complicated than my own. The idea of home resonates with people everywhere, but it connotes vastly different ideas depending on one's circumstances. Home has a unique meaning for each of us.

In my roles as an educator and lighting designer, I began to travel extensively nationally and internationally during the 1990s. It was during these travels that I began contemplating home as a theme for a collection of performance pieces. I was witnessing situations that were often depicted in novels and essays but never reflected on stage. Unlike me, who always sees home as a location of safety, belonging, and comfort, so many people in the United States and elsewhere experienced home as a source of uncertainty, dislocation, and pain. I came to understand that a person's idea of and feelings about home are contingent on myriad factors, including their community's attitudes about gender, sexual orientation, social class, skin color, religion, history, ritual, and politics.

The idea for this collection seriously took root in the early 2010s. The news of the day was inundated with stories of people around the world leaving their countries of birth because of natural disasters, war, political upheaval, religious persecution, or other traumatic events. That decade witnessed one of the largest mass movements of people in history. It was also during this period that I began including more international material in my non-western theatre courses, much of which was drawn from my travels, and using video conferencing to invite writers from around the world into my classroom. These initiatives excited my students. They found that reading a play from a writer in Ghana, China, or South Africa and then actually speaking with the author was fascinating and stimulating. Students began to ask if I planned to publish a collection of international works like the ones they were studying in class.

Telling Our Stories of Home, a collection of eleven performance pieces by and about women from Brazil, Haiti, India, Lebanon, Palestine, Uganda, United Kingdom, United States, and Venezuela, is the result. These stories reveal the impact that emigration, slavery, death, natural disasters, and discrimination have on home—its physical location as well as its emotional significance. They provide insights into the complicated experience of home.

While there are many oral stories and books by women on the theme of home, I had a difficult time locating performance pieces originating from a wide variety of countries. I also wanted to include writers who were still residing in their country of birth or who had strong connections with their places of origin because they are often from countries whose theatrical voices are seldom heard on the global stage. Despite such challenges, narrowing the collection to eleven writers was difficult as there were several others whom, space permitting, I would have loved to include.

I knew some of the writers represented in this anthology; others were new to me. I was greatly helped by friends and colleagues who introduced me to works from places like Brazil, Haiti, Venezuela, Lebanon, and Palestine, where works in English are not very accessible. Six of the eleven stories have been translated into English, three specifically for this anthology. Having invited two Siddi (Indians of African descent) artists to a 2016 festival I co-produced around the theme of home and women from Africa and the African Diaspora, I knew I wanted to include their unique story in the anthology.

My initial idea was to call these stories "plays," but I have decided to use the term "performance pieces" to include all forms of storytelling, including plays. To me, performance is any form of presentation to an audience, even if it is an audience of one. Also, in many cultures playwriting is viewed as a western concept and connotes a proscenium or indoor stage and a dramatic structure. Performance piece, on the other hand, suggests work that can be presented in museums, theatres, classrooms, community centers, and other accessible locations, including outdoors. In addition, in those instances where work was specifically created for this collection, I wanted writers who do not identify as playwrights to create freely without the anxiety of dealing with stage directions or the mechanics of formal playwriting such as rising action, climax, falling action, etc. I wanted the writers to be able to focus on their characters and their characters' journeys.

Many of the works in this anthology are relatively short and employ small casts, making them wonderful performance opportunities for classroom use. Performance times range from 20 to 100 minutes with most allowing ample time for class discussion. Six pieces have just one character; the other five have casts of two or more. As these pieces speak to situations in specific countries or unique circumstances, they offer the possibility of inviting scholars with expertise in a broad range of fields as well as the writers to join the class discussion via the Internet. When I teach works by non-US artists, I always have students conduct research on the country and its culture.

This anthology is not arranged by theme, yet there are topics that are common to several of the pieces. Fleeing dangerous situations at home is one of them, and it is an aspect of the notion of home that has preoccupied me for nearly three decades. I have seen the cheerless faces of wary refugees and read their stories in the media, and during my various travels I have witnessed their willingness to risk their lives to reach America, the United Kingdom, or another country in Africa—anyplace that seemed a haven from their birthplace.

On my first visit to Cuba in 1995, I met individuals who had lost loved ones trying to reach America by boat, and a woman who tried to convince me to obtain a black market passport for her. On my visits to various countries in Africa, I encountered people being persecuted for their sexual orientation or for having albinism, which is considered a bad omen. I traveled to countries where women were driven from their homes for having children without being married or relationships with men outside their ethnic groups. I have even had marriage proposals from men in the desperate hope that my citizenship would grant them entry to the United States. Four of the performance pieces included here focus on this type of desperation: Évelyne Trouillot's *The Blue of the Island,* Jacqueline E. Lawton's *So Goes We*, Lupe Gehrenbeck's *Leaving, but Can't Let Go*, and Zodwa Nyoni's *Nine Lives*.

The Blue of the Island by Évelyne Trouillot (Haiti), or *Le Bleu de l'île* as titled in French, takes us on a journey to the Dominican Republic in the back of a truck with twelve Haitians who are risking everything to flee their country for a better life. The piece was inspired by an actual event and was introduced to me in 2015 by a colleague whose work focuses on women writers of the Caribbean. My class on Women from Africa and the Diaspora read the play, and we invited Trouillot to speak with us via Skype from Haiti. What my students and I found so fascinating about *The Blue of the Island* was that we got to know those twelve fugitives not as "illegal aliens" or "wretched immigrants" but as people – people with families, with complicated personal histories, and with dreams for their futures and the futures of those they love. Trouillot humanized those individuals and made us understand on a visceral level why someone would surrender everything to leave the familiarity of home for the unknown, fully aware that they might die in the process.

So Goes We by Jacqueline E. Lawton (United States) is another play that involves fleeing Haiti. I contemplated the need for presenting two pieces focusing on one country, but decided to include Lawton for a number of reasons. For one, Lawton describes *So Goes We* as a choral drama, and she uses an ensemble cast to tell the story by stepping in and out of characters and in and out of the chorus. Another intriguing factor was that one of the central characters is a college professor who is fleeing Haiti for America for political reasons, not economic ones, and she is escaping with her child. These plot elements show another social class and motive for fleeing home. It also illustrates the difficulties immigrants have once they reach the post-2016 US with its policy of separating children from their parents. Lawton is a playwright for whom I have designed lighting, and I admire her focus on social issues, current political events, and history, all of which inform *So Goes We*.

Nine Lives by Zodwa Nyoni (United Kingdom) introduces us to Ishmael from Zimbabwe who, along with his lover, David, has been "outed" as homosexual. Ishmael flees to the UK to escape the humiliation and mistreatment of LGBTI people only to learn that trying to establish a new home in a new country is not as easy as he had thought it would be. While situations are better for Ishmael on certain levels, he is still so haunted by the fear of "being himself" that he hides his real name and authentic self when he finally makes a friend. I was drawn to this play because of my own visits to Zimbabwe when homosexuality was illegal. In fact on my first visit in 1996, I was advised to not discuss the topic with anyone. A couple of years later, a director/producer/playwright with Alternative Savannah Arts Township Theatre in Harare created a performance piece in an attempt to challenge the government's laws and encourage audiences to openly discuss homosexuality. The play, *Simphosimi*, received national attention and performed to sold-out houses. This was a perfect example of theatre being instrumental in helping to shape public opinion and policy. Still, I was not aware until recently of how little had changed in Zimbabwe regarding homosexuality, except that it is no longer a crime. Unfortunately, the country's LGBTI community continues to experience tremendous discrimination, violent attacks, and mental health issues.

Leaving, but Can't Let Go by Lupe Gehrenbeck (Venezuela) invites us into the home of sixty-five-year-old Elvira. She has made the painful decision to move from the bustling city of Caracas, Venezuela because of its escalating poverty, food shortages, and gangs, problems made more daunting by her advancing age. Now she is wrestling with another difficult decision: should she go to live with the daughter who lives in another part of Caracas, or with the one who has migrated to New York City in the United States? Elvira is torn between the fear of leaving the country and life she knows and the fear of what her life might be like in an unfamiliar country. In truth, she wants to leave as much as she wants to stay. I once had an older student who had migrated from Venezuela to the US nearly twenty years earlier and who shared with me her stories of the difficulties of life in her home country. When a friend told me about Gehrenbeck's play, I knew that it had a place in this collection.

Playwright Louella Dizon San Juan (United States) describes how a natural disaster changed her view on the meaning of home. Written as a two-part monologue, *Letting Go and Moving On* takes us on the harrowing real-life nightmare of surviving one of the worst natural disasters in New York City's history, Hurricane Sandy. As San Juan pieces together her family's trauma before, during, and after the hurricane, she poignantly describes how a dwelling becomes a home. San Juan often deals with the theme of home. I have always enjoyed her plays and other writings, and this is my second time publishing one of her pieces. Originally written as a blog, San Juan rewrote it as a monologue specifically for this collection.

The notion of home as both a physical location and an emotional space comes into sharp focus when a family member dies. Two works in the collection explore the complexities that arise in the aftermath of death: *The House* by Arzé Khodr and *On the Last Day of Spring* by Fidaa Zidan.

In Arzé Khodr's (Lebanon) *The House*, the mother has died and left the house to her three adult children. Nadia, the oldest, has always lived in the house and wants to keep her childhood home. Her sister, Reem, wants to sell it because it represents too many painful memories. Their younger brother, Nabeel, is caught in the middle. He is unable to make a decision and unknowingly heightens the family conflict. *The House* was sent to me in 2010 by a friend who was teaching in Qatar. She was aware of my interest in international women playwrights and thought that the anthology *Plays from the Arab World*, published in 2010 and one of the earliest to be translated into English, would be a great addition to my class. She was right. The students read *The House* and were surprised that people on the other side of the world encountered the same issues that their families did. This play triggered a great deal of discussion as most of the students had stories about how the deaths of grandparents and other elderly relatives had fractured family ties.

Fidaa Zidan (Palestine) classifies *On the Last Day of Spring* as a theatrical monodrama. Inspired by Sophocles' *Antigone*, the piece is a personal story centered on the death of Zidan's brother. He was killed while serving in the Israeli army and, consequently, was buried in the Israeli Military Cemetery. In the monodrama, Zidan's family attempts to return her brother's body to his ancestral homeland in Palestine for re-burial. In addition to the difficulties that such a move entails, the story explores the complexities of what we consider "home" while we are alive and where we want "home" to be when we die. Similar to the circumstances surrounding *The House*, I was not aware of many plays from the Middle East because of the paucity of works translated into English. A circle of friends who publish and produce plays from Palestine introduced me to Zidan. I am thankful to them for the introduction and for translating this monodrama for this collection.

Another complexity of the experience of home can arise when one returns after living elsewhere. The task of what might be called "reconciling home" is addressed in *Questions of Home* by Doreen Baingana (Uganda). In this monologue, a woman returns to her home country of Uganda after spending eight years in the United States. Having adjusted mentally and emotionally to life in the US, she now must readjust to the rhythm and rituals of life in Uganda, bringing her face-to-face with the existential question: which country is really home? This dilemma is a common one that I have heard from many friends and other people who have migrated from one country to another and even from one part of the US to another. I was introduced to Baingana by a friend during a visit to Uganda in 2018. He wanted me to know her collection of short stories, *Tropical Fish*, and I fell in love with "Questions of Home." For this anthology, Baingana rewrote her short story as a monologue.

A few of the performance pieces in this collection deal with what may be one of the most traumatic experiences complicating the notion of home – slavery. In *Happy* by Kia Corthron, *Antimemories of an Interrupted Trip* by Aldri Anunciação, and *Those Who Live Here, Those Who Live There* by Geeta Siddi and Girija Siddi, we get to see how slavery around the world affects the ways that enslaved people experience home.

Happy, by Kia Corthron (United States), was originally written as part of a short play festival. In this intriguing piece, the main character, Happy, recounts her life as an enslaved woman, chuckling throughout her story. Since her childhood, her owners have passed her from one generation in the family to the next, and always with the promise of freedom. It is a promise that Happy cherishes because she wants to live as a free person in her own home, and she is willing to do whatever is required to achieve that dream. Corthron is a playwright whom I have known for over two decades, and I have both designed and published one of her plays. A number of her works deal with young people or social issues. I contacted her nearly ten years ago looking for a play to introduce students to slavery in the US, and *Happy* proved to be a perfect piece, generating a lot of thoughtful discussion. When considering pieces for this collection, I realized that *Happy* was ideal for inclusion.

The only male writer in this collection, Aldri Anunciação (Brazil) offers *Antimemories of an Interrupted Trip*, a story of an African woman who was thrown into the sea off a slave ship en route to Brazil in the 1800s. Since that traumatic day, she has lived at the bottom of the ocean in lonely confinement. There, she retrieves a never-ending assortment of objects from modern-day life as they are discarded and drift down into the sea. These objects are often welcome distractions that prompt her to ruminate on life in general, but they also trigger vague, disturbing wisps of memories. In 2001, I traveled to Brazil looking for works by Afro-Brazilian playwrights only to return empty-handed. When colleague Viviane Juergo, a Brazilian playwright, informed me of Brazil's first collection of plays by Afro-Brazilians, *Dramaturgia Negra* (2018), I was ecstatic. Juergo was one of the contributors to the volume, and she graciously translated a synopsis of each of the fifteen plays to show me the range of stories. While my preference was to include a female playwright, I was enthralled by Anunciação's story, which Juergo translated from Portuguese for this collection.

In *Those Who Live Here, Those Who Live There*, sisters Geeta Siddi and Girija Siddi share personal narratives about their lives as members of the Siddi ethnic group in India, showing us the contrasting experiences of living in a tight-knit community within a broader, unwelcoming country. Siddis (all of whom take Siddi as their last name) are descended from Africans, an indeterminate number of whom were enslaved by Europeans and brought to India in the sixteenth century. During and after slavery, many Siddis escaped to the forests along the west coast to create their own communities. The highest percentage of Siddis in India still resides in those areas. Because of their complexion, hair texture, and African origin, Siddis experience social, political, and economic discrimination from many of their fellow citizens. Siddis do not know their countries of origin. India is the only home they know, yet they do not feel "at home" there. Most people outside of India as well as within the country are unaware of the Siddis, who are often referred to as "India's lost tribe." I am thrilled to include Geeta and Girija's story in this collection as this will be the first known publication by Siddi women.

This anthology was finally completed during the Covid-19 pandemic of 2020–21, when the global lockdown afforded me the time to return to this project. Ironically, the one thing that connected each of the writers on this project was that we were all working in isolation. Many of us were also experiencing political turmoil in our respective countries, making everyday life and maintaining home that much more complex. I am indebted to all the writers and other contributors for making this collection possible under such difficult situations.

The House

Arzé Khodr

Translated by Khalid Laith

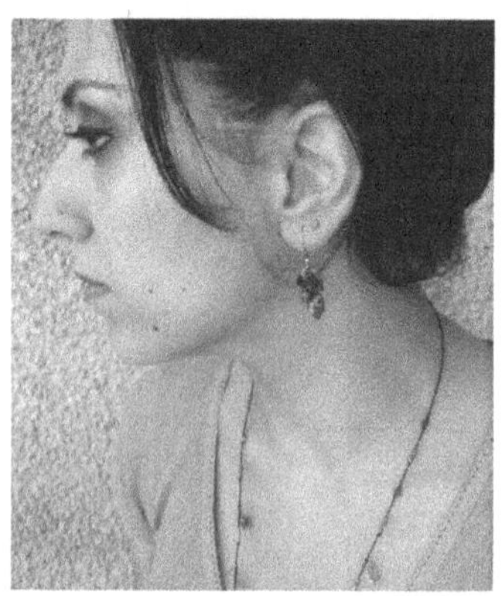

Arzé Khodr was born in Beirut, Lebanon in 1976, and graduated in theatre studies from Saint Joseph University (Beirut) in 1999. She has taught theatre, translated plays from English, and currently works as a writer and content creator for television. Her first play, *The House* (2008), was published as part of the 2010 collection *Plays from the Arab World* and has been translated from Arabic and published in English and French. It was presented as a staged reading at the Royal Court Theatre in London (2008), at Espace El Teatro in Tunis, Tunisia (2009), and at the Martin E. Segal Theatre Center in New York City as part of the PEN World Voices Festival (2010). It was also translated into German and staged at the Zimmertheater in Tübingen, Germany (2014). In 2018 *The House* was performed in Beirut, and Khodr won the award for best playwriting at the Lebanese National Theatre Festival. Her short play *Beirut Masnaa* was commissioned by the Royal Court Theatre and performed in London in August 2011 alongside other short plays by Arab writers. Khodr's *Sometimes We Remember* was selected for inclusion in the 2016 International Playwriting Festival.

Setting

After her mother's death, Nadia wants to remain in the house where she grew up. Her sister, Reem, wants to sell it because, for her, it is filled with painful memories. As a result, the old house becomes the scene of a merciless fight between the two sisters.

Production History

First production at Zimmertheater in Tübingen, Germany, January 18, 2014.

Cast and Crew

Nadia	Nicole Schneider
Reem	Agnes Decker
Nabeel	Johannes Karl
Director	Axel Krauße
Set and Costume	Christian Glötzner
Lighting	Werner Schmid
Sound	Thomas Demmel
Dramatic Advisor	Michael Hanisch
Assistant Director	Sophia Léonard
Stage Manager	Florian Leiner
German Translator	Sandra Hetzel
Manager	Axel Krauße

Act One

Scene One

2007. A living room in an old Beirut home. **Reem**, *in her mid-thirties, is seated.* **Nadia**, *in her forties, comes through the kitchen door. They are both dressed in black.*

Nadia I finally finished cleaning the kitchen! What a day it's been, I've been on my feet since seven this morning.

Reem You do enjoy the exhaustion . . .

Nadia What do you want us to do? Leave Mama without a forty-day memorial?

Reem I didn't say that, but we could've just had something intimate, without the extended family. A simple lunch. I don't think there's anyone we know who didn't come by today.

Nadia So, let them come . . .

Reem I just want what's best for you! You've worn yourself out!

Nadia It's nothing.

Reem Fine, it's nothing.

Nadia Did you see Nabeel's wife? A layer of foundation on her face this thick . . . (*She indicates a thickness of five centimeters with her fingers.*)

Reem You know her. Full make-up no matter what the occasion.

Nadia She really gets on my nerves! But then I think, if Nabeel's happy with her . . .

Reem He seems happy . . .

Nadia Happy, living under her thumb . . .

Reem Oh, Let them be. Sit down, I want to talk to you.

Nadia, *very carefully, sits down.*

Nadia I know . . .

Reem What?

Nadia You want to leave . . .

Reem Yes. I think it's time. I have to get back home.

Nadia This is also your home.

Reem Nadia, do me a favor . . .

Nadia You do me a favor. You know I can't live alone.

Reem Why can't you? You'd be better off!

Nadia No, I wouldn't. Please don't leave so soon after Mama's death.

Reem I've been here for forty days. Longer, two months, ever since Mama went to the hospital!

Nadia Two months. Seems like only yesterday. I can't believe it, she was fine . . . and in a blink she's ill, then she's gone . . . (*She starts to cry.*)

Reem I know. I can't believe it either. Every time the phone rings, I expect it to be her. I even catch myself saying "what does Mum want now!" . . . How life unfolds . . . (*Silence.*) You know that in six weeks I'm going to Qatar, right?

Nadia Yes.

Reem I'm signing a six-month contract.

Nadia You told me.

Reem And my contract might get extended, I'll be away for quite a while.

Nadia I know!

Reem So whichever way, I won't be able to stay with you.

Nadia You could stay until it's time for you to travel.

Reem I don't want to. I want to go home. I want to leave. I can't stand it here.

Nadia Ah well, you could have said it in the first place. Just say that you can't stand me.

Reem For God's sake, did I say I can't stand you?

Nadia Just for a few more days . . .

Reem Nadia. Nadia, why are you doing this? It's been ten years since I left this house, and I'm always hearing the same thing. Not once did Mama call me without asking when I'd be coming back, when I'd be sleeping here again . . .

Nadia Well, she's dead now. What else do you want?

Reem What else do I want? You think I wanted her to die? You think I'm happy now?

Nadia I didn't mean to . . .

Reem No go on, say it. For God's sake . . . Enough. Listen to me, Nadia, I have to go back to my house, I need to prepare for my trip and organize my life. I'm leaving tomorrow.

Nadia No, Reem, please. I can't, I just can't stay in this house alone.

Reem But sooner or later I'll have to leave. And you'll go back to work . . .

Nadia And you expect me to sleep on my own?

Reem And? I sleep on my own.

Nadia I can't!

Reem Well, then, get the neighbours' daughter, Nina, to sleep over.

Nadia Really?! And what am I supposed to say to her? Pack your things, you're moving in with me?

Reem What do you want? Hire a maid, she'll stay with you all the time.

Nadia I don't see why you want to live alone when the house here is empty. What's wrong with living together?

Reem I don't want us to live together.

Nadia Mama's gone now, and I certainly won't get in your way.

Reem Enough, Nadia. I've got a million things to take care of. I need to go back home tomorrow.

Nadia Oh, I get it. You have a boyfriend you don't want to bring back here. That must be it.

Reem Whether or not I have a boyfriend is simply none of your business.

Nadia So it's definitely that. Why else would you have left ten years ago? Except to go and sleep with your Shi'ite boyfriend and do whatever you want?

Reem Ah, so that's what this is about. God forbid I'm sleeping with someone, God forbid a man even touches me. Of course, I'm living alone because I want to be free to get fucked. That's why. And ten years ago, I left because I'm a whore, not because life here is unbearable. To fuck around I left home. As if I was fifteen and not twenty-six when I left. And I'll have you know that, yes, I was sleeping with my Shi'ite boyfriend, whenever and however I wanted. And I was very happy to not have someone pestering me about where I was going and when I'd be back.

Nadia I don't want to know anymore.

Reem Of course you want to know. You want to know if now I'm sleeping with someone. You can relax, I'm not. And if I want to go home, it's not so I can get fucked whenever I want it. It's to have some room to breathe and live, because this place here is killing me.

There's a knock at the door.

Nadia Someone's at the door, I hope they didn't hear you.

Reem Let them hear. I couldn't care less.

Nadia *opens the door.* **Nabeel**, *in his early thirties, enters.*

Nabeel I came back, thought I'd check on you, see if you needed anything.

(*To* **Nadia**.) You alright? You look tired.

Nadia It's been an exhausting day.

Reem I told her we didn't need such a big event.

Nadia Oh shut up, you're shameless.

Nabeel What's wrong? Have you two been fighting?

Reem Oh, it's nothing. I'm a slut and Nadia can't live on her own, that's all.

Nadia I don't want you staying here anymore. Go to your own house.

Reem You sure?

Nadia I'm sure. There's no living with people like you anyway.

Reem God forbid you should live with people like me. Careful you don't stoop to this level.

Nabeel Just calm down a minute. What exactly happened?

Nadia I was just asking her to stay with me a little bit longer. I can't be in this house alone. You know me, Nabeel. I can't sleep alone, I stay awake all night.

Nabeel I know.

Nadia But she wants to leave because she has more important things to tend to.

Reem Of course I want to leave. I have to leave. I've got to be in Qatar in six weeks, Nabeel.

Nabeel Just stay here for these six weeks, and then God will sort it out.

Reem How's he supposed to do that? Now or later, it's all the same.

Nadia You can't force her if she doesn't want to. (*To* **Reem**.) Just leave, I'll be fine.

Nabeel Reem, just stay for two or three more days . . . What's the worst that can happen? You'll be in another country soon enough.

Reem I've got so much to take care of before I leave . . .

Nabeel Well, then, take care of it during the day and sleep here at night. That's not too difficult, is it? (*Teasing*.) And you, Nadia, stop torturing her.

Nadia Me torture her? She'd torture the whole world!

Nabeel I know. I swear, I know.

Reem Really? You too, Nabeel?!

Nabeel Just relax, Reem. We know your mind is made up, you live alone and you don't care about anyone. But you can soften a little. Mama's only been dead forty days. Nothing will happen to you if you stay with Nadia a little longer.

Nadia Listen to me, Reem, you know I want you to stay with me with all my heart, but I'll tell you this: You do whatever you want.

Scene Two

Inside the house. **Nadia** *is standing on a chair in front of a large cabinet, polishing the silverware. There's a knock at the door.*

Nadia Just a second. (*She gets down.*)

Reem (*from the other side of the door we hear*) It's me . . . Nevermind, I found the key.

Nadia *gets to the door just as* **Reem** *opens it.*

Reem Hi.

Nadia Hi.

She helps **Reem** *carry some bags in.*

Reem No it's alright, I'll take them up to the room in a sec.

Nadia No problem, we'll do it together. (*She heads for the stairs carrying a heavy load.*)

Reem (*sharp*) I said I'll take them up myself!

Nadia Okay, fine. If you don't want my help I won't help you.

Reem *sighs, carries the bags up the stairs, enters the room, and comes back out again.*

Reem Anything left downstairs?

Nadia (*looking around*) No.

Reem *comes down and checks outside the front door.*

Reem God! I must've forgotten them by the bed!

Nadia What is it?

Reem My beige shoes. I went all the way back to my house just to get them. I wanted to wear them tonight. I got everything except for the shoes.

Nadia Tonight? Are you going out?

Reem Yes, in an hour or so. (*She sighs.*) I've had enough, I swear I'm sick of carrying stuff around!

Nadia (*placing the chair she was standing on away*) Do you want to have a bite to eat before you go?

Reem What have we got?

Nadia There's salad in the fridge, and I can make you steak.

Reem No, no, my friends will want to eat, I'll have dinner with them. (*To herself.*) What am I going to do about the shoes?

Nadia Wear something else.

Reem I can't keep track of what clothes I've got here and what I've left there.

Nadia I told you we should have just moved everything here. You'll be leaving that house eventually. Right?

Reem I don't know, Nadia. I just don't know.

Nadia What do you mean? Aren't you off to Qatar? You want to be paying rent on an empty house?

Reem But I already paid in advance. Four months still left on the lease.

Nadia Then what?! You want to pay for a house in Beirut while living in Qatar?

Reem I was thinking of just letting the lease run out. By then I would know if I'm staying in Qatar for more than six months. In case I'm coming back to Lebanon, I'll renew the contract with the landlord.

Nadia I see.

Reem What's that supposed to mean?

Nadia You can do whatever you like. It's none of my business!

Reem Yes of course. It's none of your business. It's not like I've been moving my things every day, running between two houses, not knowing where I am, just to make you happy.

Nadia What does that mean? Should I be thanking you for sleeping here? What have I done to you? You have a good life here. You don't have to answer to anyone. I even wash and iron your clothes . . .

Reem No one asked you to wash or iron anything.

Nadia It's alright. You don't owe me for it.

Reem Of course, you're the good one and I'm the bitch.

Nadia I didn't say that.

Reem Oh yes, I'm the heartless bitch who left this house. The one who always fought with Mum. I had a Shi'ite boyfriend. I don't care about anyone. Even Dad, I was the one who killed him.

Nadia That's enough, no one said that!

Reem You think it all the time. Mum used to think it too.

Nadia No she didn't. You're the one who blamed her for everything.

Reem I did blame her for everything, eventually. But she started it. You know what she once said to me? "If you weren't that spoiled, your father might still be alive." Who says that to an eight-year-old child?

Nadia She didn't mean it . . . She was devastated.

Reem She meant every word. She mourned him for the rest of her life, but there was never a day when they lived like a normal happy couple. She made his life miserable, and ours. She only got worse after he died.

Nadia Don't be so coldhearted.

Reem Well, I am. I wish I could go back in time to be even more coldhearted. Maybe it would have made things easier today.

Nadia Calm down . . . All this because you forgot the shoes?

Reem Oh I wish . . . If only it was all about the shoes!

Nadia No need to get upset before you go out now. I've got a pair of beige shoes. Do you want to try them on?

Reem We're not the same size.

Nadia Try them. Maybe with insoles . . .

Reem It won't work. Forget it. I'll just wear something else.

Scene Three

The house is empty. There's a knock at the door. **Reem** *comes down the stairs. She looks through the spy hole then opens the door.*

Reem Don't you have a key?

Nabeel I do, but I don't know where it is. Is Nadia gone?

Reem Just left for work. Want some coffee?

Nabeel No thanks. I had one at home.

Reem Well, sit down, I need to talk to you.

Nabeel As long as it's quick, I've got an appointment at nine.

Reem Oh Nabeel, you're always rushing off. I asked you yesterday to give me half an hour of your time!

Nabeel Fine, I'm sitting. What's up? Still fighting with Nadia?

Reem Yes . . . Well, no. Poor thing, she's doing her best not to disturb me, so I don't leave . . . but I'm suffocating, I can't stand it . . .

Nabeel It's alright. How long till Qatar? Barely a month. A little patience. If she got along with my wife, I'd ask her to stay with me for a while, but I don't even dare to bring it up, she'd never shut up . . .

Reem Neither would your wife . . . Anyway I'm not telling you to take her in. I'm talking about something else. If I stay here till I leave, then, when I come back, where do I come back to?

Nabeel What?

Reem Where do I come back to when I come back from Qatar? Where will home be?

Nabeel Where will home be? What do you mean?

Reem Don't play dumb, Nabeel. I'll be in Qatar for at least six months. My lease ends in four. I either pay rent on an empty house, or move all my things and come back to this one.

Nabeel Fine. Move your things and come back here. Isn't that cheaper for you?

Reem Nabeel, my dear brother, concentrate with me here—Haven't I just told you I can't stand living here! If I move out of my place completely, I'll have to stay here for good!

Nabeel Says who? Move your things in here now and when you get back, rent a place if you want. Is it that complicated?

Reem It is complicated. Haven't you heard Nadia: "I can't sleep alone, don't leave I won't be in your way, what do you want to eat, what do you want to drink . . ." You think she'd let me leave that easily?

Nabeel She'll get used to living alone while you're away.

Reem No, she'll be forced to live alone because I'm away. And when I get back, she'll force me to stay with her.

Nabeel Reem, honestly. We'll cross that bridge when we come to it. Besides, when was anybody able to force you into anything? You have always done things your way.

Reem But now it's different. Nadia's been laying on the guilt, thick. Every time I come back here, I decide to speak to her about leaving, but she won't let me. She starts asking if I'm hungry or thirsty, if I'm too tired . . . Every time I lose her, I find her crying in Mum's room. Honestly, it's driving me mad. I feel like I'll be trapped here forever.

Nabeel Trapped here forever?

Reem Yes, yes, trapped. Forced to live in this house with Nadia for the rest of my days.

Nabeel And . . . let's say you have to live here with her for the rest of your days, what's wrong with that?

Reem What's wrong with that? What do you mean? I'd suffocate, go crazy, I'd die . . .

Nabeel Enough already! What do you want?

Reem I want to sell the house.

Nabeel What?

Reem Sell the house and split the money. That way I can buy my own place, Nadia can have her own place, and she will get a housekeeper to stay with her so she doesn't feel so alone. You take your money and do what you like with it.

Nabeel Oh God!

Reem It's the best option.

Nabeel How did you come to think about this?

Reem Are you telling me it has never crossed your mind?

Nabeel No, honestly, it hasn't.

Reem Well, think about it. It's a big house, in the centre of Beirut. You know that property prices have been rising . . . I asked a real estate agent I know, we could get two and half million dollars for it. That means eight hundred thousand each. Have you finished paying for your place?

Nabeel Still paying the bank loan.

Reem Perfect. One less thing to worry about.

Nabeel Yes but . . .

Reem But what?

Nabeel I don't know, I'm a little shocked. Are you serious about this?

Reem Yes. I'm very serious. And I have no time to lose. I've been talking to you for an hour now. I'll be away and when I come back I want to come back to a place of my own.

Nabeel And did you talk to Nadia about it?

Reem No, I'm talking to you about it now. What do you think?

Nabeel To be honest, it has never crossed my mind. I know it is a big house, and of course we'd get a good deal of money for it, but I've never thought that we might sell it, especially with both of you living here.

Reem I am not living here, and I don't want to be. That's why I want us to sell it.

Nabeel Tell me the truth, do you need money? Do you have debts or a bank loan you need to pay?

Reem No, really no. I want us to sell the house because it would be better for the three of us, and for the house! Look how much work needs to be done . . . The walls need repainting, the roof leaks, the plumbing has to be replaced, someone has to take care of the garden . . . I'm going away. Do you really think Nadia can handle all that on her own? Anyway she doesn't have the money, and you can barely pay your bank loan.

Nabeel It's a fair point. I'm with you. But you do realize we'd be selling our parents' house, the house we were born and raised in . . .

Reem Yes, I realize that. Why are you talking to me as if I lost my head? The whole point is to sell the house we were born and raised in.

Nabeel God! You do like trouble!

Reem How dare you! Two months I've been eating shit and shutting up, when you know damn well how much I hate being here. I like trouble if I want to sell the house and get a place of my own? I like trouble if I want to make good use of our only inheritance? I like trouble if I want to have a good life?

Nabeel That's all you care about, you having a good life, everything else can go to hell. Do you know what selling this house would really mean? Have you considered Nadia at all? Did you try imagining what would happen?

Reem Yes I did, and I know very well Nadia won't accept it initially, that's why I spoke to you first, so we convince her together.

Nabeel Bravo, Reem, bravo. Always getting your own way. And if there isn't a problem, you create one just to find a solution that gets things your own way.

Reem My own way? But you seem to like the idea . . .

Nabeel Don't you understand that all my life I've tried to stay out of your problems? Don't you understand that I left this house too? Of course I like the idea, why shouldn't I? But do you know what it's going to cost? Can you imagine the headaches, the problems, the hysterics? Of course you have no problem because it's you who create problems in the first place. And if someone tries to stay out of trouble, you provoke him just to feel better. But I can't take it anymore, Reem. I am always trying to cool things down, to stay away from this atmosphere of hysterical women that I've had up to here, I'm trying to save what can be saved. I am the one who wants to have a good life. I am the one who wants the house to leave me the hell alone, not you. And this idea of yours could stir up endless trouble. Of course you'll get what you want, and who'll be stuck in the shit? Me. Who'll be in the firing line? Me. Who has to mediate between you two, talking to Nadia, patching it up with Reem? Me. Both of you have always been like this, and I say to myself, "It's ok, they're your sisters, you're all they got, you're the only man in the family". . . And now what? You want to start a war and you want me to be on your side? You're very much mistaken!

Reem No, Nabeel, no. Do me a favour and listen to me. I'm not trying to get things my way, or cause trouble, please believe me. I just can't stand the idea of living here anymore, you know that. And I want something good to come out of this house for once, instead of the doom and gloom it's given us.

Nabeel And this is your idea to get rid of the doom and gloom?

Reem Let me finish. If we sell, at least we'd have some money to spend. And each of us can have the house they want. You do have a point, I know it could be difficult at first, but just think of getting rid of our problems once and for all. The thought of this house not existing anymore makes me so happy I could fly.

Nabeel Are you listening to yourself? You are losing your mind.

Reem No I'm not, I've never been saner. I've done my research. Do you know that if Nadia refuses, the two of us could file a suit to oblige her to sell? And we would win.

Nabeel What? File a suit against your own sister?

Reem Yes, if she gives me no other choice.

Nabeel Reem, for God's sake, have mercy on us! You want to fight your own sister for her share of an old shabby house, and get us involved in an ordeal with courts and lawyers? And for what? The house will stay yours. You don't need the money at the moment, do you?

Reem No, I don't.

Nabeel If one day we need to sell, we'll do it, why not? Real estate never loses its value. But do you have to cause friction between us now? Do you have to open those closed doors? Aren't you the one who always moves on and never looks back? Forget about the house now, go on with your life and let me go on with mine. If the house needs to be sold someday, we'll find the right time to do it.

Reem That time has come.

Nabeel It's your final decision?

Reem Yes.

Nabeel Listen to me, I'm not getting in between you and Nadia. Don't even dream of it. But I'll tell you one thing, if both of you agree to it, we'll sell. If you don't, I won't be getting involved in your dirty games, dragging this through the courts. You hear me?

Reem I hear you. You're a coward.

Nabeel You can say what you like, I don't care. But don't think you can manipulate me.

He leaves.

Reem 'Course . . . Only your wife can do that now . . .

Scene Four

Reem *is in the house. We hear the keys in the front door, and* **Nadia** *enters.*

Nadia Well! You're home before me today . . .

Reem Yes. I thought I'd come home early. I've boiled us some pasta and bought tomatoes so you can make some of your "Nadia's Special Sauce."

Nadia "Nadia's Special Sauce"! How come you remembered it?

Reem I can never forget it! I never have a plate of pasta anywhere without thinking that yours is the best.

Nadia Really? You've never told me.

Reem I have. I aways tell you I Iove your cooking. And you always make fun of me because I can't cook.

Nadia Well, you can't. You remember what Mum once said? "The way you cook, it's a good thing you don't poison yourself."

Reem She never said it to me. She told you and you told me.

Nadia That's right.

Reem So how about that Special Sauce?

Nadia It's a bit of chore. I'm tired, I don't feel like chopping onions and tomatoes . . .

Reem Nevermind. I'll juice a lemon, we can have the pasta with lemon and olive oil.

Nadia No, come on. I'll make the sauce, if you're craving it. I just need to rest a little first.

Reem Don't worry about it. I'll eat anything.

Nadia No, no. Just let me rest a little.

Reem It's alright, you can make it tomorrow, or Sunday. I just wanted us to have a meal together, so we could talk.

Nadia Ah, so there's something to talk about.

Reem Yes, and it's rather important.

Nadia Come on, tell me . . .

Reem I've been thinking about making our lives easier . . .

Nadia In what respect?

Reem In all respects . . . You come home from work tired, only to do more work at home. You do the cooking and the cleaning. Sometimes the roof leaks, sometimes the toilets overflow, the garden needs tending . . . And now I'm leaving, you'll be here on your own . . .

Nadia Well, what can I do?

Reem I'll tell you what we can do . . . I was thinking that houses have increased in value tremendously, and this big place of ours is very centrally located, it could make us some money. We can sell it and share the money. We'd get around eight hundred thousand dollars each.

Nadia What? You want to sell the house?

Reem I was thinking about it. Why not? Nabeel could pay off his mortgage. I could finally buy an apartment, instead of renting all my life. You could buy a house as well, and get a live-in maid . . . What do you think?

Nadia Have you gone mad? Are you trying to kill me?! You want to get rid of me?

Reem Me? Not at all, I just want you to breathe, to be comfortable.

Nadia What do you know about my comfort?

Reem Fine, then it's for my comfort. I want to get rid of the house. Do you mind?

Nadia Yes. Of course I do. You want to sell our house and I should just stand aside and watch? What did this house ever do to you?

Reem What did it do? It wore the hell out of me! I want to get rid of it and know that I never have to come back here again.

Nadia You don't have to come back. You're free to go. No one's forcing you to stay.

Reem Yes, Nadia, you are. Forever saying how you can't live alone. Always playing the victim.

Nadia I'll live by myself. What's it to you? When did you care about anyone anyway?

Reem Sure. I don't care about anybody. You're the caring one. God forbid you should be flawed in any way.

Nadia You expect me to be like you? Always turning your back and running.

Reem When did I do that? Because I left this house to be able to breathe? You wanted me to stay here, endlessly bickering with you and your mother? You cut out my heart, both of you! I was lucky to finally have some peace outside this house.

Nadia I never did anything to hurt you. You left us, Mum broke down, and I took care of everything all the time . . .

Reem She broke down? Her whole life was a breakdown. What about me? Wasn't I broken? Did anyone ever ask about me? Did anyone ever talk to me in this house? What it felt like to see Dad lying on the kitchen floor like that? Oh, you were very good about drumming to Mum's tune. "Your father would perhaps be alive if you weren't that spoiled." Is there any normal mother who would say that to her daughter? I've played it back in my head a million times: if only I'd got up to get myself that glass of water, instead of nagging at him for a whole hour that I was thirsty, he wouldn't have gone to the kitchen and that missile wouldn't have hit him. I would have gone to drink and come back, and that missile wouldn't have killed anyone. But that's not what happened. What am I supposed to do? I still remember feeling that gust of wind pushing me back, then running to see what had happened. I found Dad on the floor, his face white with dust, a string of blood trickling from his head, down to his chin. I cried out to him, but he didn't answer. I was scared. I ran to my room. Then there were screams. I hid under the bed, I felt something bad had happened and maybe it was my fault. We went down to the neighbors, and I heard their daughter say to her cousin "she's here because her father died". Oh, my father died. Then you came and held my hand, and we watched cartoons, holding hands. I don't know where Nabeel was then, maybe at some other neighbours . . .

Nadia Then we came home and Mum was dressed in black.

Reem And she never wore anything else.

Nadia She wouldn't stop crying.

Reem And I couldn't stand her anymore, but I didn't realize it at the time.

Nadia When did you?

Reem Much later. When I grew up a little. I started to notice the way she would speak to me. The things she said. I felt that she didn't love me, that she would deprive me of the air I breathe if she could.

Nadia That's not true.

Reem It is. If I wanted to go somewhere: "Why are you going out?" If I wanted to see someone, "You don't need to see them." If I ever bought anything for myself, "You don't need it. You've got enough already." I'm glad I was a good student, it's the only thing she couldn't complain about.

Nadia She said the same things to me.

Reem When it came to me, she didn't overlook anything. I was suffocating. I couldn't take it anymore.

Nadia You think I wasn't suffocating?

Reem You chose to suffocate.

Nadia Was I supposed to just leave her?

Reem It wouldn't have killed her! All children leave at some point.

Nadia If they get married.

Reem Even if they don't, they can leave. I am not going to wait for somebody to save me to get away.

Nadia It's over, you got away. I was the one who stayed. But it's all the same anyhow. Look at us now, in the same place we were ten, twenty years ago.

Reem What do you mean?

Nadia Just what I said. Did anything change, Reem?

Reem It's not true. I'm not in the same place. You can't say that. I'm not like you. I don't want to be like you. And I don't want to stay here and end up like you.

Nadia What does this mean? Who do you think you are? What have you done with your life anyway? You left, bravo, then what? Did you get married? Become rich? Have children? You're the same as when you were living here. Nothing's changed . . .

Reem Everything's changed. And if you think you'll make me come back here to stay with you so you'll feel better and say that nothing has changed, then you're wrong. We're not going back there, Nadia. Never! Do you hear me? I'm not growing old with you in this house so you can feel good about your life and say that you didn't miss out on anything.

Nadia That's enough. Enough with your theories.

Reem These are not theories. All your life you've been without a man. Why?

Nadia I wasn't lucky enough.

Reem Yes, of course, no luck. It was always down to luck. Me, you, auntie, mum who was miserable all her life, and who never stopped complaining about men that are worthless, unreliable and all of them liars.

Grandmother never even talked to her husband by the end of it. Ever wondered why we're so unlucky? Ever wondered if we're cursed somehow? You know? I used to think I was born with something missing, that thing that could make men love me. I was sure that all the other girls had it, but I didn't. I was sure of it. Then I realized that I wouldn't let them get close, the men who could possibly love me. I wouldn't let them get close, because I was so sure they're bad and that they'll mess my life up. I don't know if things would have been different if Dad would have stayed alive. I don't know if we would've found men useful had he been around longer. Oh God I am so tired. I've had enough of it, Nadia. This house kills me.

Nadia Leave, then. I'll live alone. Pack your things and go now, if you like.

Reem No.

Nadia I'm telling you, go. If you're tired of this, I am exhausted. I'd rather be alone than have to listen to this one more time. You're killing me, Reem. Go back to your place . . . Honestly, I won't stop you anymore.

Reem No, no this house needs to be sold. I need a place of my own, and you need one too.

Nadia I'm happy here. You go back to your place. Enough.

Reem No, I said no. This house shouldn't be ours anymore. Other people have to live in it. I never want to come back here again. You should leave too. Why can't you understand that? You have to leave as well.

Nadia That's enough. Calm down. Go upstairs and go to sleep now. You can move your things out in the morning and leave.

Reem Oh, I will leave. I will leave and this house will be sold.

Scene Five

Nadia *and* **Nabeel** *sitting at home.*

Nadia You've made it clear to her that I won't be selling?

Nabeel Yes, I explained it to her I swear. You don't believe me?

Nadia So what else does she still want? Can't she just leave us in peace?

Nabeel I don't know, Nadia.

Nadia I thought she was joking at first, talking bullshit. Thought she'd go back to her place, calm down, and just forget all about it.

Nabeel Does she ever forget anything? She's not capable of forgetting. Never lets anyone forget either.

Nadia Nabeel, please, stay true to your word, don't let her have her own way. You know how much I'm attached to this house . . .

We hear the keys in the door. **Reem** *opens the door and enters.*

Reem Good evening.

Nadia (*frosty*) Good evening, Madame Reem!

Reem What? You're still on your high horse?! Can't we at least discuss this like civilized people?

Nadia There's nothing for us to discuss. You know where I stand. I don't want to sell.

Reem This isn't just your house, you know.

Nadia It is. I'm the one who lives in it.

Reem You live in it, but the three of us own it, and the three of us get to decide.

Nadia Nabeel and I aren't selling. It's two against one.

Reem Are you sure about that? So, Nabeel? You didn't tell Nadia that you like the idea?

Nadia What?

Nabeel I never said I liked it, outright. I said I'd sell, if both of you agreed . . .

Reem Your wife too seems to like the idea . . . Very much so . . .

Nadia Your wife knows about this?

Nabeel Reem spoke to her. But it doesn't change anything. Like I said, we won't do anything until both of you agree to it.

Nadia You've enlisted your sister-in-law? You want a war?

Reem (*with disdain*) I really don't understand you, Nadia. This is an opportunity. You can be independent and comfortable and rich.

Nadia I am independent and comfortable.

Reem Well, I'm not.

Nadia That's your problem.

Reem And yours too. I'm entitled to a share of this house and I want to sell it. It's not yours alone.

Nadia Have I ever said otherwise? Or stopped you from coming here?

Reem I don't want to come here. I want to sell it and be done.

Nadia Are you hearing this, Nabeel?

Nabeel Could both of you please calm down so we can talk about this?

Reem I'm calm. Nothing's the matter.

Nadia That's right, nothing is the matter. I'm living in this house. I don't want to sell.

Reem But this house, Madame Nadia, is not yours alone. It's our inheritance, the three of us. And we all have the right to decide what to do with it. Don't you agree, Nabeel?

Nabeel Just a second here, one second. We already spoke about this, Reem, we agreed that selling can wait.

Reem No, it can't wait!

Nabeel You said you don't need the money.

Reem Right now, no, I don't.

Nadia Well, that's wonderful. You just want to sell the house on a whim!

Reem Exactly! I want to sell this place because I can't stand it, I can't tolerate it, can't tolerate its smell, its walls, or anything in it. I can't stand it. I hate it. I hate that I was born in it, raised in it, I hate that I'm standing in it now and that it still causes me problems. Never in my life could I stand this house or the life I had here. I almost didn't believe it when I was finally able to afford to move out, and not have to listen to your voices again, your voice, your mother's, your father's, your brother's. Ugh. I've never been happy in this house. Not one minute of normality. It was all doom and gloom and nagging and complaining. This house makes me sick. It suffocates me. I wish they tear this place down. I hope it burns down. All of it, with every last thing in it.

Nadia What is this madness?! You're crazy! You've lost your mind!

Reem I'm not crazy.You're the one living in a silly dream. Are you really happy now? Are you really convinced that you're living like a queen in your parents' house? You're so stupid. You really think I'd live with you? Do you think anyone can bear living with you? You'd make the devil run away! Just like your mother!

Nabeel Just shut up! I've had enough of both of you! I don't have to listen to this. I'm going.

Nadia No, stay. You stay and she can go. Insulting me in my own house!

Reem (*calm*) I'm not leaving. This is my house and I have the right to be here.

She sits on a chair at the dinner table. Some time passes in complete silence. **Nabeel** *sits at the other end of the table. Looking at the side of the table, he finds a stack of old photos. He takes one in his hand; it's a picture of the two sisters standing next to the newly bought father's car.*

Nabeel What are these?

Nadia The room upstairs has a leak, I brought stuff down so it doesn't get damaged and I found those photos.

Nabeel I have never seen this one. Where was it taken?

Reem (*gets closer to look at the picture*) Show me? Oh, that's the day Dad bought the new Fiat. He took us for a ride and took this pic.

Nabeel And where was I?

Nadia At home. Where else?You were maybe six months old.

Nabeel *and* **Reem** *continue to flip through the photos.*

Nabeel I'm not in a single one of these. It's just you and her.

Nadia They're very old. That's why they're left loose.

Reem It's true. When you were born we made you an album and we put all your photos in there so we wouldn't lose any. (*To* **Nadia**, *in a tone of complicity.*) We really spoiled him, Nabeel . . .

Nabeel That's not true. (*To* **Nadia**). You were the spoiled one.

Reem He does have a point!

Nadia Ok. But it didn't make any real difference.

Nabeel To you, of course it didn't! But to us it did.

Reem You should talk about being spoiled, the only boy after two girls . . .

Nabeel So what? I always felt that you were together and I was on my own.

Reem We were all on our own, Nabeel. I always felt like I was living on another planet.

Nadia You? Of course!

Reem Oh, shut up!

Nabeel I used to think you loved each other more than you loved me.

Nadia Seriously?

Nabeel You walked to school together, wore the same clothes, played together . . .

Reem Mostly bickering and hair-pulling.

Nadia (*to* **Reem**) You were always pulling my hair because you were always jealous of me.

Reem No, no, no . . . I pulled your hair because you were mean to me. You still are.

Nadia Admit that you were jealous of me!

Reem Never.

Nadia Just admit it.

They both laugh.

Reem Even if I was jealous, that was long ago. I grew up and realized I am prettier, funnier and smarter . . .

Nadia No no no . . . That is not true.

Nabeel You girls are unbelievable . . . You really are like children weren't you fighting a minute ago?

Reem Oh yes. Good, you reminded us. So how about it, Nadia?

Nadia I've already told you. No means no.

Reem What do you have to say about it, Nabeel?

Nabeel I told you both, if you two can agree on selling then we'll sell. If you can't, then no.

Reem Yes, but what would you prefer?

Nabeel Whatever you two want . . .

Reem I want to sell . . .

Nadia And I don't want to.

Nabeel Here we go again . . . Listen I hate these problems of yours, and if you think you will get me involved in this and make me take the responsibility for your decision, then you're wrong.

Reem Of course! Don't you make any decision in your life. Don't you ever!

Nadia Oh yes, just let Reem walk all over you. Typical.

Nabeel What is wrong with you two? You finished fighting with each other, so you ganged up on me?

Reem Forget it, Nabeel. Just go. You're absolutely useless.

Nabeel Oh, I'm gone.

He takes his jacket and leaves, closing the door behind him. The two women sit in silence.

Reem I'm leaving too.

Nadia Go, good riddance. And get the idea of selling this house out of your head.

Scene Six

Nadia *stands outside the front gate. The gate is locked. She is looking at a piece of paper hung on it.* **Nabeel** *arrives.*

Nabeel What now?

Nadia Have a look. Be my guest.

Nabeel What?

Nadia Read.

Nabeel *reads the paper stamped with a red wax seal.*

Nabeel "This property is hereby seized, by order of the Court of Expedited Cases in Beirut, until the closure of the case: Reem Khoury vs. Nabeel & Nadia Khoury." So Reem actually went through with it . . .

Nadia Did you know she was going to do this?

Nabeel Nadia, how can you ask me that?

Nadia Well, she said you liked the idea . . . so does your wife. She spoke to you first about selling the house. She tells you everything . . .

Nabeel Are you out of your mind? You really believe I'd take you to court? Are you crazy? Look, the case is filed against me too. Don't you see my name next to yours?

Nadia I can't take it anymore. . . How did we even get to this point? Where did all this come from? I don't understand why Reem is doing this, I don't understand anything anymore . . .

Nabeel Did you call the lawyer?

Nadia I was on the phone with him for an hour . . .

Nabeel And?

Nadia He says it's a scare tactic. "Expedited case," meaning she spun this web of lies to get some judge to sign off on the closure quickly, but we can get it overturned in a few days.

Nabeel Are you sure?

Nadia That's what the lawyer says.

Nabeel Fine, if it's only a matter of days, then we can handle it . . .

Nadia How can we handle it, Nabeel? Where am I supposed to go now? Can you believe this?! I come back from work to find my own house off-limits? If it's come to this, then there's no stopping Reem at all . . .

Nabeel Relax. Let's go to my place and we can talk about this.

Nadia I don't want to talk to anybody. I just want to go home . . .

Nabeel Well, Nadia, have you thought about this idea of selling? Eight hundred thousand dollars would buy you a very nice place in town and we'd be done with all these problems . . .

Nadia What?! There might have been a chance of me considering it before, but after what she has done today, not even God can change my mind . . . I know you like the idea of selling, I know . . . Your wife too. She's a crafty one that Reem, she knows how to get what she wants.

Nabeel God! I already told you, I'd never stand with her against you. Don't you believe me? What else do you want from me? Do I need to put it in writing? What a pain! I don't blame Reem for wanting to get rid of this place. I'm sick of this!

Nadia So it's come to this? You want to kick me out too? I don't believe this! Oh God! It's unbearable!

Nabeel Calm down and listen to me! I would never force you out. Never. You have to believe me. Is that clear enough?

Nadia Yes.

Nabeel Let's head to my place—you can stay with us until we get this sorted.

Nadia I'm not going to change my mind, Nabeel. Don't you ever ask me to think about it again . . .

Scene Seven

Inside the house, **Nadia** *is busy cleaning. There's a knock at the door, then* **Reem** *uses her key and enters.*

Reem Congratulations! You're back!

Nadia Can you tell me what are you doing here?

Reem I'm paying you a nice visit. I've come to see how you are, what you're up to . . . I'm flying out the day after tomorrow.

Nadia Great! We'll get a break from you!

Reem Come on, Nadia! Is this how sisters speak to each other?

Nadia Is this how sisters treat each other? You make up all those lies and you wait for me to go to work so you can have the house sealed off with red wax?

Reem You're back now. It's no big deal.

Nadia It's no big deal? What a shame . . . You want to throw your own sister out of her parents' house and it's no big deal!

Reem I've had enough of you and this house! You think I'm doing this just to piss you off?

Nadia Why else? To have fun?

Reem No, Nadia, I'm not having any fun. I'm not having fun at all! I told you I want to sell and will do everything I can to make that happen!

Nadia Bravo! You'll have to show me how clever you are then!

Reem So we're still in the same place! You insist on this torture! Shall we have this out in the courts? Is that what you want?

Nadia What do you think you'll get from taking me to court? If I don't agree, you'll never sell the house!

Reem If Nabeel agrees, we'll force you to sell!

Nadia Don't worry, Nabeel can't agree anymore . . .

Reem Really? You've got him in your pocket now?

Nadia Not just Nabeel, his wife too!

Reem Oh really?

Nadia I swear! She loves her money, and I've found a way to keep her satisfied.

Reem Liar!

Nadia Go on, ask her.

Reem Are you trying to scare me?

Nadia Suit yourself. You'll find out soon enough.

Reem What did you do? What did you say to Nabeel?

Nadia Ask him.

Reem I'm asking you.

Nadia I've signed off my share of the inheritance to him, on the condition that I get to stay here for the rest of my life.

Reem What does that mean?

Nadia It means that two-thirds of this house belong anyway to Nabeel, now or later, and in return he has to let me live in it until I die. That means, if you want to sell this house, Madame Reem, you'll have to wait for me to die or just kill me . . .

Reem But you have no right to do that . . .

Nadia Says who?

Reem I know! You just can't!

Nadia Fine, ask your lawyer about it, and then get back to me . . .

Reem Oh really? You must be very pleased with yourself. Do you feel strong and intelligent now? I will ask my lawyer and I'll take you to court and you'll see!

Nadia You will see! Do you know how long property cases take? Ten years, at least. And anyway you'll lose.

Reem No, I will not. What do you know about it?

Nadia Whatever you say, Reem. Do whatever makes you happy, if you can . . .

Reem Of course I can. Even if it means dragging this through the courts for ten, twenty, fifty years. Even if I'm dead before the judgment is issued, this house will be sold and I'll get rid of it.

Act Two

Scene One

One year later.

Nadia *and* **Nabeel** *are in the living room.*

Nadia What does that mean?

Nabeel It's over, you have to leave.

Nadia I can't even comprehend it . . .

Nabeel I know. . . But there's nothing more we can do . . .

Nadia I don't understand . . . Suddenly they want to build a new highway? All of a sudden there's town planning involved?

Nabeel Not all of a sudden, Nadia. Didn't you hear the lawyer say this project had been lost for fifty years—(*mocking*) if not since the time of the Ottomans . . . Our beloved government . . . Before, they were busy with Solidere,[1] now they just remembered there are other roads to build. Lucky us!

Nadia What have I got to do with it if they just remembered the other roads? What has our house got to do with it?

Nabeel It's right in middle of the planned highway. That's what it's got to do with it. And if your highness had agreed to sell a year ago, we would've made some real money! Now, we'll be lucky to get forty or fifty percent of what it's worth!

Nadia As little as forty or fifty?

Nabeel Yes! Because the highway is not running on all of the house, it's running just in the middle. Even in this, we are screwed!

Nadia You can stop talking about it now. Don't make it harder . . .

Nabeel I am making it harder? If you'd only accepted when Reem wanted to sell last year. But no! You wanted to stay! You wanted to hang on! You're stubborn and unbreakable! You'd never change your decision!

Nadia Now it's my fault? Why didn't you hang on? Why didn't you insist? Or you just loved it when I yielded my share to you?

Nabeel You're crazy. All I did was for you! You were breaking down. There was no talking to you . . . But you're always right, whatever you do, you're always right. Whatever happens, you're always right . . .

Nadia Don't blame me if you have no balls! If you really wanted to sell this place, you could've stamped your foot and sold it with Reem regardless!

[1] Solidere s.a.l. is a Lebanese joint-stock company in charge of planning and redeveloping Beirut Central District following the conclusion, in 1990, of the country's devastating civil war.

Nabeel Not one more word or I'll kill you!

Nadia I'll speak to Reem . . . We'll see what we can do about this. Maybe we can take it to court, appeal or whatever . . .

Nabeel The order was signed at the Ministry . . . What can you do? Go to court for nothing? Aren't you tired of this already? Or do you want to waste more time until the value drops further?!

Nadia Why are you shouting at me? Am I the one running a highway in the middle of the house? What am I supposed to do? It happened this way, let's try to find a solution, some legal loophole . . .

Nabeel There is no solution, Nadia, and I don't want to be getting into any legal loopholes with you or wasting any more money on lawyers . . . In seven, eight months, a year at the most, they'll pay us our money, you'll leave the house, they'll demolish this place and it will be over. We take whatever they offer, because, this house, no one's going to buy it from us anyway . . .

Nadia It's not about finding someone to buy it! It's about buying us more time . . .

Nabeel More time for what? You'll have to leave sooner or later. Enough! Let go! Forget about it! You wore the hell out of us with this goddamn house!

Nadia Can you please just listen to me? Reem knows many important people, she might be able to help us . . .

Nabeel Reem help you? She was dying to get rid of this place. Or has that slipped your mind?

Nadia Reem wanted to sell. I don't think she'd be happy with the Ministry running a highway through the place and screwing us with the money . . .

Nabeel It's over. Either way, we're screwed.

Nadia We have to call Reem. I'll speak to her.

Nabeel And? You want to keep on fighting? Till your last breath?

Nadia I'm fighting for my home . . . You don't live here, you won't understand.

Nabeel Of course. You're the one living here, only you understand! (*He starts to leave.*)

Nadia You're just going to sit back while they take our house away?

Nabeel There's nothing more we can do. Nothing more I want to do.

Scene Two

A year later.

Inside the house, empty of most of its furniture. Suitcases and boxes in the corners. **Nadia** *brings some bags down from the upstairs rooms. The front door is open,* **Reem** *enters.* **Nadia** *sees her, runs towards her, and hugs her.*

Nadia I'm glad you came! I missed you . . .

Reem (*quietly*) How are you? Everything packed?

Nadia Almost. The movers came and took the furniture to the new house. There are still a few things, and some stuff for you. I put them all there. (*She points to a corner.*)

Reem Do you need any help?

Nadia No I'm done. That's it . . .

Reem What about the furniture that's left?

Nadia Not enough space in the new house. I'll put them in Nabeel's garage, he can sell them if he wants to . . .

Reem *looks at the remaining furniture, observing the space.*

Nadia Can you believe it, Reem? I can feel my heart breaking inside . . . I can't believe I'm leaving this place . . .

Reem (*noticing another pile of things in a corner*) Are those mine as well?

Nadia No, they're Nabeel's. Have you seen him?

Reem No, not yet.

Nadia Have you spoken to him?

Reem Yesterday, after I got back.

Nadia What did he say?

Reem What can he say? That you're moving out in three days . . .

Nadia Didn't he say we should've sold the house, just like you wanted?

Reem Not yesterday, no. But before, when he called me in Qatar to tell me about the highway, yes. He was very upset. I told you . . .

Nadia He blamed me for not selling and was very mad at me . . . but this is the way things happened. I just couldn't bring myself to leave here . . .

Reem It's over now. No use talking about it . . . (*She starts moving her things closer to the door.*)

Nadia Will you come and visit me at my new place?

Reem Of course. If I'm invited . . .

Nadia (*smiles*) I don't know if I'll get used to it, the new house . . . I don't know how I'll do it . . .

Reem Of course you'll get used to it, Nadia! You've survived worse. What's wrong with you?

Nadia I feel as though the world is ending . . . You know? I don't regret not selling the house two years ago . . . At least I had those couple of years living here . . .

Reem You really don't regret it? With all the money we've lost? We only got half of what it's worth! (*Silence.*) Just so you could stay here those couple of years, you put me, yourself and Nabeel through hell! All the lawyers and courtrooms . . . and you don't regret it? Well, I don't regret it either, I don't regret it at all.

Nadia Of course you don't! When did you ever regret arguments and problems . . . In any case, you got what you wanted. You wanted to get rid of this place and you couldn't sell it, the government snatched it away . . . You always get what you want . . . You've always been lucky . . .

Reem Yes, Luck. You're right, it's all just a game of luck. (*She moves the rest of her things to the door.*)

Nadia What can we do? In our family we're destined for pain . . .

Reem You know what, Nadia? If you think sometimes other people have it easier, you're not mistaken. You'd be right, some people out there do get what they want in an easier way, their lives are easier than ours. But if you think this thing just fell out of the sky as a blow for you and a relief for me, you'd be very wrong about that. I worked hard to make this happen!

Nadia What?!

Reem You heard me! If you think the government woke up to a long-lost piece of town planning overnight, you'd be very wrong. They had someone to remind them!

Nadia I don't believe this! You took your twisted ways all the way up to the Ministry? You liar!

Reem No, I'm not lying! My twisted ways? In a way . . . You remember my Shi'ite boyfriend? Majid . . . Remember we wanted to get married but his parents and mum wouldn't have it? He went to study abroad and I had a nervous breakdown? Well, Majid's now an engineer working for the Ministry of Public Works. And we're still friends . . .

Nadia So it's that easy? You tell your ex-boyfriend and he tears down the house?

Reem Of course it wasn't that easy, Nadia . . . I spent God knows how long trying to convince him. He doesn't like this sort of thing, but I have my twisted ways . . . I'd heard about this piece of planning a long time ago. Remember Mum used to say there was a highway that was going to run right through the house? And Dad would tell her it would take them a hundred years to get the ministerial order signed? We dug up the highway plan, found a government official who would profit from it, we begged for an approval from there, got some support from here . . . If Majid had enough power to get this done himself, it wouldn't have taken so long.

Nadia I can't believe what I'm hearing . . .

Reem I'm sorry, Nadia. You forced me to do it like this . . .

Nadia No, of course I didn't.

Reem Can you imagine the highway cutting through this dining room? We might be left with just a corner of the kitchen. I don't know if they'll demolish the whole thing, or maybe they'll leave a piece of wall . . . I think they'll tear it all down. (*Excited.*) The cars will rip right through here (*she points in the direction of the future traffic*) at 120 kilometers per hour . . . Nice! The dining room, the living room, everything above it: your bedroom, Mum's room . . . Wow! It'll all be like a convertible, open, we'll see the sky . . . Feels so good . . . Breathe, Nadia, breathe . . . Fresh air . . . Finally . . .

Nadia How could you do this? How could you?

Reem It's the happiest ending! You know if we'd sold it, and they'd turned it into a restaurant or a hotel, the walls would still be standing. But now it's over. There will be nothing left. Do you understand? Do you understand we're done? It's all over?!

Nadia Yes, I understand . . . Now, I understand . . .

Reem Congratulations, Nadia, congratulations.

End of play.

Happy

Kia Corthron

Kia Corthron is a playwright and novelist. Her plays, including *A Cool Dip in the Barren Saharan Crick*, *Breath*, *Boom*, and *Force Continuum*, have been produced in New York by Playwrights Horizons, New York Theatre Workshop, Atlantic Theater Company, Ensemble Studio Theatre, and Manhattan Theatre Club; in London by the Royal Court Theatre and Donmar Warehouse; and across the United States. For her stage work, she has earned the Horton Foote Prize, Flora Roberts Award, Windham Campbell Prize, United States Artists Jane Addams Fellowship, Simon Great Plains Playwright Award, and McKnight National Residency. She was the 2017 resident playwright at Chicago's Eclipse Theatre, which produced three of her plays. Her most recent play, *Tempestuous Elements*, will be produced by Arena Stage in Washington, DC in 2022. Corthron's debut novel, *The Castle Cross the Magnet Carter*, was a *New York Times Book Review* Editor's Choice and the 2016 winner of the Center for Fiction First Novel Prize. Her second novel, *Moon and the Mars*, was published in August 2021. She serves on the Dramatists Guild Council, is a New Dramatists alum, and is a member of the Authors Guild.

Setting

This monologue takes the form of a slave narrative told by Happy, an eighteenth-century enslaved woman in New York City. She recalls her life in bondage with surprisingly good humor as she awaits her long-promised freedom.

Note: **Happy***'s laughter is always genuine: never sarcastic, ironic, or maniacal.*

Happy First they call me "Mary," but somewhere it get changed: "Happy" they say, "Happy" always laughin! (*Laughs.*) I was! My mother dies hatchin me seventeen and thirty-eight, and the Hennesseys gimme "Mary," then "Happy." Summer they work us till ten, eleven at night, then right back to work two in the mornin! Winter they let us sleep till four, then work till ten, only a eighteen-hour day but still feel too much, the tiredness make everybody else solemn but reckon the sleepies gimme the chuckles! (*Laughs.*) Just the four a us, New York City the masters don't got no plantation, no need for a battalion a slaves. Handful'll do em.

Tell ya, I did *not* wanna be touchin them Hennessey children when they all come down with the smallpox! (*Laughs.*) But I nursed em like I was told, hopin not to get the sick myself. I did! Them Hennesseys all better from my nursin, then *I'm* down with the fever, bumps, bring it home to my *own* two children who dies of it! And somethin happen to my insides, no more children I could have. God got some sensa humor! (*Laughs.*) Oh but I weren't laughin then. And little Gracie Hennessey: "Happy, why you not happy?" I tell her bout my buried babies, she say, "You saved me from dyin, Happy. When I grow up, I'ma free you." (*Laughs.*) Little Gracie Hennessey weren't nothin but five years ole! And me jus nineteen, still plenty a life I got so I say, "I'ma holdja to it, Miss Gracie! I'ma holdja to it!" (*Laughs.*)

Miss Gracie was seventeen when she wed Mr. Edgar Warren, age twenty-four. I was given to Miss Gracie, passed on from her parents, weddin present. I mention to Miss Gracie her little girl promise to free me cuza nursin her back to health from the smallpox. She pat my arm, "Oh Happy, I was just a child. You didn't really take serious the promise of a child? I plan on havin plenty a babies! How we part with you?" (*Chuckles.*) Well I never figured she keep her ole promise, I's jus *usin* the promise. "Well, Miss Gracie, since you ain't gimme my freedom like you *promised*, then how bout you sign a *per*mit sayin my half-Sundays free time I can travel, see my husband?" My husband Isaiah recently sold to a doctor three hours' walk, I weren't much more n thirty, my legs still easy strong enough. Well, Miss Gracie turn beet red! Huffin, puffin: "Impertinent!" She make it clear I'm goin *nowhere* my half-Sundays free, "So you can run off? So you can *escape?*" Now I'm plannin escape, why I'm gonna let her onto it? (*Laughs.*) Later though, she soften up. "All right," say she, "you can visit your husband. Every Christmas." And *that* measly promise she stuck ta! (*Laughs.*) Every 25th of December I walk the three hours there, three back. Cep one Christmas Eve Miss Gracie got s' drunk, gone to sleep fore she writ my permit! But that fine. Never was unlawful for Northern slaves to read and write, and the latter I learnt from copyin her handwritin. Identical! (*Laughs.*)

When the war come there was black fightin for the redcoats, England offerin freedom in return. Thirty-seven then, figured I was still young enough, strong enough. And them Hennesseys was big loyalists lovin the British, why not ask? Maybe the Englishmen need women for the cookin, washin. Well Miss Gracie and Master Edgar stared at me like I gone crazy! And maybe I had! A whole brood a little Gracies, five or six she'd had by then, and me nerve to ask for leave! (*Laughs.*)

Sometimes Miss Gracie and Master Edgar and the whole horde took trips to the seaside, but no rest for me then: they jus loan me out to Miss Gracie's Connecticut cousins, so I ain't had more n a half-Sunday off since I was five years old. After they refuse me the British fight, I'm thinkin hard on my nex move, which between you and me was escape, when two days later Miss Gracie and Master Edgar come back, say I could go! I don't know what changed their minds, I didn't ask! (*Laughs.*) Off I went! Mendin the Brit soldier uniforms, stirrin the stew. There was some cold frostbite days. Hungry days. Blood. Death. And still: excitin time. Happy time! Till the British lost. (*Beat.*) The British general was Sir Guy Carleton. Wantin to keep his promise, free the slaves fought for the Brits, but ole George Washington prefer to get his slaves back. (*Chuckles.*) And figurin the rebels won the war, all them oughta reclaim their slaves too, who's the Brits to make the rules? In the end: compromise. November 30th, seventeen and eighty-two: date a the first peace treaty. You wanted your promised freedom, you had to prove you was in New York before. Which I was! New York City my whole life! But ole Miss Gracie. Get her lyin Connecticut cousins to lay claim to me, hire theirselves a lyin lawyer! (*Laughs.*) But Isaiah went free. Turns out Isaiah also fought for the Brits, though I never seen him when we was both on our battlefields. He not wantin to leave without me, I say, "Go, Isaiah! I be along directly!" So he gone on to Nova Scotia waitin for me, crossed on over to Canada with all them other slaves. With all them other *free men and women.* And I stay and care for Miss Gracie's newborn twins. And later care for Miss Gracie's grandchildren, her great-grans. By the time the new century roll around, I'm lookin at my sixty-second birthday, fifty-seven of those years slavin for Hennesseys! (*Laughs, shakes her head.*) But ole Miss Gracie say she gonna gimme a present. My birthday eighteen hundred, she gonna set me free! This she told me two weeks before. Fifty-seven years' labor since I was five make me kinda feeble by then, reckon not much use to em anymore. But after all my life wantin free, now I tremble to think about it. Isaiah's letters stopped a few years back, he surely died. No husband, no children, how I gonna live? Few years before Miss Gracie finally decide I'm too old to run off, she leeme build myself a little house where the free blacks was, and I walk to her and Master Edgar's every day. So I got myself a roof, garden. Reckon I don't need much else, I get by.

And Miss Gracie say they gonna have a little sendin-off for me, dinner honorin my retirement! That touch me, and I think, Ain't been such a bad life. Nobody never whup me, nobody sell me. Passed down but not sold. Miss Gracie's children and grandchildren's grown then, I raised em all, and her son Ebenezer and his grown daughter and son come home to celebrate me, five at the table, six includin myself! But as Miss Gracie givin me the final instructions, somethin come to me. This occasion ain't gratitude to me. Only five place settins, them Hennesseys startin to see the direction things goin in the North, come a day soon *all* North slaves be free and they ain't a bit pleased on it, no, I ain't guest a honor. They all jus come to taste slave cookin one lass time, they brung me as a teary farewell to days gone past, *I'm* the one doin all the slavin for the dinner party!

Goin in n out kitchen to dinin room, I take note that this a special family meetin. That's why ain't no children, only grown peoples come, grown-people talk. I'm the only slave Miss Gracie and Master Edgar got left. But these Hennessey descendants all got their own slaves and Miss Gracie and Master Edgar brung em here so they all make plans bout sellin em down South, *now*, before Northern freedom come and too late. The shock of it upset me s' much, I'm in the cellar gettin the wine and drop a bottle, somethin I ain't never done before in fifty-seven years a slavin, praise God they's all arguin upstairs, never heard it. I stare at them little tiny pieces a glass. I sweep em up, bury em in the ground I figure, what else to do with em?

She stops, thinks. Smiles.

I give em all a good hearty meal. Turkey, yams. The buttered sparagus. Then the apple cobbler. My cobbler got a funny feel, crumbly feel. After I serve dessert I wait outside, the orchard. Then I hear it: the chokin, cryin, screamin, screamin my name, I hear it a little but most a the sound get lost in the wind. When all go quiet I walk back in the house, fine me some paper. I write a note. Bout how awful it all is, enda slavery. Bout how lass week, *lass* week, Miss Gracie freed Happy, her lass slave. Bout how Miss Gracie brought her slavery-lovin family together for this suicide pact, Miss Gracie's handwritin I'm expert on. I get caught they hang me, but I figure ole as I am, I be dead soon either way. Well the authorities take that note I made for true! Guess I make a pretty good writer! (*Laughs.*) So I go home, *my* home, here, to start my dyin. Cep now it two years later, two years free, steada gettin weaker, as time go by I'm feelin younger! Kep some a Miss Gracie's paper, them Hennesseys don't need it, bein dead. (*Chuckles.*) And every day I tend my garden, every day I write a little. The gal nex door tell me I oughta write a slave narrative, like all the people been doin nowadays. You be famous! I tell her I want no fame. But, looky here, I keep my story in this drawer, you can publish it after I die. Happy, you so humble, my neighbor says. (*Nods.*) That must be it. (*Laughs.*) That must be it! (*Laughs.*)

End.

The Blue of the Island

Évelyne Trouillot

Translated by Robert H. McCormick, Jr.[1]

[1] I wish to thank the following people for their insights and helpful suggestions. First and foremost, thanks to the author for repeated readings and invaluable suggestions. I would also like to thank Charles Ridouré, Professor Patrick Saveau, and the translator's former research assistant at Franklin College Switzerland, Lindsay Hodgman, for their various helpful contributions.

Évelyne Trouillot was born and resides in Port-au-Prince, Haiti. She has published four story collections: *La chambre interdite*, *Islande suivi de La mer entre lait et sang*, *Parlez-moi d'amour*, and *Je m'appelle Fridhomme*; two poetry collections in French, *Sans parapluie de retour* and *Par la fissure de mes mots*, and two in Creole, *Plidetwal* and *Yon kòd Gita*. Her first novel, *Rosalie l'infâme* (2003), received the Prix Soroptomist de la Romancière Francophone and has been followed by *L'Œil-Totem* (2006), *Le Mirador aux étoiles* (2007), *La mémoire aux abois* (recipient of the 2010 Prix Carbet de la Caraïbe et du Tout Monde), *Absences sans frontiers* (2013), *Le rond-point* (2015), and *Désirée Congo* (2020). Trouillot's play *Le Bleu de l'île* (*The Blue of the Island*) was awarded the Prix Beaumarchais by ETC Caraïbe, read at the Théatre du Rond-Point in Paris, and performed in Port-au-Prince at the 2009 Festival Quatre Chemins. Trouillot has published a book of children's stories, *L'île de Ti Jean* (2004), as well as an essay on the situation of children in Haiti, *Restituer l'enfance*. Her work has been translated into German, Italian, Portuguese, and Spanish. Her published English translations include two novels, nine short stories, and various poems.

Setting

This play recounts the journey of twelve Haitians fleeing to the Dominican Republic. It was inspired by the true story of Haitian migrants who were killed while attempting to cross the frontier in 2000 by Dominican guards.

Production History

Readings at Théâtre du Rond-Point in Paris, France, 2005; subsequent readings in Martinique and Guadeloupe.

Performed at Sainte Cecile Auditorium in Haiti, September 24–25, 2009

Theater Company	Dram'Art
Director	Rolando Etienne

Act One

Scene One

Ronald'*s house.*

The twelve passengers are reclining, on their knees or bent over under a blue tarpaulin. The background is composed of various sets, but, according to the dialogue, only one is illuminated at a time. The sets: **Ronald**'*s house, the streets of the village, the market, the streets of Port-au-Prince, a slum of Port-au-Prince, the interior of a bourgeois home, a corn field. From time to time, one hears a sigh, a passenger complaining, or a passenger pushing another, uttering a name, bursting out laughing. In the background there is the noise of a vehicle that is being driven wildly on a dirt road. From time to time, dust clouds rise. Dawn is breaking.*

Francine (*doing various household tasks*) I don't have any power. Some say women have all the power over their husbands, but I will always be weaker than misery . . . She can take you and lead you far away from me, and I won't be able to do anything about it.

Ronald (*approaches her, but cannot touch her—it is as if she were transparent*) Let me inhale the scent of your skin! Don't say anything because the silence is allowing me to stock up on you.

Francine Don't forget our first "Good mornings," with my warm posterior against your loins and the odor of coffee between our lips. Don't forget my skin!

Ronald Its radiance struck me from the very first.

Francine The first time, in the church courtyard, a few meters from the market behind the elementary school. On wet grass. My bundles of cloth made a rainbow-colored blanket for us.

Ronald (*an emotional smile*) We ruined a couple of them.

Francine (*dreamily*) At home, I told them I had sold them. I think that Carlo is the only one that suspected anything . . .

Ronald Why do you have to mention his name?

Francine I'm sorry. My brother will always be between us, stickier than poverty, more resistant than rust.

Ronald Francine, don't ruin my attempt to keep you in the deepest confines of my memory! Tell me about Roberto.

Francine Listen to the beat of his feet on the dirt road. He is running toward you, with open arms, his smile already at the corner of his eyes before it reaches his lips. He's throwing all the tenderness of his five years against your chest.

The child seems to throw himself against **Ronald**, *but, with* **Francine**, *there is no contact.*

Ronald His smile tickles my heart. It really makes you feel good! . . . I promised him protection and security, too. Bread on the table, mornings without the anguish of hunger, and a future with a well-delineated path. I know, a parent can't foresee everything and a child will find, in spite of everything, potholes along his way, puddles of water, and red lights from time to time. But I want him to have some idea about a possible path, not a series of traps so he won't even know where to put his feet.

In the background, the sound of a child laughing and of the pitter-patter of a child running.

Francine My father has been living in Miami for such a long time that I don't even remember his face. He's a human being without a form. If I look too closely, I don't recognize him anymore. He sent us greenbacks that we converted into stacks of gourdes, into food, into shoes, into little extras that made us the envy of others, but the absence of one's father weighs heavily.

Ronald I know that better than you. My father left us before I had even turned four. But, for my part, I don't plan on spending an eternity in Santo Domingo. You'll see, honey, I'll be back in five years, at the most, perhaps even sooner, if only to see the baby.

Francine She'll be born while you're gone.

Ronald She'll be born thinking of me because my love is already with her, in you. When she's born, remember the name I chose because she'll have almond-shaped eyes like my mother. My daughter, my Amandine-to-be . . .

Gestures as if putting his hands around the stomach of **Francine**.

Francine (*appearing to detach herself from* **Ronald**, *she shrugs her shoulders and turns away*) In September. While you're away.

Ronald Francine, don't criticize me, especially when I'm clinging to you in order to forget this truck that's taking me away from everyone I love. To forget the dusty dirty people I have been bouncing around with since dawn, under this blue material as artificial as our breathing, controlled, measured, so we don't make any noise. It's as if all our life, we were condemned to not making any noise.

He lies back down. He is sandwiched in between two women. He wriggles about trying to find a more comfortable position. The movements of the vehicle jostle the clandestine passengers. One hears protests, sobs, and then the voice of a woman.

Lorette Stop crying, Marie-Jeanne!

Another voice, the voice of a strong, ironic woman, responds.

Romaine Leave her alone, Lorette. Not everyone can plunge themselves, like you, into silent depression. It's the privilege of the rich, the unhinged.

Evariste Shut up! You are going to get us caught, you idiots.

Josaphat And you! The barber that didn't make it. You were so anxious to get in that truck this morning. Don't tell me you're already afraid.

Many Voices Shut up! Be quiet!

Ronald *speaks without getting up. He is plastered against* **Lorette**. *Little by little the set representing the streets of the village of Piment lights up.*

Ronald Oh, my dear Francine, how can I feel attracted to Lorette when your memory fills me with softness? Does what men have between their legs obey its own laws? And yet, Lorette is not my type. The coldness of her stare reminds me of the icy calm of a river after the rain, but the movement of her buttocks against my loins reaches deep inside me.

Lorette *frees herself from* **Ronald** *and gets up. She starts to speak monotonously as if she were recording her own voice.*

Lorette My dear sister, I am sending you this cassette from Port-au-Prince. I don't know when I will be able to return. I couldn't scrounge up enough money to pay for courses this semester. I lost the part-time job I had as a cook in a restaurant on the Grand-Rue. Under normal conditions, I would finish this year, but with all these delays, if I finish next year, I'll consider myself lucky. Send what you can. I didn't want to ask you, but I didn't have any choice. Say "Hi" to my friends in Piment. Kisses, your little sister, Lorette.

Lorette's sister *is energetically doing the wash. The scene takes place inside a dilapidated house.*

Lorette's sister (*in a tone that becomes more and more emotional as she speaks*) You finally returned after taking classes sporadically for three years. Three years for a program that usually takes eighteen months. If you knew what they cost me, your famous courses at the School of Home Economics, "A Woman Who Has Her Ten Fingers." But I had promised Mom to take care of you. Everyone made sacrifices for you.

Lorette You've repeated that so often, I could never forget it. I should give you back one hundred times over what you have given me. By the way, your sacrifice was not without ulterior motives.

Lorette's sister We were so proud, so happy when you opened your bakery, "The Happy Mouth." You made all sorts of pastries: the Mickey Mouses for kids' birthdays, elaborate constructions for baptisms and communions. On top of the wedding cakes, a married couple, all pink, was holding hands. You even made cakes for burials on which you'd write "May Your Soul Rest in Peace" in purple letters.

Lorette *gestures mechanically as if she were kneading dough and putting cakes in the oven.*

Lorette How much pastry can one sell in a small village like Piment? If one's relative in Miami doesn't promise to send off the money for the dress and new shoes, the first communion is postponed until next year and the order for the cake is cancelled. I did try. I borrowed money to start my business, bought the molds, the beaters and, of course, a special oven to perfect my cakes.

In the background one hears the sounds of "Happy Birthday"—with a strong Kreyòl accent—and then "Sak pa chante pap manje."[2]

Ronald (*sits up to speak*) For Mother's Day, Fifi and I ordered an amazing cake from "The Happy Mouth" bakery. With flowers all over and on top, Lorette had written in beautiful, rounded letters: "Happy birthday, dear Mother, from your two children." Man Etienne trembled when she read the inscription, and she thanked us from the depths of her endless grief. As Fifi says, Mom put a veil over her joy after the death of the twins, and she has never taken it off. We haven't purchased a cake for her since.

Lorette Anyway, no one buys pastry for anyone anymore. I can't make any more. I developed an aversion to the smell of melted butter and eggs, to everything that reminds me of the long years of study and solitude in the capital. I'm allergic to flour and to vanilla extract. My hands are covered with boils. At the crucial moment, they shake like the hands of an old woman. I break eggs in the wrong bowl, I mix, without wanting to, the egg whites with the yokes, mess up the cream, and frost the cake with my failures.

Lorette's sister (*wringing her wash angrily*) And now, you'd like me to pity you. I neglected my kids to support you in that rotten Port-au-Prince. I worried about you so much that I couldn't sleep. I sent you everything I possibly could. And then today, Mademoiselle decides that she can no longer stand the smell of flour. After all that schooling, you embarrass me by opening under an arbor, between two trees, a wretched fried-fish joint. You can't even make a go of that. And you are surprised that I am kicking you out of the house.

Lorette (*while lying back down*) From all my years at school, the only thing that lingers is the persistent smell of vanilla that I can't get rid of. Why stay here? I'd prefer to take my chances across the border. Nothing is holding me in this town where you all think I'm a strange beast.

Lorette's sister You intimidate people and you irritate them with your fits of depression. Do you think unfortunate people, the real unfortunate ones, have the luxury of feeling depressed? Hunger doesn't care about equivocation.

Lorette (*moves awqy from* **Ronald** *and the others and lies back down curling into a fetal position*) In the name of misery, you even deny my moods.

Ronald Your vanilla smell reminds me of Mom and the twins. Fifi and our youth. I don't want to think about it, though. My big little sister, she, too, is buried in this truck driven at breakneck speed. My sister pregnant with her second child. Oh, God! Please make sure that nothing happens to them! I couldn't bear it.

Back to **Ronald's** *house.*

Fifi *and* **Ronald**, *as children, are running around a tree singing "Yon ti pye lorye." They're playing hopscotch. One sees two smaller girls dressed identically.* **Ronald**'*s mother appears as well. All the children are surrounding her, and she is smiling as she gathers them around her.*

2 "Whoever doesn't sing doesn't eat."

Ronald Mom! You are so beautiful when you smile. I had forgotten the sound of your laugh. You have changed so much since the death of the twins. The epidemic of dysentery that ravaged the town almost got Fifi and me, too.

Man Etienne *stops playing with the kids and turns toward* **Ronald**.

Man Etienne But you survived. Please forgive me, and the Everlasting Lord knows I love you, but each time I see you, I think of my two babies. Scarcely six years old. I did everything to save them. First, the school's dispensary run by the Sisters. Then, old Rosa, famous for her herbal remedies and then the vodou priest, Zachary. Dear Lord, please forgive me if I have offended You, but, at that moment, I would have sold my soul to the devil to keep them. I have since repented. At the Church of God, I gave an account of my aberrations to the faithful.

She lowers her head in repentance; then, she sits down in front of an old sewing machine.

Ronald Mona died during the night. Monique, who we thought was healed, passed from life to death in the early morning. Her *marassa* lays claim to her. It's normal.

Man Etienne I sewed their last dresses. I wouldn't have let anyone else do it. I took out the material that I was saving for their seventh birthday, netting of pink cotton with soft green daisies. I put green lace on the collar and the cuffs.

Ronald Yes, we heard you all night on your old sewing machine. Until dawn.

Man Etienne All night long, I cut, pinned, and sewed. I didn't need to take their measurements. I knew each centimeter of their bodies, the length and thickness of each tiny limb, rigid forever.

Ronald In the morning, the dresses were waiting properly on a chair in the living room. You broke down after the funeral. And your grief has cut you off from us ever since.

In an outburst of anger, **Man Etienne** *throws a frame, with the picture of the father of her children, to the ground.*

Man Etienne Your father, who disappeared two weeks after their birth, didn't show up to bid them adieu. I could have forgiven all those women who started swaying their hips when they saw me as if to let me know that he had placed his snoopy hands on them, the stench of *clairin* that accompanied his return in the middle of the night. But he would not, until their death, acknowledge their existence. That was what hurt me the most. I know that my brother, Ferdinand, had informed him . . . Your uncle thought he was doing the right thing.

While **Ronald** *is speaking, the children mime a spanking. They try to avoid the blows of Uncle Ferdinand. A silhouette behind the tarpaulin.*

Ronald My Uncle Ferdinand has always wanted to do the right thing. He hit us, Fifi and me, on the back with his bull's skin riding crop. On the most sensitive part of the shoulder, where the hollow of the flesh reserves its softest, and most painful sensations, as well. In Dad's absence, he took it upon himself to punish us, and, each time he visited Cap-Haïtien, he inquired about our misdeeds. Only the twins escaped his correctives.

Without wanting to admit it, the big man was afraid of the supernatural powers of the *marassa*. He always invented a reason for not punishing them. Magnanimous and malicious, my two little sisters took the blame for our wrongdoings, and, even when Uncle Ferdinand suspected subterfuge, he didn't dare deal with them severely.

The four children are playing in the background. There is a joyful and happy atmosphere around a tree.

Man Etienne I was never afraid of my little angels. So soft and cuddly, they snuggled up together against me, giving me a double dose of tenderness.

Ronald You know, Mom, I loved them, too. The day of the funeral, you didn't realize that Uncle Ferdinand was carrying one of the caskets, or that he made me carry, with cousin Antoine's help, the other one. How could two small caskets made of planks of light-colored wood weigh so much? From the church all the way to the cemetery, I was waiting for Monique to ask me to let her out. For two nights, I thought I heard their tiny fists beating against the planks demanding light.

Man Etienne (*makes a gesture as if to touch the cheek of her son before she disappears*) I heard you crying the whole night, you and Fifi, but I couldn't break the shell of my own sorrow. It benumbed me until my death.

Ronald *lies back down. The passengers are becoming agitated. The truck is moving faster and faster. Grunts are heard. And kicks. The sun has risen.*

Lorette (*offstage*) "Move over, Ronald!"

Marie-Jeanne *is crying softly.*

Lorette (*offstage*) "Stop crying, Marie-Jeanne."

Madeleine We have plenty of reasons to cry; otherwise, we wouldn't be here.

Evariste In any case, that Dominican drives like an idiot. He will kill us before we even get to Dajabón.

Josaphat Ah. Now the coward begins to moan: "We're all going to die. We're all going to die." So, Evariste, death is not made for dogs.

Violetta It's not for nothing that they call the driver La Volanta.

Enzo Gabriel Shut up, shithead! You'll bring our little truck bad luck.

Romaine Bad luck! It hasn't waited for our words to show up. She's the one that led us under this blue shit where we can all kick the bucket.

Abruptly, a voice in Spanish demands silence.

Scene Two

Moans and whispers. Suddenly the crazy escapade of the truck stops with a screech of its tires, sending up clouds of dust. A formidable explosion arouses the benumbed passengers and gives them the right to yell. Immediately, prayers, cries, shouts, litanies and oaths come from all directions, criss-crossing and inundating the blue tarp with a grief-filled cacophony.

Jesus Mary Joseph
Anmwe[3]
We are all going to die
I want to return to my country
This driver wants to kill us
Help
God damn it

Mauricio Rafaël Perez (*shaking the tarp. The noise of a chassis being hit.*) Calm down! A tire burst. That's all. *Silencio*. You're crazy! *Silencio!*

Enzo Gabriel (*gets up, throws himself to the ground, and pounds the earth.*) *Mierda. Mierda.* Ma Carmencita is waiting for me. When are we going to arrive in Dajabón? The border guards brought me back here six months ago, and I have been trying to get back to my family for six months. What has happened to my wife and my three *hijos* without me.

Josaphat (*ironically*) That Haitian is crazy. He thinks he's Dominican because he speaks Spanish.

Romaine He did live there for ten years.

Madeleine Leave him alone, Josaphat. I know what it is to have a love on the other side of the border. I know the pain of waiting.

Madeleine gets up and relives the farewell scene with her husband, Charlot.

Madeleine (*with a serious voice*) My husband, my man, my Charlot, you are madly in love with me; yet, you are leaving. Your little hardware business is dying out. You can't stand dragging it behind you anymore like a piece of rotten flesh. Begging people to buy: five gourdes for the rusty lock, twenty gourdes for the screwdriver, but I will give it to you for fifteen. When you left, you didn't know that I was pregnant with your generous love.

She addresses the other passengers, all the inhabitants of Piment.

My man will come back, I'm telling you. He's not like those fathers who leave forever. Charlot will return and my two loves will meet without saying anything. I'll see them dancing under the blue of the sky for love scoffs at borders.

She is wandering about with her son, who is holding her hand. Knocking from door to door, they march up and down the streets of the town. The set of the streets of Piment.

The Child Have you seen my father?

[3] "Help!"

Madeleine Have you bumped into my man, the handsome Charlot, in Gurabo?

The Child In Santiago?

Madeleine In Santo Domingo?

The Child In Dajabón?

Madeleine (*talking to the* buscones *that are recognizable by their ridiculous guard apparel: boots, helmets, rifles, and big mustaches, swarthy complexion*) Are you the ones who have come to harass my Charlot, to take him to Santo Domingo? Tell me where he is! What have you done with him?

With little Leo, **Madeleine** *circles the village twice.*

Madeleine I'm afraid. If he were OK, Charlot would have written. So many disappearances in the *bateyes*, the hills, and the countryside. From the agricultural farms of Navarette, from Villa Gonzales to the intersection at Botancillo. Who has the courage to begin counting the dead that are still standing?

The child is looking in the direction of the border.

Madeleine No, we won't go there. I didn't have a child in order to give him, like mincemeat, to the Dominican guards. Come here, my son! I am going to tell you a story. When you see your father, you'll have so many things to tell him that the time will become longer so as to allow you to get to know each other well.

Suddenly, she lets out a horrible cry. Little Leo moves away from her slowly and then disappears.

Charlot, our son is gone. After a week's vigil, fever, then meningitis, took him away. I rushed him to Cap-Haïtien where the doctors, in spite of their efforts, couldn't save him. He is dead, that's it, and the sun doesn't rise anymore. The others tell me life is unjust: if it is beautiful, they are suspicious of it, if it is cruel, they curse it, for it never relents except when you break its neck. I wasn't expecting that blow. Madness is contacting me. Only you can keep it away.

She turns straight towards the east.

I'm coming toward you, Charlot. With tears in my eyes, I'm leaving behind my son's corpse, the son you never knew. In Piment's cemetery, in this village where you and I grew up, I have decided to leave him, and nevertheless to come and find you, Charlot my man, and bring you back to us. I left one dead in the West. Will I find another one in the East?

Ronald (*leaning on his elbows, he distances himself from* **Lorette**) Madeleine is so strong! A bleeding scratch with the harsh smell of wounds too fresh, a green vine, suddenly bent over, but standing up to misfortune. I feel so weak in her presence and so cowardly.

Madeleine (*lies back down after having spoken*) It's not courage that makes me act. I have no other choice than the truth. With what's left of my good angel, I charge straight at my grief. I am ready to welcome madness because it's the only thing that can save me.

Voice of Enzo Gabriel *Nada importa ahora. Nada.*

Jean-Marie (*with a cold, incisive voice*) If you don't shut that idiot up, I'm going to punch him in the face.

Romaine You think you can scare people, you well-dressed *zenglendo*.[4]

Ronald That Romaine! Nothing, nobody frightens her. A slip of hot-tempered energy difficult to keep in one place. I wonder how she manages to stay immobile and quiet for so long in this truck of grief.

While **Ronald** *stands up and speaks, the set of the streets of Port-au-Prince is slowly illuminated.*

Ronald I remember the first time we met. My first trip to the capital. I was still full of illusions when I got on the bus. After having completed my studies to become a mechanic, I was going to return to the village to set Man Etienne up in a decent house. Finished with rents and farms. Done with those end-of-the-month anxieties, that feeling of powerlessness when confronted with an arrogant, vulgar proprietor.

The background noise of a bus station with the voices of the passengers and the driver: "Move to the back! There's space for everyone. Hurry up if you want to get to Port-au-Prince before nightfall!"

Romaine *gets up and hails* **Ronald**.

Romaine (*mocking smile*) First time in the capital, little guy? Be careful! You're wearing your story on your face. You aren't, by chance, Man Etienne's boy, are you? She's the one who sewed my first communion dress. A good woman, your mother.

She sits down authoritatively near **Ronald** *on a bench and nestles up to him in a teasing, yet very sensual way.*

Romaine Are you timid, little guy? Stick with me and I will show you how to conduct yourself in this city full of traps. Port-au-Prince is a monstrous book with pages ripped out, missing parts, and gaping holes. Even if you know how to read, you can lose your bearings. The Rue des Fronts-Forts is a den of gangsters. On Grand-Rue, a car can cut you down in front of the police station, a thief can take your gourdes, and another your shoes and your pants, before a policeman arrives. Lalue,

4 *Zenglendo* is Kreyòl for murderer, robber, rapist or any other violent criminal. It was coined during the first waves of political terror and violent crime that followed the dissolution of the Tonton Macoutes. The word is derived from *les zenglens*, the secret police of the Haitian emperor Faustin Soulouque (1847–1858). The term connotes more than a criminal, but rather a thug with a political dimension. Many *zenglendos* are former Tonton Macoutes.

Avenue John Brown, for chauffeurs, guides, and foreigners, if you are in a hurry, don't go there on school days. In a procession of air-conditioned automobiles, the parents come to drop off their spoiled daughters at the Sisters' academy. Their long braids swing from left to right, and from right to left. The chauffeurs wait. The girls who are escorted on foot weave their way in and out quickly, proud to have been admitted to such an important school. Too bad if they are despised by the other children! Be careful in Jardine alley! It's the authorized place where, for decades, governments cut down rebellious young men with impunity.

Ronald I fell in love with her before we got to the capital. She put me up in her two-room apartment on the Rue des Casernes during the first three months and taught me how to satisfy a woman. I would have eaten at her feet, covered her with kisses, or written her long passionate letters on white paper without squares. But she didn't believe in it . . .

Romaine Love is good for young girls. I was a woman well before the arrival of my first period. At fifteen, life had already given me my identity card. I wasn't about to let myself be mistreated anymore. The talk-to-me-of-loves, the love-mes, the be-faithful-to-me-till-deaths, I arrange them nicely on a shelf and look at them from a distance. Ronald is not nasty. I could have become attached to him, but he would have held it against me later. He used to say that he liked my cheeky airs, but he paired up with the gentle and docile Francine. Just the opposite of me.

Ronald I still dream of her sassy legs, of their stranglehold around my loins. Oh, I love Francine. She's the mother of my son, Roberto, and of my Amandine-to-be, but Romaine, she's the complete woman, the woman who could have calmed all my extravagances and attacked my weaknesses, could have given me the desire to take life by the horns when she's too nasty and put my hands around her neck when she is cuddly. She didn't want me.

Romaine *and* **Ronald** *act out the gestures of love while they are speaking; then,* **Romaine** *separates herself from the young man.*

Romaine If you only knew, my man, how much I would have wanted to be able to love you, how my body will always remember your tenderness, how my head, on its own, sometimes turns toward a shoulder that resembles yours.

Ronald After making love, your voice was always clothed with depression in a destabilizing dispute between anger and pleasure. You would immediately jump out of bed to reestablish the distance, reaffirming your role as cynical, detached initiator. My gestures of tenderness, incomplete and unnoticed, were thrown back at me, at my loins and my heart.

Romaine *disengages herself despondently from* **Ronald**.

Ronald We had continued to see each other even after I moved to Delmas with the other mechanics. I would go to see you at least twice a week, sometimes more. Then, one day, you weren't at your apartment. No one knew where you went. I looked for you everywhere, like crazy, for months.

Romaine If you only knew how it hurt me to leave you. I would have loved, still today, to snuggle up against you and absorb your tenderness in large gulps, but I cannot be happy for too long. Bitterness always gets me right in the gut and reminds me that life and I have some scores to settle.

She casts a last sad glance in **Ronald***'s direction.*

Romaine (*with her eyes misty and a subtle gesture toward her abdomen*) You'll never know what I almost kept of yours.

Scene Three

In the distance, a rooster crows. Under the blue tarpaulin, gradually there is more light. The passengers slowly begin to move about. Some stretch; others yawn. His straw hat on his head, **Josaphat** *gets up. He makes exaggerated movements with the machete he took from his sack. His gestures and his facial expression reveal his rage. The others seem to move away from him and look at him in alarm. He spits his disgust and his disdain.*

Josaphat We let ourselves be disarmed without saying anything, and now we can only escape, leave our land, and run towards the unknown. We know well that in the East they will treat us like dogs, but we all go there. As for me, I assure you that I won't let them push me around.

Josaphat's wife (*strong and dressed in white, grabs the stick*[5] *with him, a miming revealing pride, pain, and grace. A cornfield in the background suggests work in the fields. Images of peasants, both male and female*) Then, why are you going, my man? I am already dead and buried. You avenged me quite nicely. You killed our neighbor's wife. You demonstrated your strength, but I am dead, and you can't do anything about that.

Josaphat Yes, you are dead. You, my wife with whom I wooed the earth from dawn until dusk. They killed you for a patch of land and some stolen plantains. Our son, the only one of our children to survive, to escape the thousands of diseases that kill the kids of poor people, they turned him into a zombie. You and I saw him, grey and spiritless, incapable of thinking, laughing, or loving. Like a plant that's going to rot soon. One only has to look at it to understand that no treatment will save it. And you want me to keep my machete cold and useless under the mattress.

Josaphat's wife (*with an angry movement of the stick*) But now, today, you have to leave the country to escape the police.

Josaphat (*dodges the stick deftly but almost excusing himself for it*) I'll return when things have calmed down. Watch over your tomb and that of our son. I will return.

[5] "Tirer le bâton" is a ritual of martial arts practiced in certain regions of Haiti. Peasants, for the most part, use the stick to play amongst themselves, to defend themselves and to attack when necessary. [The author]

Man can't hide behind the trees of his neighbor; their shadow won't recognize his silhouette and will denounce him sooner or later. I will return.

Josaphat's wife (*disappearing*) I'm going back to my tomb, Josaphat.

Josaphat I hope to see you some day, but not too soon. Don't come and disturb my sleep if you don't know how to get home.

The noise outside intensifies just like the bouncing of the vehicle. Several voices are heard.

Romaine He's going to crush our guts, that Volanta.

Madeleine He should let me get off if he's intending to have an accident!

Evariste Your mouths are full of bad luck, ladies. Shut up!

The voice of **Edgar** *is heard for the first time.*

Edgar Fifi, snuggle up closer against me. Put your stomach next to my loins to protect the child.

He gets up holding his wife's hand who, until then, had remained in the shadow. One sees the couple advancing, but, as they get closer to the front of the stage, the distance between them becomes greater. The set of the streets of the village is illuminated.

Fifi (*her voice starts as a murmur, then get progressively stronger like a torrent*) It's hard to bear the love you're overwhelming me with, Edgar. I decided to live my life with you like one chooses the straightest road, wearily, while one's heart turns toward mysterious paths and the fragrant underbrush. I carry my affection for you like a burden inside me since I can only show you the part of me that is smooth like a stone and clear like river water.

Edgar (*his look directed away from the young woman*) I always knew, even on the day of Christelle's birth, that your presence at my side was nothing but a reprieve from your real life, that you often escaped into thought and that I would never be able to rejoin you. Sometimes, you leave me your tenderness as security, in order to distance yourself from me even more. Behind that gaze, serene and calm, you hide reservoirs of seething and tumult. I would have given my life to dive in there with you, but your smile, so full of affection, became a wall to keep me at a distance.

A musical fanfare fills the stage. The hymn to the flag. The narrow streets of Cap-Haïtien appear in the background. **Fiji** *effectuates grandiose gestures with her arms and pretends to blow into a trumpet (the sounds of the fanfare are heard), and she marches in step. In the meantime,* **Edgar** *goes and sits down on a corner in the shade, and* **Ronald** *approaches his sister.*

Fifi Cap-Haïtien has always fascinated me. Do you remember, Ronald, when we saw it for the first time on Flag Day? I had never seen houses so high or streets so narrow. It seemed to me that it was a magical place where the sea slid in to rock the city to the rhythm of the water. Each house hid its mystery and whispered to passersby stories both gentle and ancient. After you left for the capital, I frequently returned to

Cap-Haïtien. Just because, for no specific reason. I didn't tell Mom, for she wouldn't have understood. It seemed to me that I was going adrift and that nothing made sense. As soon as the sewing orders gave me a bit of pocket money, I would take the bus and spend hours at the port. I avoided Uncle Ferdinand's street; otherwise, he would have told Mom. I took my notebook of fashion designs, but, after a while, I wasn't able to design clothes anyone would ever wear. In the end, I only knew how to sew, to complete the prototypes conceived by others. I learned, like Mom, to faithfully follow the patterns of the dog-eared catalogues clients brought me. At that time, I still had orders that were regular enough, but clients gradually became more and more scarce. What dressmaker can compete with the clothes coming from the United States? Even if they're used, they give off the smell of money, of societies overwhelmed with things to buy. They're much cheaper and always much better than the tailored clothes with their foul smell of the poor. One day, while watching the boats, I ripped up that notebook. It no longer served any purpose. Yes, I lied when I told you I had misplaced it.

Ronald We all need a space to hide our deepest sorrows. It's as if expressing them fully exposes them and makes them more real. I lied to you about something much worse, little sister.

Fiji *places a soft kiss on her brother's forehead.*

Fifi Oh, little brother, the guilt that grows in us is so inhibiting. I have never spoken to you about Gérard even though you have always been, besides being my brother, my best friend, the friend I chose around the family table, before the mischievous faces of the twins, over the sad silences of Mom and Dad's desertion. But how could I explain to you what I didn't dare contemplate deep inside myself? At that time, I even arranged it so that our paths never crossed. It's true that you have always known how to read me and to figure things out. But most of the time we all control that part of ourselves we present to others. Except when misfortune makes us different, and we become moans and wounds. That's what happened to Mom. The death of the twins shattered her world as a pious woman, a woman superbly impassive when confronting life's misfortunes. Generally, she would filter what got to us by only allowing to experience what she deemed capable of making us better and happier: moments of joy, satisfaction with work accomplished, her faith in God. She protected our emotions from all pain that was too raw. Until the death of the twins when her suffering, stubborn and brutal, reached us without any buoys for our infant hearts.

Ronald I can't be angry with her, sis. Now that I am a father and that Francine is expecting little Amandine-to-be in September, I wonder how Mom was able to survive the death of the twins.

Fifi I'm not mad at anybody. Somewhere inside the circle in which you are born, you choose your life. I wanted to choose mine, but I lied to myself so many times. I am so afraid of hurting others that I bruise myself. I thank Mom for having given us a happy childhood . . . until the death of the twins.

Ronald I would like to provide that same happy childhood for Roberto, for Amandine-to-be, for my goddaughter, your daughter, Christelle, and for the baby you are carrying inside you.

One hears the voices of children playing, the clickety-clack of **Man Etienne***'s machine. Then,* **Edgar** *gets up and takes* **Fifi***'s hand. They mimic a marriage procession.*

Ronald Mom was so happy to see you married. Me, too. Edgar is a good guy and he loves you madly. The only problem is his brother, Jean-Marie, with his desire to be the big black man, ready to sell his entire family for something with four-wheel drive and a gold watch.

Fifi You forgot the light-skinned wife with long hair who is supposed to symbolize his social success. We aren't very lucky with our brothers-in-law. Me with Jean-Marie and you with Carlo . . .

Ronald Don't talk to me about him! I know I'll have to mention his name one day before this lousy truck drives us to our death, but give me another reprieve. Tell me about Cap-Haïtien, about its mysteries and about your adventures. I get the feeling that that city is at the heart of the secrets living in your eyes.

Fifi Have you ever discovered someone else, besides yourself, in your thoughts and in your gestures? It's as if a stranger had taken possession of you and that, from a distance, you were following a film, the lead actor of which you'd recognized, without questioning the climax of the plot. When Gérard touched my arm that morning at the port, I sensed a stranger under my skin. I didn't know she was living there. I heard her wake up with her movements, both languorous and quivering. I felt the chills even in my toes. He was staring at me as if he were waiting for me at the peak of my desire. Without rushing. (*While talking,* **Fifi** *mimes the encounter with the man she's talking about. In the background, the sounds of a religious service can be heard. The thundering voice of the pastor and the enthusiastic responses of the believers, punctuated with curses.*) "Repent, the end of the world is near. You will be punished if you don't follow in the path of the Lord." We would meet near the cathedral. Sometimes, waiting for the appointed time, I would kneel to pray inside. It's true we're not Catholics, but, at that time, it didn't seem especially important to me. Sin had never seemed to me so inevitable and so easy to bear. On Sundays, I would accompany Mom to mass. Without fail, the pastor would return to adultery, fornication, all the filth the human body, inhabited by the devil, is capable of. Sometimes, men and women would come to bear witness to their depravation. I would bow my head to hide the pleasure that moistened my memories. I would close my eyes to escape into those sensations that defied any sort of absolution. The fervor of the hymns intoxicated me immoderately. That lasted three months and four days. Then, he left. A week later, I realized I was pregnant.

Ronald *goes closer to his sister. Together, they dance around in a circle. Then, they stop abruptly, and, putting his hand delicately on her abdomen,* **Ronald** *embraces the young woman.*

Ronald I never even suspected it. You could have talked to me about it, little sister.

Fifi At that time, you and Francine were trying to have your second child. How could I tell you that I was aborting a baby that you would have loved as your own? But I would never have been able to lie to Edgar and have him raise the child of another. The truth would have caused him too much pain.

In the silence that follows, the voice of **Edgar**, *still in the shadows, is heard.*

Edgar I suspected as much, but I would have never, at any price, broached the topic. And take the risk of losing you. Ask you to choose between that man that put sparks in your eyes and our love, too comfortable and placid to be a substitute for the attraction of fire.

Fifi (*turned deliberately toward* **Ronald**) At six weeks, it was easy to get rid of the flesh, but more than two years afterward, my abdomen still deplores its emptiness. Every hug that I give Christelle bears the nostalgia for that unknown baby. The one inside me now is Edgar's. It's also my way of giving my body the chance to heal its wound.

Ronald (*in an aside*) I feel even guiltier for the mistake I still can't talk to you about because the shame fills my mouth like wet sand. You took off with your child in your womb, your husband at your side. You left little Christelle with your mother-in-law, and perhaps I could have spared you all that. When you know the truth, little sister, will you be able to pardon me?

Fifi (*aside*) Ronald will never understand that nothing would have stopped me from leaving with Edgar. Not because, as the pastor of the Church of God says, a wife should accompany her husband.

She turns toward **Ronald**.

Fifi I wonder what would have become of us if Mom had followed Dad when he abandoned us. I saw our father again, you know. Something else that I haven't told you. One fine day in Port-au-Prince, without advance notice, he showed up while I was working in that swimming suit factory in the Industrial Park. God knows how he found me. I recognized his voice when he articulated my name. "Michelle," he said. He had never called me Fifi. He always had to distinguish himself from everyone else. For a second, I thought he had returned for good after all that time. The first thing that came to my mind was that Mom was wrong; *he* hadn't forgotten us. Then, seeing his eyes, I understood that he was only passing through. He was going to leave for the Northwest illegally, on a small wooden boat, with Miami as his final destination. Immediately the big act. The misty eyes and the hoarse voice. To bid me farewell. To ask me to pass along his greetings to you, his only son. To tell me how much he cried when he'd heard about the twins. *It's not necessary to say anything to Solange. She won't understand.* It took me a while to realize that he was referring to Mom. As if I were going to acknowledge to our mother that her husband had given a sign of life, after more than fifteen years, only to announce his definitive departure for Miami. I would have liked so much to not think of that long absence anymore. It's crazy how, sometimes, I want him to hold me in his arms and throw me up in the air like when I was a kid. I would tighten my lips and close my eyes, but I felt my heart expand so that I could take in the whole world, everything shaking behind the clouds. I would never cry, even when he tossed me way up and my head would turn, because I didn't want Mom to come and snatch me out of his arms.

Ronald Poor Mom. She mistrusted Dad's bursts of laughter. No doubt she saw them as bombs ready to hurt her children.

A loud noise is heard that makes all the passengers tremble. The screams start up again. The truck stops with an abrupt jerk that throws the passengers into one another.

Act Two

Scene One

After that noise, a deep silence sets in. The stage takes on a grey tint. Little by little, voices, like scarcely audible murmurs, are heard. "He hit a goat." "Are you sure? It made such a racket!" "What a nightmare!" The stage becomes progressively more and more grey. A fine powder seems to cover everything. A young woman bent over, dressed in grey with a scarf on her head, slowly comes forward. She is shaking her head from left and to right with an air of desperation. She's beating her chest and counting out loud. The set of the village is illuminated during the whole scene.

Marie-Jeanne One, two, three. I left my three small ones at home. One, two, three, Johnny, Charlemagne, and Gabriel. At this hour, each of them must have received three thrashings from their father. My mother-in-law will not be able to protect them. My man shows more tenderness for the shoes he makes than for our sons.

Suddenly she screams and rushes forward.

Let me off so I can find them!

Romaine *jumps up and encircles her with both arms.*

Romaine Calm down, Ma-Jeanne, calm down!

Marie-Jeanne Leave me alone, Romaine, with your female scent that goes to men's heads, young and old, well-behaved young men and registered criminals. Without prejudice. They all want to breathe it in. As for me, I have been a charcoal vendor for too long. Even if I wash myself with peach-scented Camay, the foul smell of grey smoke remains on my skin and in my hair. It gives my fingers the color of crushed ashes. My poor kids have inherited, how I don't know, the same smell and the same dust. Don't tell me that you didn't notice that their hair is always full of ashes, that their skin is always pale and their eyes grey. Their father whips them as soon as he sees them, by habit or by principle.

Romaine Their father beats them because it's easier to direct his anger towards the weakest. It's not your fault if used shoes coming from America the Beautiful have invaded the sidewalks.

Marie-Jeanne Almost no one orders shoes from him anymore. Formerly, at home, the smells of the leather and glue of a shoemaker dominated; they even surpassed that of charcoal. The kids played with the small bits of leather strips. Johnny, the oldest, had even acquired the habit of going to bed with a small piece of leather in his tiny hand. In his sleep, he brought it close to his cheeks and his nostrils quivered with happiness.

She gives a start as if someone were hitting her. She stumbles and protects her face with her hand and her arms. She gestures as if to position her children behind her back.

Romaine I know, we all know that he beats you, too, sometimes when he returns, irritable and execrable, from his workplace next to the old chapel with his pockets empty and his fists clenched.

The sounds of children crying, of moans, and of a loud voice, full of anger, their father is giving them a talking-to: "Band of imps, I am going to maim you. Your mother's the one that can put up with you." "Stop whining! It will be good for you to get used to beatings. Lift won't be giving you any presents."

Marie-Jeanne (*lowering her head*) I am ashamed of leaving my kids at his mercy, but I had to do something. I can't stay until Francis gets his clients back. The streets are filling with more and more used shoes everyday. There are shoes in every color, size, and style: leather pumps, plastic sandals shining like Christmas tree ornaments, lace-up combat boots for soldiers, shoes for sports, Adidas basketball shoes, and I don't know what else. When school started around September, there were no more orders for a good, solid pair of black shoes with laces. No, parents buy used shoes with strange names that come straight from the garbage dumps of Miami or New York.

Romaine Does that give him the right to beat you or your kids, Marie-Jeanne? You don't have to justify what you're doing.

Marie-Jeanne When I left my kids, I told them to be as quiet as possible. Not to contradict their father, not to cough, not to smile too often, or for too long a time. Everything exasperates him. He would have wanted me to stay and take care of the kids, but he didn't want to leave. He wanted his life as it was before, when the whole village got their shoes from him, when the orders were piling up in his shop, when he employed apprentices to help him. He didn't want me to leave just like he hadn't wanted me to become a charcoal merchant. As if I had had a choice!

Romaine Don't blame yourself. He doesn't have the right to transform you and your kids into punching bags to compensate for his frustrations as a permanently unemployed shoemaker.

Marie-Jeanne (*as if to convince herself, but tears are streaming from her eyes*) I'll come back as soon as I have come up with a bit of money, enough to change my place of residence. There are five of us in only one room. The dirty walls are falling in on top of me. I'll come back with enough money to open a small grocery store. I'll send money to the kids and to Francis's mother, so she can take care of them in the meantime.

Romaine If ever your man doesn't spend it on rum or on *petit trempé*.[6] We know he comes home drunk, that the little money he earns repairing tired soles is spent at the

6 A Kreyòl term for rum or *clairin* in which extracts of plants, bark, roots, or flowers are steeped for a long time.

tafia shop and that he returns to your place with foul breath, fists clenched ready to strike and a mouth full of insults. We know that.

Marie-Jeanne *suddenly straightens up*

Marie-Jeanne (*shouting, insultingly, at* **Romaine**) Yes, I know that you are all aware of the blows I take, the lickings my three sons and I get during the course of Francis's angry outbursts. One, two, three, a slap for the repair work that hasn't been picked up for three weeks, a blow for the new woman who has set up shop selling secondhand shoes just two blocks away, a clout for the feeling of powerlessness that reddens my eyes, three blows for my inability to awaken his desire. Yes, did you know that, for five years, he hasn't touched me except to hit me with his fists, with insults and with humiliations? We don't make love anymore because the word doesn't have any meaning anymore. You all know that my lowered eyes hide my scars, that my slow-moving steps conceal my desire to flee, but you don't say anything. You have never said anything.

One hears the passengers' voices, like murmurs, like whispered discussions: "Husband who beats his wife, that's a private matter." "Child scapegoats. Really, that's not normal!" "A blow, or a clout, never killed anyone." "Beating a woman is okay, but beating the mother of one's children is intolerable!" In the meantime, **Marie-Jeanne** *sinks down and regains her place huddled up on the floor. The voice of* **Evariste** *is heard as he moves forward.*

Evariste My father never raised his little finger against anyone. He spent his whole life respecting people, and what did he get for it? His only son, me, is forced to go to the neighboring republic. His barbershop didn't last.

Ronald (*remains sitting, cross-legged*) Oh! Stop your lamentations, Evariste! You continued in your father's footsteps because of your sense of duty or rather because of the simple reflex of ownership, but you have never understood anything about Mario's talent.

Evariste I should have let you pile up debts, cut your hair for love without demanding my due? Play you the records of Tino Rossi while I cut your hair? I didn't inherit my father's naivety.

Ronald Don't ruin my memories for me. I remember my first visit to Chez Mario. If I returned so frequently, it was because your father was more than a barber. All the men of the village appreciated the power of his steady hand. Their shoulders and necks would recount to Mario the disappointments of the day. The fights with the wife over those minute things that, on payday, make fingers move up the length of legs in a gesture full of sensuality, but that are transformed into get-out-of-heres when one's pockets are empty. The failure of the oldest son at school was so similar to yours that you pummel him and feel spiteful and alone at night. The humiliations swallowed because the children have to eat and go to school, the injustices in the face of which one feels powerless and that weigh on one's shoulders a bit more each day. Mario would move his hand and the cut hair would tell him the story and the struggle, each day more difficult than the last. Since the death of the old barber, Chez Mario is nothing but a cold salon where scissors, deft and disdainful, glide right over the depressions of others.

Evariste My father taught me technique. I know how to cut hair as well as him. Moreover, I'm sure that they'll recognize my talent in Santo Domingo. Don't forget that three years ago I did a seminar there on *hair design.* [*"Hair design" is pronounced with ostentation in English as opposed to the French of the original text of the rest of the play.*]

Ronald How could I forget it! You shape, you cut, and you arrange thinking about Santo Domingo. In a loud voice or a low voice, it doesn't matter. La *ciudad* oozes from all your pores and extends itself in monotonous melodies all around you.

Evariste Yes, my burning desire is to return. My two-month stay remains like a painful red rocket in my memory. I must have it plunge into my flesh one more time to be liberated from it.

Ronald You have chosen to forget the billy clubs, the raids, and the *bateyes*. You only think of la *cuidad*, the asphalt and the hotels, the public spaces and the avenues, the streetlights and the sidewalks. That scent of shaving cream, calming and purifying, that Mario carried with him is gone along with the old barber. You have not been able to create your own. Your stares, tormented and bitter, have been oriented toward the east for so long that you have forgotten where the sun sets.

Evariste You are all criticizing me. But who is with me in this truck of misfortune? Who, like me, met the *buscones* to negotiate the clandestine crossing? Who was tempted to go look for a better life on the eastern part of the island? I am not alone in this vehicle.

Ronald You are right. You are not alone. But do you know that with every kilometer covered, I feel my heart contract like a painful lump, an abscess condemned to cause pain because it can never burst?

Evariste As for me, I'm leaving this country like one closes a wound that reeks.

Ronald God damn it. Shut up, Evariste! I am going to tell you something without hoping you understand anything at all from it because I still don't understand it myself. In Port-au-Prince, I worked at the international airport for two months scouring the urinals and stalls, mopping the floors, and cleaning the sinks in the lounge for departing passengers. I envied those travelers, in a subdued way, without any ill-will, persuading myself that one day I would leave, too. *Don't worry be happy. Life is beautiful.* I had gleaned enough English words to give me the impression that I belonged to America the Beautiful.

While he is speaking, all the other passengers, their legs tucked under them, congregate around him in the form of a circle to listen to him.

Being so close to the planes, to the runway that took them so far away, reassured me about my destiny. One morning, while I was carefully picking up the scraps of paper left on the floor, I surprised a man furtively drying his eyes in front of the sink. I had heard stories: of false papers, of falsified passports, of pregnant women anxious to give birth, in the United States, to a little American. I had seen many passengers, but I had never seen a man cry. He was probably someone leaving behind his wife and children, an old mother or a beloved father. The eyes of the man met mine above the handle of the mop.

He assumes the voice of the man. He speaks like a recording.

"I have been waiting to leave for five years. I spent so much money for this visa; I invested everything in this departure. It's finally happening, today! In four hours' time, I will be in New York City. I have been dreaming about this for five years . . . No, don't congratulate me. I feel bad. I should be happy today, but I feel bad. You are a young man. One day perhaps you will understand. It's like a woman you're seeing, you aren't getting along with her, she makes all kinds of trouble for you. (*The song of TiCorn is heard in the background.*) So, you decide to break things off, you tell her, "It's finished between you and me." And you find yourself miserable, so miserable that you would like nothing else but to see her one more time, to run your hand through her hair, to caress her lips and to make love to her while crying. That's how I feel today! I know that I won't be able to come back. I have a simple tourist visa good for only three months. Unless the Americans force me back, I know that I will not return that fast. Maybe I will even die away from home with the whites, and that hurts. It hurts to have to leave under those conditions. Oh, deep down, I am happy. I will be able to help my mom and my family. Besides, I know that there are thousands of people who would love to be in my shoes, but . . . Do you know the song 'Ma prale'?[7]"

The song gets louder and louder.

Ronald (*continues simulating the man's voice full of repressed tears*) "I forgot the name of the singer. Listen to that song! It's sad and beautiful: distress without a solution, a wound without a cure. Listen to it if you have the time!"

The song continues in the background.

Ronald (*continues with his own voice, shaking himself as if he were coming back from a dream*) I used to consider the man a bit strange. Then, one day on Grand-Rue, a traveling music vendor found me that singer's, TiCorn's, song. "Ma prale." In the midst of the cacophonous chaos on Jean-Jacques Dessalines Boulevard, next to the garbage overflowing from sewers, face to face with men and women rushing toward an already overcrowded minibus, I made up my mind to the leave this country at all costs, felt my eyes sting nonetheless. At that moment, I thought I understood the bittersweet nostalgia of the song. Today, reclining under this blue tarp, getting hotter and hotter beneath the rising sun, I know I have only grazed misfortune. I'm leaving without knowing if I can really return. The mornings of fleeting dawn vanish under the demented tires of the truck, *Ma prale*, the stars of December, the stardust of dreams, are scattered over the black sky.

The others continue, like a long, sad suite, without completely drowning out the singer's voice.

Romaine The rustling of leaves decomposes in the humidity of a rainy morning.

Fifi *Ma prale* the feet that leap from rock to rock without being able to avoid the chilliness of the evening mist don't leave any traces.

7 *Je m'en vais.* The words and the music are by Jean-Claude Martineau, also known as Coralen. [The author]

Laurette The gentleness of the wind that rises at dawn to say "Good morning" to me before everyone else, I am leaving it forever.

Josaphat The generous smile of a stranger at the foot of the hill and his white teeth in the yellow flesh of a recently picked mango fade. *Ma prale.*

Madeleine I am staring, one last time, at the flowering *flamboyants*.

Ronald *Ma prale.* I salute you, my country. My love for you is too impossible to live. It always gets me in the gut.

Scene Two

The scene changes abruptly. The song stops. The quiet, nostalgic atmosphere is suddenly replaced by chaos, noise, and screams. The passengers return to their places. Curses in Spanish and Kreyol are heard. The truck speeds up and suddenly the countryside is flying by at an infernal rhythm resulting in dust flying every which way. The voice of **Enzo Gabriel** *rings out.*

Enzo Gabriel *Madre. Mis hijos y Carmencita.* I don't want to die without seeing them again. I left my wife and children there six months ago. After fifteen years on the eastern part of the island, I couldn't expect to be deported like that since I have my house there, livestock, fields where the ears of corn take on, in spite of everything, the color of modest bliss. That's where my Carmencita and our three sons, Pedro, Felipe and José Gonzalez are waiting for my return. Barely one year old, little José Gonzalez says "Papa" when I come back from the fields. Felipe is three years old and speaks Spanish like I never will, and Pedro, who just turned six, must start the *escuela* in September. I have to go there now to prepare for the beginning of the new school year. My Carmencita is probably worried about that, she, who, at any price, wants to have a daughter, a *muñeca* as beautiful as she is. We have already chosen the first name: Rose Isabela. If I can't see them again, may I die right now. *No importa. Nada importa ahora.*

Romaine As they say: "No news is good news." Those are words from the French dictionary for those who believe in the stories of alphabets and proverbs. Go tell that to Enzo, who has had no news from his wife or from his children. All those sent back home, they know that the absence of news often signifies disappearance in a refuge camp, an unexpected departure, and a separation without the formality of saying "Farewell." "No news is good news." For us, all news has a tendency of being bad. Those new means of communication, rapid and instantaneous, the Internet on the corner of the street, those cyber cafes with their cheap calls, serve only to communicate emergencies. From the funeral of the elderly grandmother to the first communion of the little sister, the news begging for some kind of financial support runs rampant across the waves, without worrying about good manners, and one hangs up either relieved or disappointed. (**Romaine** *takes on a weak, high-pitched voice.*)! Yes, dear aunt. Yes, I learned about September 11th. It's horrible. On television, they showed the towers falling. That's not good. Nothing happened to you, right? Thank God! We were afraid when we learned that those buildings were in Manhattan. For, what would become of us without you? Who else would send us that small money order for the ends of the month? We were afraid, you know! Luckily you were *off* that day! Those damned terrorists wanted to cause problems for us."

She shrugs her shoulders in order to say, for the last time, "No news is good news." She addresses the public.

Some of those sent home are incapable of taking back up the slice of life that had been attributed to them. Too many loose ends left unresolved. Information doesn't reach the frontier.

Madeleine Enzo, you would like to send information there, and I would like to receive some. We are at the opposite ends of a silence that kills.

Suddenly **Jean-Marie** *emits a derisive laugh and separates himself from the others with violent gestures.*

Jean-Marie You're pissing me off with your whining. You wanted to leave, and now you are acting like children who change their minds for no real reason.

Edgar *runs over to his younger brother and tries to pull him toward him, but* **Jean-Marie** *pushes* **Edgar** *away.*

Edgar Before we left, Mom asked me to keep a watchful eye on you.

Jean-Marie (*laughs sarcastically and stares at his brother with contempt*) You watch over me. You, who can't even control your own wife. You, who follow her like a well-trained dog.

Edgar (*suddenly furious and resolved to make his brother be quiet*) Don't talk about my wife! I forbid you. You hoodlum! Yes, Mom asked me to keep an eye on you. Oh, she knows full well that you have no need of me to settle the business of your gang. She knows how you'll get along without me organizing thefts, rapes, and burglaries of all sorts. Mom has tears in her eyes when she thinks about it.

Jean-Marie (*imitates mockingly the voice of his brother*) "Mom has tears in her eyes when she thinks about it." Then tell me how she feels when she sees you, her eldest son, become more faded every day. Only traces of you remain, like one of those texts that the French professor in sixth grade would put on the blackboard for us and that the math professor would erase with an air of mockery as soon as he arrived. You are erased, my brother, in Port-au-Prince where you try to play the mason and where you can only get wretched jobs, eliminated from the blackboard in the eyes of your wife who tolerates you and whom you can't satisfy, even in this pick-up truck where you crouch down playing the protective husband.

Edgar Shut up! You will never understand anything of love, of the need to inhale the same air as another, of the need to be the air that the other breathes. To become a simple leaf, a tiny speck of dust in order to cling to her flesh, so as to never be separated from her. You will never know that.

Jean-Marie No, I will never know it, and I am completely indifferent. I reject your timid lives, that dignity and honesty that stick to your skin and lead you, very soon, and poor like Job, to the grave. I tried to make Mom happy, to take courses in classrooms packed with students as disillusioned as me, and I only reaped failure after failure. Then, she insisted that I sign up for a computer course in Cap-Haïtien.

Edgar You abandoned it three months before the course ended. You came back with a gold ring and a wristwatch of dubious origins. Is that where you met your new friends with sinister-looking faces?

Jean-Marie My stay in Cap-Haïtien was good for quite a few good deals. But how would you know, you with that bad luck that weighs you down? Do you think that I was going to fight against life with the same weak arms that you and Mom chose, honest hard work that doesn't bring in anything. Collect diplomas from mediocre schools, slave away for a boss who's unfair, when so little suffices to obtain a big stack of green bills.

Edgar So little, you say, even though you scare Mom, my wife, and all our family. Everyone in the village knows about your dirty dealings and is afraid of you. They are ashamed of you and afraid.

Jean-Marie In any case, before reaching the age of twenty-five, in less than three years, I will have a motorized vehicle, a cell phone, and a beautiful wife. The vehicle will be a Jeep with four-wheel drive! With the rocky rundown roads in this country, a small car wouldn't do the trick. A cell phone, because only pathetic people don't have them now. How can anyone communicate otherwise? And a beautiful light-skinned woman with hair as long as possible. Not that artificial hair that is sold by the piece, but real hair. With money, you can pay for anything. I swore to myself that I'd own a house by my thirties. A big house with a swimming pool, a terrace, a garden and air-conditioning in every room. In Port-au-Prince, of course. Holing up in this forsaken place is out of the question!

Edgar I don't know why Mom wanted so much for you to come with us. As if Dominican earth had redemptive power or the power of expiation.

Jean-Marie Oh, I am not complaining. It's an opportunity for me to make some contacts on the other side of the island. As a result, I'll be able to organize my own dealings and not be dependent on others anymore.

Ronald (*gets up and pushes* **Jean-Marie** *forcefully*) Tell him to shut up or I'll break his neck. He disgusts me, this guy. Remember your poor mother, you thug. She's going to die of grief.

Jean-Marie Like yours!

Ronald *rushes over towards* **Jean-Marie** *and is restrained by* **Fifi**, *who grabs him around the waist.* **Edgar** *and* **Jean-Marie** *return into the shadow.*

Fifi Let him talk, little brother. He's a good-for-nothing. Twice, he brought drug dealers to the house. I told him straightaway never to do that again.

Ronald You should have told me about that. How can I protect you if you hide things from me?

Fifi It's clear you were born in January. Capricorns think they can control everything.

Ronald Oh, I know that hunger often imposes its choices and that we have to suppress our predilections and stifle our desires. I hate masonry; yet, I had to accept working at a construction site with Edgar at Cap-Haïtien. That's where I received the news of Man Etienne's death. You had sent a neighbor to tell us that Mom was getting worse. I understood immediately. "Getting worse" in our language had always meant death. "I'm kind of okay," Mom used to say as if she didn't dare stick her neck out by boldly declaring she was doing fine. Confronted with calamities, you have to be prudent so as to not overtly defy them, but cope with them, and pass alongside them until the end: "getting worse" in place of "dying." Three years after her death, I still can't think about her without the impression of jumping into the abyss without any wall where I could hang my appeal without response. Sometimes, the surprising wish still comes to me, so much more so in that it comes spontaneously and naturally, to run toward Man Etienne and tell her those sweet, stupid little anecdotes that make no sense except for the links they create between people. Midway, the idea freezes, and my acknowledgment of the absence destroys the flight. Mom is no longer there to listen. How does one get used to nothingness?

Fifi *becomes all playful speaking to* **Ronald**. *One senses that she wants to raise his morale.*

Fifi Think rather about the body shop you want to open upon your return from the neighboring Republic. Tell me once more what you plan to call it.

Ronald *looks at his sister, then smiles indulgently and begins with a mocking tone as if he were telling a fable. Gradually, his tone becomes more serious.*

Ronald I will open it near the square, and I will call it Garage Etienne and Company. Francine advised me to add "It's in God's Hands" to attract divine benediction. Since one should have all the forms of chance on one's side, I'm not saying "No." It will be painted a beautiful green, and I'll write the letters in white in remembrance of the twins, like the dresses they wore the day of their funeral. Yes, I'll add "It's in God's Hands" to please Francine and our Good Lord.

He stops, pensive.

However, boss Wilfrid's hardware store was called Hardware Store God is Great, and every client who entered had to listen to boss Wilfrid preach the words of the Lord: "Repent before the Last Judgment. Listen to the Word of the Gospel before it is too late, my brothers." When the hardware store caught fire one night last July, we all helped Wilfrid put out the blaze, but not much, except the crude masonry, remained. All the merchandise was reduced to twisted fragments of rubber and red-hot metal, a sinister entwinement of cables and charred electric wires. "God is great," muttered boss Wilfrid, but we saw clearly that he said it by habit, with a new tinge of gloom in his eyes.

Fifi (Garage Etienne and Company) It's in God's Hands since Francine wants it that way. It sounds good in any case. Like something important and serious. You'll bring it off, you'll see.

Ronald My dream was just within my reach, and that Carlo ruined everything. I have to resign myself to mentioning his name, sis. He did me a lot of harm. I suffer from not being able to trust like I could before. I see his smile again when we were playing dominos. I see the emotion in his eyes upon hearing Roberto's first words. I feel the crude warmth of his hand against mine holding the crank for an exceedingly difficult repair job. And then, he renounced everything. He took everything, my trust and our business, sold our tools, the spare parts, to leave for Miami. He left me with the debts and the shame of a person that has been duped.

He dries his eyes furtively before continuing.

I had always known that Carlo wanted to leave for Miami, but I can't figure out exactly when the scale turned against me, against my family, and my friendship.

In an aside, he adds:

I, too, fell. I betrayed my family, my mother's dead body, and the trust of my sister who had grown up with me. I also betrayed my Francine whom I had sworn to protect. Do I have the right to judge?

He continues for **Fifi**.

Ronald Francine doesn't mention the name of her brother anymore, but it surges up between us like an acidic belch. Like a leak in the heart, the drop-by-drop dripping, terrible and throbbing, of a disintegrating friendship.

Fifi You'll rebuild your garage. I'm sure.

Ronald I have to. The important thing is getting started. That's worth the sacrifices. Like the one of staring, for hours on end, at that dirty blue tarp that makes you want to punch holes in it in order to rediscover the true blue of the sky. The people seem different, for sure, the language is unknown, but it's the same blue, the same sky. The blue of the island.

Fifi (*continues along the same lines as her brother and with the same tone, both sad and full of light at the same time*) Not that dirty, anemic indigo blue soaked too long in water and bleached in an irregular manner, but the real blue, the one that makes my heart skip. In the morning. Without reason. In a few short hours, it will be over. We will be able to see it. Rub our eyes in the light of day. See the blue of the island again.

Scene Three

Violetta*'s voice rises like a whip.*

Violetta I knew this Daihatsu was going to bring us misfortune, with its pooh-yellow color, definitely not a color one can trust, a color of treachery, raw and hard. Don't pretend that you don't see me, Ronald! You know I'm here. Don't ignore me!

She is still not visible. One only hears her voice. **Ronald** *doesn't turn in her direction.*

Ronald Memory is like a balloon that soars: one cannot always control its trajectory. Sometimes, it makes three-dimensional rainbows re-emerge, but when you would like to linger there, it gets stuck between two tree branches, and you find yourself a prisoner of your fears. Take pity on me, Violetta. Don't clog my memory. Your imitation Opium perfume is already irritating my nostrils.

Violetta *gets up slowly. She moves forward with a sensuality filled with aggression, both vulgar and pathetic at the same time.* **Ronald** *turns towards her and addresses her.*

Ronald How could I have slept with you even if it was only that one single time? So many things sparkle on you like false glimmers and then disintegrate as soon as one touches them. Your long reddish hair, your eyelashes outrageously curved, even your name transformed from Viergéla to Violetta.

Violetta You think I was going to find a good position as a governess in the city carrying on my back all the debris of this dying village? The name of a coarse peasant woman, a dubious primary school diploma from the national school of the village. One has to distance oneself as much as possible from everything that resembles too much the misery you left behind; otherwise, it clings to your steps. I learned how to please ladies of high society in order to adroitly worm out of them old shoes, used handbags, clothes put aside. It's true that the patrons come sometimes to pull up my skirt, panting like pigs being skinned, but one needs to know when to push them away and when it's profitable to consent. The supplementary dollars are worth a few tedious moments to guarantee that madame will not informed of monsieur's proclivities.

Ronald And yet, accused of theft and taken to court by your former patroness, you had to take refuge here in this village you detest so much. In the end, your friendship with a police officer wasn't that useful to you. Your patron forgot everything and supported the accusations of his wife. The couple banded together against you and so did the judiciary system. You spent five long months in prison. Upon your liberation, the village, accustomed to the desertion of its children, welcomed you accommodatingly back and allowed you to set up your little business of low-priced beauty products even though your facial expression and your gestures indicated coolly, to the whole community, that you didn't give a shit about them.

Violetta So? I wasn't going to play the role of the repentant, full of remorse for a life of sin. Yes, I have slept with many men who have given me something to eat, something to keep me from kicking the bucket, a roof over my head. I wasn't going to wait, whining, until life passed me by. I made the first move so that I wouldn't find myself out on a limb.

Ronald But ultimately, you lost because now you are a prisoner, trapped in this truck with us.

Violetta I'll try my luck elsewhere. Without a bad conscience. I couldn't give a damn about the blue of your island. It has never helped me out, never adorned my dreams with light. I am not like you, full of remorse, regret, and hope. That's the reason I followed you that day. You seemed so desperate that I immediately wanted you. That's my sadistic side.

Ronald Shut up, if you don't mind. Do you have to make me relive that moment of weakness? That was the infamous day of Carlo's treason. I fled my house, unable to sustain Francine's gaze, full of consternation and shame. I had been walking haphazardly for a long time, pacing up and down muddy paths without paying much attention, mechanically acknowledging the locations of the stumps of trees uprooted by cyclones or by men's arms.

Violetta (*retrospectively*) Actually, I had felt that desire since that distant day when, for the first time, I saw you approach Francine.

Ronald You caught up with me near the old cemetery. And you spewed your spite over me in grandiose, vindictive deeds. Telling me your story without worrying about how it might affect me.

Violetta Finally, having had enough, you threw me on the grass, and you entered me sobbing like a baby.

Ronald Everything is coming back to me now. The wild image of our two bodies. Our feet intertwined and our cries. My God! Never would I have thought that I could, in that way, have lost myself three times in a row on the half-scorched grass of that old cemetery.

Violetta (*with a mocking smile while rolling her hips in front of* **Ronald**) You wanted to flee afterwards without even zipping up your pants. You were mumbling awkward excuses. Uttering the name of Francine, of Fifi, and of your mother. Your feelings of guilt were pouring out all over.

Ronald Don't make fun of me, Violetta.

Violetta I made you discover all the violence inside of you. Through me, you were hammering Francine, Carlo's sister, as guilty as her brother in your eyes. You were hitting her by sleeping with me because you hadn't dared to tell her that the sight of her reminded you incessantly of Carlo.

Ronald Francine figured it out. Since Carlo's betrayal, I often surprise her staring at me. She knows that if I am leaving today for Santo Domingo, the shadow of Carlo weighs heavily on my decision.

Violetta (*an aside and with the weary voice of an old woman that contrasts with the movements and the clothes of a young woman of an active, vulgar sexuality*) Poor Ronald! You also want me to pity you although, all my life, I have never stopped fighting against bad luck so that she forgets me. My twenty-five years seem so arduous to me today. The only thing I have left to keep me from crying is the strength to be hard and spiteful.

She sinks down and regains her place. Caressing his stomach, **Fifi** *rejoins her brother.*

Fifi The baby moved for the first time. He chose his moment well. Was it to ask me which wasp's nest I led us into? Little brother, I'm afraid.

Ronald *takes his sister's hand and both turn toward the set representing the village.* **Fifi** *continues in a tone marked by gentleness and nostalgia.*

Fifi Fear of dying without having spoken to you as I often do deep inside myself. It's as if we were on the same side of the mirror, staring into one another's eyes and at the mirror. Unique yet together. Like the twins. Do you remember how one would defend the other in every situation? Little brother, I know what happened when Mom died, I know that you feel guilty, but Mom wouldn't have been mad at you. We all have our secrets mixed up with our feelings of guilt cutting us off from the rest of the world, keeping us in solitude. I am afraid to leave without saying "Farewell." Put simply, I am afraid to die.

Both speak without looking at each other. They hold each other's hand and look elsewhere. It's as if the presence of the other served solely as a pretext to speech.

Ronald I would like to have the courage to confess my mistake to you. I am so ashamed of what I did that day while you were waiting for me next to Mom's corpse at the funeral parlor.

All of a sudden, the shots of firearms are heard. The voice of **Mauricio Rafaël Perez** *orders the driver to slow down.* **La Volanta** *is indifferent to the injunctions of the organizer and to the ricocheting bullets around the truck. Nothing seems capable of stopping the Daihatsu. Its swerves becoming more and more dangerous, throwing passengers from one end of the small truck to the other. The tarp becomes taut, then loose, like a blue monster breathing spasmodically. Throughout this scene, the different sets follow one another, illuminating each other in a disorderly manner, as if the thoughts of the passengers were intermingled.*

Romaine (*shouts*) Are we going to accept dying like dogs?

A second-long silence demonstrates the impact of her words on both men and women. Then the babble of the unleashed fears picks up all the more and the insults, the prayers and the litanies clash.

Jean-Marie (*in a grating voice*) Shut up, bitch!

Josaphat (*brandishing his machete energetically*) As for me, they won't take me alive. If I have to, I'll kill some of them before I die.

Ronald *notices, with fear, the ferocious movements of the man who, with a machete suddenly surging out of his tool bag, seems to defy death. As much as possible, the passengers nearest him move away. Jostled together and moaning, men and women become entangled with one other.* **Ronald***'s attention is attracted by the person sobbing right next to him.* **Evariste** *howls and beats his chest with his clenched fists.*

The body of **Edgar** *is bent over as if he were stumbling, and* **Ronald** *approaches him. With a firm, hard grip,* **Edgar** *pulls* **Ronald** *toward him.*

Edgar If I don't get out of here alive, take care of your sister and your goddaughter.

His voice makes **Ronald** *tremble, and he would like to tell* **Edgar** *to shut up, God damn it, to stop saying stupid things. But around them, the blue inferno doesn't allow for any more tricks. He responds in the same broken voice.*

Ronald For Roberto and Francine, I am counting on you.

One hears **Fifi** *'s voice, which gradually fades. Around her, the commotion continues, but in silence. People are moving, hanging around, trying to escape. Arms and legs are convulsing, but only* **Fifi** *'s voice can be heard. When she finishes speaking, her inanimate body will be seen near* **Edgar** *'s.*

Fifi Mom often said that one shouldn't be afraid of dying, that a Christian is always prepared to encounter his God! I believe I am a good Christian, but I don't feel ready. I would like to stay on Earth a little bit longer. Up till now, it seems I have been playing hopscotch with life and that I have never reached Paradise. I've encountered so many obstacles along the way. The devastating sadness of Mom, who forbade all laughing and outbursts of joy, and the poverty that encloses our ardent impulses in a grey, rectangular space. The village, too, where all eyes confine you to the life that they think is right for you, as if they were keeping themselves ready to take it back from you if you ever decided to change directions and to not appear before them. Life. I haven't known it. I caught sight of it once in Cap-Haïtien, between two episodes that I haven't shared with anyone. Like an appetizer of the happiness that I could never have! Christian or not, I could have lived a little longer.

The terrible, deafening noise suddenly returns. Vehicles brake violently. The blue tarpaulin twitches and contorts, then caves in and disappears. The violent noises of doors and the echo of shoes on the ground precede detonations of firearms nearby. Fearful screams are heard. Arms and legs are shaking violently. **Ronald** *gets halfway up and looks around panic-stricken. Like the others, he attempts to protect himself from the gunshots. He doesn't know yet who is shooting, but the necessity of protecting himself and finding* **Fifi** *render him suddenly calm and lucid.*

Romaine (*snuggles up against* **Ronald** *and whispers*) Those Dominican military pigs want to kill us. We have to escape. Come with me.

The young woman's expression takes on a newly acquired emotion. **Ronald** *looks around, searching for his sister he has yet to see. His eyes stop at the corpse of* **Evariste**, *whose head is strangely contorted.* **Ronald** *pushes* **Romaine**, *who is staring at him regretfully, gently out of the way before venturing forth. Without worrying about the ricocheting bullets, the noise, or the screams,* **Ronald** *advances haphazardly.*

Ronald Fifi, where are you?

He steps over **Marie-Jeanne**, *who is moaning and examining her injured leg.* **Josaphat** *'s big hand knocks him off balance. Traces of blood stain the old peasant's pea coat. He is staggering a bit, but his machete remains vibrating against him. Bent over to avoid the bullets,* **Josaphat** *dodges in and out without worrying about the men and women kneeling, sprawled on the ground or, like him, trying to escape.*

Josaphat Let me pass, I'm telling you.

His machete in hand, **Josaphat** *runs off into the distance.* **Ronald** *hesitates an instant and reels before the cadaver of* **Madeleine**. *He bends over and closes her eyes, which had remained open. Dominican soldiers seize* **Jean-Marie** *and* **Lorette**, *who defend themselves with their hands and feet, but in vain. They are pushed off unceremoniously.*

Ronald *stops abruptly, for he has just spotted the bodies of his sister and his brother-in-law. The two bodies are stretched out on the ground.* **Edgar** *has his arm placed on his wife's hip.* **Ronald** *kneels down next to* **Fifi***'s corpse and takes her hand. He runs his fingers over her skin as if he wants to wake her up, but she doesn't move. Her palm is still moist and tender. He places his forehead on top of her rounded belly.*

Ronald (*raising his eyes toward the sky*) Oh, mercy! Oh! Mom, mother, m . . .

After having cried, he is silent for an instant. Then, with great tenderness, he places **Fifi***'s head on his knees. His voice becomes like a murmur, like someone confiding a secret.*

Ronald I had planned on returning the money to you. Without fail. The first few pesos earned in the East, I would have sent them to you and explained what happened. You would have understood. For sure. When Man Etienne died, I had found 10,509 new gourdes in her box. You know the one in which Mom kept the family papers wrapped in rubber bands. Ten thousand five hundred and nine new gourdes, (*He enunciates distinctly the numbers in a tone of amazement.*) a windfall, a miracle, as if upon dying, Mom had made known her wish to see me accomplish my dream, the body shop project with Carlo that had been dragging on lamentably for such a long time for lack of money. I wasn't expecting it, I can assure you. I was numb with grief. I opened the box for no reason, as if to bid farewell to Mom by touching the most secret part of her life, a life with almost invisible perforations. A piece of material with a floral pattern from the twins' last dress, a black and white photo of her father and mother, our school report cards. Then, between the certificates of birth and death, I came across an envelope full of wads of bills. My only excuse remains that I hadn't planned on doing what I did. I couldn't get over seeing all that neatly arranged money. I counted it several times before taking it.

Around **Ronald***, the movements continue. The soldiers conduct the prisoners* (**Enzo Gabriel**, **Marie-Jeanne**, **Lorette**, **Jean-Marie**, *and the organizer,* **Rafaël**)*, who bend down over the cadavers: the driver* **La Volanta**, **Evariste**, **Fifi**, **Edgar**, **Madeleine**. *Isolated, the young man remains alone with his sister's lifeless body.*

Ronald I didn't tell you anything. I let you take charge of the funeral. No one was surprised at that. After all, you were the oldest and you inherited Mom's sewing machine. At the last minute, as if in spite of myself, I gave you two thousand gourdes. You took care of everything: the funeral, the wake, your clothes for mourning. After a long while, I found out that you had hocked all of your few possessions at the pawn shop in the neighboring village: the dishes still in boxes, and the new sheets, a bedspread, that Violetta had sold to you a few weeks before, still in its plastic cover. An immense bedspread, shiny and pink, with large red flowers that we had all admired without daring to touch.

Fifi (*her voice is heard, monotonous and dead*) The same with the beautiful white tablecloth embroidered by Man Etienne herself that always adorned the table on festive occasions before being wrapped back up in its covering of transparent plastic and relegated to the back of the closet. I got the tablecloth back, but I have never been able to get back the bedspread. Too many emergencies, one after the other!

Ronald I had promised myself that I would buy you a bigger and more beautiful one in Santo Domingo. A blue one with large white flowers. Blue, that's your favorite color.

Fifi (*still lying down*) It's only a piece of material like any other. I knew you had taken the money because Man Etienne had spoken to me about it months before her death. She had made me promise to use it for her funeral; in no way, did she want her burial to be a burden for us. I didn't say anything because you needed it to get on your feet. That's what dreams are for, that burning sensation that gives us wings, that makes us forget we are mortal. We all had our dreams, and I would have wanted so much that at least one of us could see a part of theirs realized.

From then on, the echoes of the voices of children are heard in the background. One sees the silhouettes of children playing, jumping rope and laughing. Gradually, the voices become louder and the silhouettes more distinct.

Ronald I was well punished. I don't have anything anymore. That bastard Carlo sullied my dream with his stain. I feel even guiltier. I would have wanted to give you so many things. The blue bedspread . . .

Fifi It doesn't matter if it's blue or pink! It will never be anything other than a makeshift substitute for real happiness.

Ronald I didn't have the right to deny you those things to satisfy my own needs. I would have given anything to keep you with us a bit longer.

Fifi On which side of the island?

Ronald A part of me will stay here with you. With you, with Edgar and your baby who moved today for the first and only time. A part of me will stay here with you forever.

At this point, the song hummed by the children can be distinguished. It is a popular Haitian song, "Haïti chérie Mwen konnen yon bèl ti peyi . . ."[8]

Fifi Promise me you won't forget the blue of the island. Promise me to come back from the other side of the island and take care of my daughter and your son. And of your Amandine-to-be . . .

Ronald So many things to do. It seems to me that we wanted to find a solution and we forgot that the blue sky doesn't change crossing the border.

Fifi Take everything with you that might help: Madeleine's dignity, Romaine's zest, Edgar's quiet determination, and my baby's innocence.

Ronald I am taking with me that part of our childhood that makes me invincible. Your tenderness and your drive toward happiness. I will need them on the other side of the island

8 "Dear Haiti I know a beautiful small country . . ."

Fifi Take care of Amandine-to-be . . .

Ronald In September, on our side of the island.

Fifi So many children to be born under the blue of the island.

Ronald So many things to do.

One last time, in spite of the pokes pounding his ribs, **Ronald** *stares at the corpses of his brother-in-law and his sister. One sees him stand up and salute the dead. Then, he heads off towards the West. Gradually, as he advances, the stage becomes blue, more and more blue, an almost unbearable blue. The dead rise and accompany him. Finally, the silhouettes of the children become enormous and invade the back of the stage. They, too, head off towards the West.*

Nine Lives

Zodwa Nyoni

Zodwa Nyoni is a Zimbabwean-born playwright, poet, screenwriter, and director. She has toured her poetry nationally and internationally with performances at the British Museum, Venezuelan Embassy, Latitude Festival in England, Ekhaya Multi-Arts Centre in South Africa, National Gallery Bulawayo in Zimbabwe, Nuyorican Poets Café in New York, and Historic Hampton House in Florida. She won the Channel 4 Playwrights' Scheme with her play *Boi Boi Is Dead* (2015) and was a finalist for the Susan Smith Blackburn Prize 2014/15. Her other theatre credits include *Nine Lives* (2014, Leeds Playhouse/Òran Mór), *Phone Home* (2016, Upstart Theatre), *Ode to Leeds* (2017, Leeds Playhouse), *Borderline* (2017, Young Vic), and *Duty* (2018, Paines Plough). Her radio credits include *Love Again* (2016, BBC Radio 3), *A Khoisan Woman* (2019, Drama on 3), and *Conversations on a Bench: Leeds* (2020, BBC Radio 4). Nyoni's short films are *Mahogany* (2018, National Trust and 24 Design Ltd) and *Notes on Being a Lady* (2019, New Creatives/BBC Arts). She is currently in production with her third short film, *The Ancestors* (BBC Films/BFI Film Hub North). Nyoni is a guest lecturer in playmaking at the University of Manchester in England.

Setting

Ishmael has fled Zimbabwe to seek sanctuary in the UK where "there are queens [and] rainbow flags." Humor and humanity are woven together to tell the personal story behind the headlines of political asylum.

Production History

Produced at Òran Mór in Glasgow, United Kingdom on May 19, 2014.

Cast and Crew

Ishmael	Lladel Bryant
Director	Alex Chisholm
Composer	Jonathan Girling
Mbira (soundtrack)	Kudaushe Matimba
Sound Designer	Ed Clarke
Stage Manager	Emaleigh Pightling
Design Associate	Emma Williams
Producer	Milan Govedarica

Characters

Ishmael, *twenties, Zimbabwean asylum seeker.*
Cyrus, *fifties, Iranian refugee living in a shared flat with Ishmael.*
Bex, *late teen, born and raised in Leeds. Single mother to Bailey.*
Mother, *sixties, Ishmael's mother.*
Ricky, *mid-teen, Leeds lad with a pitbull called Razor.*
Miss Marie Monroe, *sixties, nightclub drag queen.*
Cath and Brian, *both fifties, married café owners in Armley.*
David, *forties, Ishmael's lover (voice only).*

Scene One

Spotlight. **Ishmael** *enters carrying a suitcase and wearing a sports jacket, jeans, t-shirt, and trainers. He places the suitcase down. This is his new accommodation. A flat in Armley, Leeds. He takes in his new surroundings. A soundscape of an angry mob is heard. It takes Ishmael back to the incident which led him to flee Zimbabwe. He starts running as if being chased. The sound intensifies. His pace quickens. He tires out and tries to catch his breath. Soundscape ends. Beat. Mbira music is heard.*

Ishmael (*speaks in a Zimbabwean accent*)
Some of us were running.
Some of us were fleeing.
Some of us know wars that will never cease.
Some of us were persecuted.
Some of us were stripped and beaten.
Some of us have scars that will never heal.
Some of us were broken.
Some of us were thrown into prisons.
Some of us were sent back.
Some of us were dispersed.
Some of us were alone.
Some of us felt invisible.
Some of us felt time slow in our wait.

Music ends. He takes off his jacket and puts it aside.

Burnstall Heights, flat 46, twelve floors up, third door on the left. Temporary accommodation, not home. This is Section 95, not leave to remain. This is where you will wait. This is all that you'll get.

There's a stranger in my house, or I think that I am the stranger in his house. This conveyor belt of a system moves us from place to place. You'll never know who you'll find here. You'll never know how long they have been here, in these concrete cocoons where we live in limbo. We would be perfect metaphors for change if we didn't emerge so scarred. Something happens to us in our metamorphosis. We shed the past to acquire new inflictions. It is traumatic to be an immigrant.

Beat.

In the first month I start to feel the walls closing in. During the day, I fear sleeping in case the laws will change overnight and this country will vomit me out. The Home Office doesn't tell you how long the wait will last. It feels like there is no point in keeping time. I avoid the clock so much the hands go limp. (*He puts his jacket back on.*) To keep my mind busy, I start taking walks.

Traffic and chatter are heard.

On Town Street, I see men laughing with full pint glasses at 11 a.m. in Malts Pub. St Bartholomew's stained-glass windows. Pink tracksuits, red tracksuits, black tracksuits. Young girls on phones, babies on hips and pacifiers in mouths. Mike's Carpets boarded up. Fridges dumped in streets. Pit bulls on leashes. Grandmothers with little broaches pinned to their coats. Pop music blaring out from car speakers. Fish and chip shops. Tattoo shops. Charity shops. Betting shops. Turkish shops. Russian shops. Tower blocks. Back-to-back houses. British Heart Foundation. Cancer Research. St George's Crypt. (*He notices engravings on the pavement.*) Barbara Taylor Bradford written in stone. (*Takes a step.*) Alan Bennett written in stone. (*The sound of a bus rushing past.*) Number 16 bus to Stanningley Road . Prison walls. Greggs. Body builder. Two for ones. Call to prayers. Mosque. This is Armley.

I want to learn everything. I want to remember it. I want it to remember me. I want it to climb inside me and build a home. I don't want to feel strange and distant in this place. I don't want the nightmares of the past.

Beat. **Ishmael** *takes out a mobile phone from his pocket. He dials a number. A ringing tone is heard. It goes straight to voicemail. He tries again but is sent to voicemail again. He puts the phone back into his pocket. Beat.*

Scene Two

A café soundscape is heard.

I've started checking Facebook for news from those I left behind. I give up bread and milk and save enough for two hours on the computer in Cath's Café. Cath is married to Brian. Brian always stays in the kitchen. I've never seen his face. All I've ever seen is a forearm with a tattoo of a white flag with red cross passing plates of full English breakfasts to his wife. As each plate comes through Cath is forced to peel herself away from the weekly *Take a Break* magazine that's spread open on the counter. I sit in the corner every Thursday and for the hours that I'm there, their marriage unfolds for us to hear.

Ishmael *becomes* **Cath** *and* **Brian**. *They both speak in a broad Yorkshire accent.* **Ishmael** *switches between the couple and himself.*

Ishmael *as* **Cath**.

"Bri, you won't believe it. Listen to this: Grandma falls in love with long-lost grandson. There are some right sickos out there! I bet they're Americans."

Ishmael *as* **Brian**.

"Yes, love. They can only be Americans."

Ishmael *as* **Cath**.

"I mean, what are you doing falling in love with your grandson? The Jeremy Kyle Show is low but even that would be too sick for him. There's got to be a limit even for the bottom feeders."

He tells her not to be so judgmental. They start arguing again. Cath's Café has been open for twenty years.

Beat.

I sit at a computer and scroll down David's page. I'm checking for updates on his whereabouts. His last post was an interview that he did with Star FM. It was the last time I'd heard his voice, before all the trouble began. Above it are posts telling him to never come back. (He reads the posts.) "Good riddance to them all. A disgusting import from the colonial days. Un-African and ungodly!"

I write him messages. I write him many messages asking him to tell me if he's alive. I tell him, "If you don't want to do it here just call me. Here is my number. Please confirm, are you in England?" (*Beat.*) The messages are read, but he hasn't replied.

We spoke of one day living abroad together. But when the incident happened, fear threw out all of our plans. The newspapers outed David and he ran. I followed. I ran out of Harare, out of Zimbabwe and into South Africa. I continued to England following rumours of David's movements. I arrived at Heathrow with one bag packed in a hurry and a recount of what had happened. The Border Agency officers said my story wasn't true. They asked me to prove that I am gay. They asked me, "Was David real? What does a penis feel like? Why do I like it?" We weren't dirty. We were real. We were in love. I needed David to tell them so.

Beat.

I look at my page last. After three months, I haven't called anyone. I don't know what to say to them. My friends Muzi and Deejay post every day asking where I am and why didn't I tell them. They are (*Beat.*) were my boys, ever since we were this high. (*Ishmael gestures. Beat.*) We never thought we'd exist past the good times. We were the blood brothers. The three musketeers riding together for life! The boys all the ladies loved!

I thought about telling them many times. When I was thirten, I knew for sure. But I was worried about my friends seeing me differently. At eighteen, I was worried they wouldn't see a man. At twenty-one, I was worried what drunk mouths would say.

I spent years practising what I'd say to my father, if I ever told him.

Ishmael *plays out the scenario. He clears his throat.*

"Listen, can we talk? . . . I think I'm . . ."

Beat.

I wished he'd listen. But I'd probably be killed there on the spot. Not his only son. Not the one who's supposed to carry his name. Not in this family. Not in this house. (*Beat.*) I thought about telling my mother, but she'd probably die there on the spot, and then be resurrected to drag me to church to receive a healing.

He takes out African shells from the suitcase. He becomes his **Mother**. *He shakes the shells back and forth.*

"Yes Lord!"

Shakes the shells.

"Cleanse him!"

Shakes the shells

"Heal him!"

Shakes the shells

"Save him!"

Shakes the shells. Beat

They needed a good son. I tried to be a good son for as long as I could.

Beat. He places the shells back in the suitcase. He takes out a flyer from the suitcase. Beat. There's a soundscape of people talking and children playing indoors.

In the library I find a flyer for a place called Sanctuary Point. On Mondays, in a church between 5 p.m. and 8 p.m. there is a gathering of refugees and asylum seekers. The words "hot meal" call out to me. It's not been easy rationing £36.62 a week for food, clothes, toiletries, transport, and chasing an overstretched London solicitor who has all of my files. He stopped representing me when they moved me out of a convenient radius. I've been living in my head for so long I wondered if I'd remember how to speak to another person.

Beat.

I stayed at Sanctuary Point until the drop-in session ended. I walked back to the flat thinking of what I'd do until the next Monday. I wondered if the young Nigerian man will be there again. Would he sniff out more secrets from me like he did my Africanness, when he yelled out from across the room, (*in a Nigerian accent*) *"My brother, welcome!"* His handshake was fast and acrobatic. It was like we are performing a traditional dance of salutation. During our meal of rice and curried chicken, he said there were four more Nigerians, one Ghanaian, and six Libyans. But I was the only Zimbabwean. (*Beat.*) I thought about that moment when one of them turns to ask me the reason for my immigration claim. Even in our collective misfortune, my brothers and my sisters could shun me. A citizen of the unwanted being excluded by the excluded. Would I lie to them?

The sound ends. He puts the flyer in his pocket.

The night's darkness was over me when I got back to the flat. I pressed the button for the lift. It was slow coming down. (*Beat. A vicious dog bark is heard. He cowers back.*) The dog barking came out of nowhere. I cowered into the corner. Urine and fear filled the small corridor. The dog's leash snapped back and the young boy laughed.

Ishmael *becomes* **Ricky**. *He moves fast and intimidatingly. He repeatedly tugs at a dog leash.* **Ricky** *speaks in a Yorkshire accent.* **Ishmael** *switches between himself and* **Ricky**.

"This here is Blade, short for Razor Blade cos of his teeth, innit. He's a good pitbull. I'm Ricky. We saw you up near our street, walking all lah-di-dah from church. It's all good for you lot, innit. Free food, free clothes, and free laptops. Maybe you can borrow us one of those laptops one day. You know, give back to the community and all that."

Back to **Ishmael**.

Ricky couldn't have been more than fifteen years old.

Back to **Ricky**.

"Blade ain't eaten today. I ain't got money to feed him. Are you going to feed my dog?"

Back to **Ishmael**.

The dog was already digging its nose into my spilt food parcels.

Back to **Ricky**.

"What else do you have?"

Back to **Ishmael**.

I empty my pockets. Give him all of my money. He lets me keep my keys.

Back to **Ricky**.

"Cheers, mate. We'll be seeing you same time next week."

Back to **Ishmael**. *Beat.*

I don't go back to the drop-in center. I don't go out at night. I don't go out for over a week. I don't want to know the streets anymore.

Beat. **Ishmael** *puts the flyer back into the suitcase. Mbira music is heard.*

Some of us found others like us.
Some of us found them seething.
Some of us were called leeches.
Some of us were dirt beneath their shoes.
Some of us broke our African names.
Some of us erased our histories,
Some of us conjured up secret identities.
Some of us couldn't recognize ourselves anymore.

Music ends.

Scene Three

The sun comes out for the first time in a long while. I decide that this will be the day that I will bravely leave the flat. I walk to a little park and sit on a bench and watch the leaves fall. A little boy comes running up to me, making the sound of a racing car. He rolls the wheels along my arm and takes off running again before his mother can catch up.

Ishmael *becomes* **Bex**, *a young mother who speaks very fast in a Yorkshire accent.*

"Bailey, get the fuck back here! *(Beat. She notices* **Ishmael**.*)* Hiya, you know he takes them toy cars everywhere, drives me crazy."

He takes out a cigarette and lighter from his pocket.

"I aint seen you here before."

Back to **Ishmael**.

I tell her that it's my new favorite place. But its beauty has long been lost to her because she says,

Ishmael *as* **Bex**.

"Dog shit park is your favorite place?"

Back to **Ishmael**.

It's the space. It doesn't feel like we're all squashed together.

Bex *laughs.*

"It's always looked the same to me, love. Anyways, what's your name?"

Beat. Back to **Ishmael**.

The lie rolls off my tongue before I can even catch it.

Ishmael *as* **Bex**.

"It's nice to meet you, Sam. I'm Bex and that's Bailey."

Back to **Ishmael**.

Bailey runs up to her and buries his face into her thigh. He pulls at her Nike jacket, beckoning her to bend. He speaks softly. His words are secrets only for his mother's ears. Her bleached blonde hair falls forward revealing a letter "B" tattooed on the back of her neck. **Bex** pulls out a lollipop from her pocket, Bailey snatches it and runs back to the swings.

Beat.

In two weeks, we see each other three more times in the park. Sam is funny. Sam is studying Business at college. Sam wants to be rich man one day and never have to worry about struggling. Sam likes Stormzy. Sam doesn't have a girlfriend, it's a bit complicated. Sam has an older brother. They used to wrestle a lot when they were boys, play fighting, nothing serious.

Ishmael *as* **Bex**.

"My mam never wanted more kids. She said I was handful enough. I think about giving Bailey a little brother one day. I like the thought of my two boys looking out for each other, you know."

Back to **Ishmael**.

I have become someone with her. When Bailey falls asleep holding a sausage roll in his hand, I realize that I have become someone that she can trust. She asks me to carry him home for her. (*Beat.*) As we walk I ask her about his father.

Ishmael *snaps into* **Bex**.

"Dickhead ain't worth talking about. He left before Bailey were born."

Beat. Back to **Ishmael**.

I put Bailey down on his bed, he curls up and sticks his thumb in his mouth.

Ishmael *as* **Bex**.

"Listen, yeah, you can stay for a bit if you want. Relax, Sam, you don't have to be so nervous. I'm not asking you to marry me. *Strictly*'s on tonight."

Back to **Ishmael**.

She clears away the clothes on the sofa. In the mess there's a new fire engine still in its packet. She holds the toy in her hand like it's something rare and precious. She sighs deeply.

Beat. **Ishmael** *as* **Bex**.

"I was hiding this. It's Bailey's birthday in a couple of weeks. I mean it's not like he bloody needs another one, but I like how happy he is when he's playing with them. Here, sit down. I'm thinking of giving him, like, a right big party and invite all his friends. I'm going to get some balloons with a big '4' on them and put them all round the house, hang them out the window; so that everyone knows that something special is happening. I'm going to make a right fuss over him. I do it every year. God knows why I'm not in debt over that boy. (Pause.) His dad didn't even want him. He wanted me to get rid of him but I couldn't. It just seemed cruel to get rid of something that was, you know, like, living. (Beat.) I remember the day so clearly you know. I woke up really early. I put on my school uniform and told my mum that we had a school trip. When I got to the hospital, they put me in a room with another girl. She was moaning and wriggling all over the bed. Her sister was telling her that she was going to be alright. I was only fifteen then, so the nurse asked me if someone over eighteen was going to come and pick me up. They couldn't let me go, afterwards, without an adult. I was, like, yeah, yeah, sure my boyfriend is coming. When she left the room, I called him like a bunch of times, but it kept going into voicemail. I couldn't believe that he wasn't there, you know. He'd been the one saying that we couldn't do this, we couldn't have it. I waited and waited but when the nurse came back, she was, like, listen, love I've got to start. I've got other patients to see. (Beat.) It hit me. He really didn't care about me. I jumped out of bed and I was, like, no! No way, I'm not doing this. The nurse thought I'd proper lost it. I thought there's no point. If he doesn't want to be with me to raise it, and he doesn't want to be with me to kill it, then why am I even with him? I'm not better off anyways. But if I keep it at least then I'll have something that cares about me. (Beat.) So, I jumped out of bed and I put my clothes on. I went down to his mum's in Chapeltown and started banging on the door. I screamed, Leon get the fuck out here! Leon, you think you can just leave me on me own! His mum flung the door open. I thought she was going to kill me. She was all, like, my son this and my son that, he's a good boy. What will he be doing with a little white girl like you? (Beat. She kisses her teeth.) She knew nothing about me. She had no fucking right to talk to me like I was shit. I told her, your son is having a baby with this little white girl. Her jaw fell to the floor when I said that. I went up to her face and told her that I didn't do it. I didn't kill our baby and I'm finished with him. (Beat.) I wasn't even gone two minutes before Leon called me screaming down the phone. He was a right coward when it came to his mum. She'd always threaten to send him back to Jamaica. I told him to grow up. He was going to be a dad. I hung up the phone before he could say anything. (Beat. She sighs.) I knew we'd never get on from that point. (Beat.) I told Leon he could come over whenever he wanted to, but him and his mum never bothered. I thought it was alright because Bailey at least had another grandmother. But when Bailey had just turned three, my mam got a new boyfriend. He'd never had kids so he couldn't cope with Bailey crying all the time and didn't want us around. I came back from doctor's one day and found all of mine and Baileys things packed up. He stood at the door telling me I couldn't stop at my mam's anymore. She didn't bother saying anything. They'd only been together a few months. I thought forget it, do what you want, Charlie will put us up. And she did, she's always been a good mate. Six months we were there and then we got this flat. Our own little place. Mine and Bailey's place, just the two of us."

Beat. Back to **Ishmael**.

She finally looks up and pulls herself back into the room with me.

Ishmael *as* **Bex**.

"I talk a lot don't I?"

Back to **Ishmael**.

I don't mind, I tell her.

Ishmael *as* **Bex**.

"Well, then, I think we're gonna be right good mates you and I."

Back to **Ishmael**.

She leaves, puts the TV remote in my hand and heads to the kitchen.

Ishmael *as* **Bex**.

"Do you want some tea? I've only got fish fingers and wedges. Bailey won't let me buy anything else. Is that alright? I was gonna tell you something actually. A mate of mine Garry sells fridges. He's done his back in and is looking for someone to help him with deliveries. I can't imagine it's much but it's something. He's hardly breaking bank so it'll be the odd job here and there. D'ya want me to ask him? (*Beat.*) Sam, did yah hear me? (*Beat.*) Sam? Where'd you go?"

Beat. Back to **Ishmael**.

I didn't know what to say to her. I quietly slipped out of her flat. I wasn't allowed to work. Sam was trapped by Ishmael. Sitting in her flat with her truths laid out in front of me made my lies a heavy stone in my heart. Selfishly, I wanted to sit with someone and be just normal. Bex saw me. I tasted something that I was not allowed to have.

Mbira music is heard.

Some of us wear our secrets
Like a cloak around our shoulders.
Some of us don't know what to say
When they label us greedy foreigners.
Some of us don't know how to be
When limbo comes with every morning.

Music ends.

Scene Four

Ishmael *takes out a family picture of an Iranian man and his family from the suitcase. He props it up. The sound of a door closing is heard. It startles him.*

I don't see shadows around when he walks. There are goodbyes with no words. At times I forget that he is in the flat. Our life together is a constant attempt not to meet, not to touch, and not to connect. But his body tells a story. Hard steps on floors, humming in the bathroom and deep breaths at night. I want to know who this tale belongs to. All day I listen out for him. When the shuffling and thuds stop, and the front door slams shut, I sneak out of my room. Tiptoe towards his door. I knock and wait. Then push the door open, just enough for me to peek in, scan for a letter and finally learn his name.

Cyrus comes into the kitchen. There are no boundaries today. He looks me straight in the eyes and says:

Ishmael *become* **Cyrus**. *He is heavy-set and speaks with an Iranian accent.*

"What do I tell them? What do I say to my wife? No more appeals. Denied, last time. They send me back. I don't want to go. Two years they have me wait and just like that they say it's over. My family is waiting for me to bring them here. We all suffer in Tehran. There, there is no life. They don't want us here, but we cannot go back."

Back to **Ishmael**.

I don't have any answers for him. I don't have any answers for myself.

"You wait and see; they do to you what they do to me. You apply, they reject, you appeal, they reject, you beg, they tell you there's nothing more they can do. Well, they won't get rid of me. My friend tells me if they take you to the airport you cry, you scream and you fall on the floor. Pilot won't fly with crazy man. They not allowed. I do everything by the rules and hope for fairness but it not work. So, I make trouble. I don't care. This is England, but in here it is slum. She fix nothing because she think we nothing. We don't deserve anything, not even her kindness!"

Back to **Ishmael.**

I see his anger building. He clenches his fist and punches a hole into the kitchen door. I don't even have to ask, I know he means Angie, the landlord. The one who makes us feel like we've fallen into a crack and no one is looking for us. When I first met her, I held out my hand. "I'm Ishmael," I said. She grunted. She doesn't need to say it, but I know it. She owned everything in this flat, including my dignity.

Ishmael *as* **Cyrus**.

"Kitchen sink have mould when I move in. Carpets stained, I get down on my knees and scrub. My bed break six months ago. She give me stick, wood from fence outside, and say here, fix it. Go, go see bedroom. The wall is wet. It's been wet since I come here two years ago. I tell her and tell her my daughter Susann have asthma, it is bad for her. She says, I see no children here. I tell her, they're coming! She laugh at me. She laugh at my children. She laugh at my appeals. She laugh at my rejection. She laugh at my deportation. I hold my tongue and she laugh. I say please and thank you and she laugh. I read my Bible and she laugh. She come in with own key and check your room when she want. I suspect she take what she want, but who will believe foreigner over British. She come in bathroom, to check shower with me inside. Home Office give people like her money to rent property. Two years ago, I get my first rejection and they give me Azure card. She free to do what she wants with money but I can only use card at authorized places. I cannot use bus with no money. When they give me I ask, how do I get back to Border Agency office to report? The first time I go, I walk two hours to Kirkstall. I get there late and the officer give me a warning. I tell him I had to walk far but he doesn't care. I swear, they teach them not to be human. Two years they treat me like this. Two years I walk. Two years I shop where they tell me to shop. Two years I buy what they want to me to buy. Two years lady at the till laugh at me when card don't work. She talk in microphone to everyone in Tesco and call manager. I don't know what this card is, she say. (*She shouts.*) Yes you know! (*Beat.*) I come here every week. Everyone in line look at me like I ruin this country. She make me feel small. (*Pause.* **Cyrus** *goes to the window.*) Look at them out there, living their lives. They don't know. The dogs at the gates are not how they protect this country. They do it in this flat, my friend. They do it in here. (*He points to his chest.*) They break spirit and make you want to give up before they tell you to go."

Pause. Back to **Ishmael**.

The days following, the flat is quiet. We are both alone with our thoughts, knowing the inevitable is soon. Unexpectedly, one morning, Angie opens the door, followed by three men. They barge into his door and start packing his belongings. He tells them that this isn't right, but they don't stop. I don't go out to look. I pull the blankets over my head. (*Beat.*)

Ishmael *as* **Cyrus**.

"Let me dress, just let me dress."

Beat. Back to **Ishmael**

And just like that, he was gone.

Ishmael *puts the picture frame back inside the suitcase. Beat. Mbira music is heard*

Some of us didn't cheat.
Some of us held on to our integrity.
Some of us held on to our honesty.
Some of us had dreams turn into boulders.
Some of us were begging for a taste of your liberty.

Music ends.

Scene Five

Suddenly **Ishmael***'s phone rings. He searches for it in his pockets. He finds it and answers it.* **David**'s *voice is heard.*

David (*voiceover***)** *"It's me, David. Don't talk, Ish, just listen. Stop sending me messages, okay. I don't know what you want from me but I can't help you. Remember it was my house that was burned down. I barely made it out. I got my asylum, Ish. I want to start again. Please just let me go. Don't ruin it for me. I hope everything works out for you, but I don't want to deal with all that stuff again. I refuse to see another application form. I refuse to answer any more of those questions. I had to explain what I do with men and why I like it. Never again! I've been degraded enough. Plenty people pay others to support their claims. Just do the same and take it to the Home Office."*

Ishmael *is desperate. He speaks into the phone.*

I'm not going to lie. I was your secret and you left me. I can't be sent back now, not after running. My family, my friends, the police will all be waiting. What will I tell them? Just tell the Home Office that you know me. Be my evidence . . . Help me . . . (**David** *hangs up.*) Hello? . . . David?

Beat. **Ishmael** *is upset. Mbira music is heard.*

Some of us were joining lovers.
Some of us left lovers.
Some of us were discarded by lovers.
Some of us felt love wither inside.
Some of us felt raging storms crashing against our chests.

Music ends.

Scene Six

Ishmael *takes out red high heels from the suitcase. He takes off his trainers and puts them on. Club music is heard.*

The city is different at night. There are creatures that wake and take over in the darkness. I want to know what it's like to become. Inner beings escaping from their cages. Free to be. I want to escape my body.

I know that it's there. But I haven't been brave enough to go. I've thought about what I'd see there. I've thought about who'd see me there. I've thought about the people back home. I've thought about what they'd think if they saw me right now. My elation soaring on the back of their pain. I've thought about being their shame. I've thought about being their outcast. I've thought about whether they'd know me now. See over here it's not like over there. Here there are neon lights. Here there are queens. Here there are rainbow flags drawn high. (*Music crescendos.*) Body, beat, Mission, Monday, bubbles, paint, night, glitter, rave, collar, cuffs, cabaret, music, body, flesh, uppers, downers, him, she, me.

It's nothing like I have ever known. It is more than I have ever seen. She takes me by the hand. She tells me to dance. To let go. I'm awkward. Is this what it feels like to not be afraid? Is this what it feels like to be free? Is this what it feels like to be yourself? She leans in and speaks in a language that is only made for us:

Ishmael *becomes* **Miss Marie Monroe**. *She is ethereal and speaks in Polari.*

"Don't be strange, darling. Just let it all go. In here, it's all fun. I'm Miss Marie Monroe. Zhoosh your riah, slap on some lippy, powder your eeks, grab a bevvy and dance. Come on, turn my oyster up!"

Back to **Ishmael**. *He starts to dance.*

I'd been holding it in for too long. It needed to come out, to break out. I gave in. Let it be, let me be me.

He is overcome with joy. The music gets louder. He shouts above it.

Some of us wanted to stop being afraid.
Some of us wanted to find ourselves.
Some of us wanted to belong.

The music fades and he gradually stops dancing. He takes the heels off and laughs. He puts the heels back inside the suitcase.

Scene Seven

Ishmael *takes a letter from the Home Office. He quickly opens it. He reads it. Beat. There's a look of disappointment in his face. He puts on his trainers and jacket. He shoves the letter into his pocket and takes out a toy truck. There's a soundscape of children playing in a park.*

In two months, Bailey looks like he's grown enough for a year. I'd missed Bex. I wanted to tell her so much. I wanted to tell her what had happened since I ran away. I wanted to tell her why I'd run away.

He puts the toy car on the floor and pushes it out into the audience. He watches it until it stops. He snaps into **Bex**.

"What you want? You know what, I don't even want to know. I mean honestly, what sort of person just walks out like that. It was weird. You could have at least said that you were going. You made me feel like as if I'd made you up. I thought I was going crazy. I started to think after you were gone that I really didn't know anything about you. I mean I knew stuff, but nothing that really mattered. You could have been a murderer for all I knew. I thought you were going to come back and kill me in my sleep. You don't just do that to people. Bailey actually liked yah. You don't show your face around here for months and you think it's alright to just turn up with your little presents. (*Shouts.*) Bailey! Bailey bring it back. Bring that bloody toy back here! Put it in the bin over there! I said put it in the bin! He's going to put it in the bin when we get back home. You might as well go. (*Beat.*) I wasn't trying to shag you if that's what you think. I definitely ain't going to shag you now. I was just trying to be your friend."

Back to **Ishmael**.

I ask her to sit down. I hand her the letter. She doesn't understand. I start to explain that I am Ishmael. She tries to interrupt. I tell her to wait and to let me finish. (*Beat.*) I shouldn't have lied, but I didn't want to be who I was. Ishmael can only dream of the freedom that Sam has. You are the friend I didn't know how to be. You reminded of what it's like to feel like person and it's silly because you didn't do anything. You just sat next to me and said hi. Not many people said hi. Not many people made me feel human. They sort of look past you, look though you, and the ones that see you only see the labels they give.

This letter says I'm a reference number. I'm an applicant. I'm circumstances. I'm categories. I'm outcomes. But it doesn't say that I'm real. It doesn't say that I exist. That I laugh. I cry. I dance. I dream. I wonder. I want. I think. I question. It doesn't say that I'm a person, Bex. (*Beat.*) I went to this club a while ago and whilst I was there, I felt seen. I chose to be there, proudly. Everything has been out of my hands. Everything still is out of my hands but for that moment I tasted it. I tasted choice and it was good. She asks why I can't have that again. (*Beat.*) It's not as easy as you think it is. You've got to prove yourself and, if that fails, you've got to start again and that's your last appeal. I'm going for my last chance. I don't know what will happen. (*Beat.*) I know you don't think it's much, but I'd rather have this park, this place as it is now, as my own. At least then I can hold it. Waiting to be allowed to live is like flickering in and out existence. Sometimes you're not even sure if you are real. You made me feel real. That is all I wanted to say. I'm sorry that I lied.

Pause.

She doesn't say anything. I can't tell from her face if my apologies are enough. She just stares at me. Then, she takes the letter, folds it, puts it into my pocket and holds out her hand.

Ishmael *as* **Bex**.

"Hi, Ishmael, it's nice to meet, yeah. I mean properly, yeah."

Back to **Ishmael**. *He smiles. Mbira music plays.*

Some of us leave pieces of ourselves
In all the places that we've been.
Some of us are still counting how many
Battles we have to face.
Some of us are just at the beginning,
Hoping to call somewhere home again.

Ishmael *picks up the suitcase and leaves. Music ends.*

Curtain.

Leaving, but Can't Let Go

Lupe Gehrenbeck

Lupe Gehrenbeck is a playwright, director, and professor whose plays have been produced in Caracas, Buenos Aires, London, New York, Paris, Montpellier, Curacao, and Montreal. Her works include *Discovered*, *The Girls of Santa Fe*, *Piñata*, *Are We Going? Or . . . Are We Staying!*, *With an A of Illusion*, *From Miracielos to Hospital*, *Gregor Mac Gregor*, *Matarile*, *Eve*, *Adam*, *Guardian Angel*, *Bolero*, *Bolívar Coronado*, *Leaving, but Can't Let Go*, *Cruz de Mayo*, *Catch Minnie*, and *The Son of the President – Family Circus.* She has developed various methodologies for theater creation such as Theater Without Borders for migrant children in Chiapas, Mexico. She teaches scenic communication for the master of social communication program at Central University of Venezuela and the summer playwriting workshop at City University of New York. Gehrenbeck has received the Juana Sujo Prize and awards from the Film Authors Association in Venezuela, London's CASA Festival of Latin America Arts, and Spain's Teatro Autor Exprés by SGAE, and was a nominee for the 2020 Gilder/Coigney International Theatre Award. She has been part of the Playwrights/Directors Workshop at The Actors Studio in New York City since 2017. In 2018, Editorial Eclepsidra published *Gregor Mac Gregor and Other Plays by Lupe Gehrenbeck.*

Setting

Among the six million people who have fled the violence and the political and economic instability in Venezuela is Elvira's younger daughter, who wants her mother to come live with her in the US. But Elvira's older daughter wants her mother to stay in Venezuela, where she believes it is possible to build a better future. Elvira is divided: she wants to leave as much as she wants to stay.

Production History

Productions in Caracas, Venezuela – Centro Cultural BOD, 2015; Teatro de Petare César Rengifo, 2016; Teatro Trasnocho, 2016; Sala Viga, Chacao, 2017; Teatro Municipal de Chacao, 2021.
And in New York, Santiago Rubio Hall, 2017.

Casts

Caracas 2015–2017

Elvira	Caridad Canelón
Candelaria	Nattalie Cortez
Alberta	Simona Chirinos/Verónica Arellano
Carolina	Gladys Seco
Director	Oswaldo Maccio
Production Design	Gladys Seco, María Alejandra Rengifo
Costume Design	Raquel Ríos

New York City 2018

Elvira	Sonia Berah
Candelaria	Mónica Quintero
Alberta	Antia Arruez
Carolina	María Fernanda Rodriguez
Tony	Samuel Garnica
Director	Lupe Gehrenbeck. Teatro de La Comarca

Caracas 2021

Elvira	Aminta de Lara
Alberta	Matilda Corral
Candelaria	Valentina Garrido
Carolina	Andrea Levada
Tony	Francisco Aguana
Director	Lupe Gehrenbeck. Teatro de La Comarca

Characters

Elvira, *Venezuelan, housewife, sixty-five years old, lives in Caracas.*
Alberta, *Colombian, sixty-five years old, works as a domestic help at Elvira's house.*
Carolina, *oldest daughter of Elvira, thirty-five years old, lives in New York.*
Candelaria, *Elvira's youngest daughter, thirty-three years old, lives in Caracas.*
Tony, *Alberta's only son, twenty-two years old.*
Gustavo, *Elvira's tenant (always off stage).*
Tania, *Elvira's neighbor (always off stage).*

To Karina

Note: A vague silhouette appears and disappears every now and then. That shadow seems to be observing everything from the darkness. Nobody notices it.

Blackout.

The sound of a Skype call. The screen from a laptop lights up.

Elvira *enters, wearing a robe and slippers. She answers the Skype call.*

Carolina *enters. She is wearing an apron from a restaurant.*

Elvira Hello, my love . . .

Carolina Did I wake you?

Elvira No, *mija*, I already had breakfast. I was reading the newspaper.

Carolina I don't know why you still read the newspaper, Mom, it only worries you.

Elvira Not knowing what happens is what worries me.

Carolina And what did you discover this morning?

Elvira *reads a piece of an old and wrinkled newspaper, she was using to wrap a glass cup.*

Elvira That "the National Guard ordered to have the fish removed from the beaches."

Carolina What? Only in Venezuela!

It surpasses any reach of the imagination . . .

Elvira That's why you have to read the paper: to know about the unexplainable.

(*Reading.*) "A pile of dead sardines were found on the beach" . . .

The pictures are terrible!

. . .

The government doesn't know if the expensive yacht clubs are responsible, or if it's the result of an environmental crisis.

Carolina And what do sardines have to do with yacht clubs?

Elvira The same fucking thing they have to do with the price of tea in China!

Carolina Mom! Remember you're a grandmother!

Elvira I'll be buried with a curse on my lips. It doesn't hurt anyone!

So tell me, what am I good for?

Carolina Should I buy your ticket for the end of the month?

Elvira For the end of the month?

No, Carolina, it's too soon! I still have so many things to do.

Elvira *goes back to wrapping the glass cup with the newspaper and places it in a cardboard box.*

Carolina What do you have to do besides pack your suitcase and Dad's? You don't need to take care of everything at once.

Elvira I can't leave things pending, because I won't be able to sleep.

Carolina Candelaria could deal with it if anything comes up . . .

Elvira You know your sister. She has no time for anything.

Carolina I know, she only has time to care for the poor . . . but not for her own family . . . When was the last time she visited you?

Elvira She always comes for lunch.

Carolina When was the last time?

A month ago, when she told you she didn't agree with you coming, right?

Elvira I talk to her several times a day, every day.

Carolina You can do that from New York too.

Elvira Don't start fighting about your sister.

Carolina Candela is selfish, masquerading as a socialist.

She only thinks of herself. But since you've always protected her . . .

Elvira Leave me alone, Carolina!

Pause. Silence.

Carolina How did the garage sale go?

Elvira I was going to get to it now.

Carolina Oh, Mom, you were supposed to do it yesterday!

Elvira I didn't have time.

Carolina It is not so complicated: you put a price on things, and that's it. It's all right if you don't sell everything though.

You could also hire someone to organize it for you.

Elvira Do you really think that just anyone can come along and decide what's important, and how much my memories are worth?

Come on, Carolina!

I already have enough on my plate just getting rid of my things . . .

Carolina You don't have to sell what you don't want to sell.

You might sell only the things you haven't used for a long time.

Elvira They're not just things! It's is my life that is being put on sale!

Even though I haven't used it in years.

Carolina Oh, no, Mom, that's too much drama.

If you're so tied to the old, to the past, you won't be able to open yourself to the future . . .

Elvira Your dad's the only old thing I'm tied to.

What other future? After a certain age, the past and the future go together, if not, you're lost. You carry your baggage wherever you go, the older the heavier.

Carolina You need to look on the bright side.

Just think that everything that happens is for the best!

I just don't want anything bad happening to you in Venezuela.

Elvira Whatever was supposed to happen to me already did, and nothing happened.

Carolina So, what are you suggesting?

That we wait until something bad happens to you?

That would kill Dad!

Elvira The only thing that worries you about me dying is that your dad dies.

Carolina Mom!

Elvira At least my wake might help you to reconcile with your sister.

You need to look on the bright side . . . right?

Carolina Why are you being so aggressive with me?

Because I want to have you close to me . . .

Because I need you, because I'm worried about what might happen to you in Venezuela . . .?

Elvira No, Carolina, I understand all that but give me time.

It is not easy to let go of the only life I know.

Tania (*off*) Elvira . . . Elvira . . .!

Elvira Yes, Tania, *mi amor* . . .

Carolina Why do your neighbors never use the phone, Mom?

Tania (*off*) There's cooking oil! But only one bottle per person.

So, you better come and stand in line—do you want me to wait for you?

Elvira Yesterday I found butter in the market down the street, and since there were no sardines, I bought meat to make *carne mechada*. I don't need the cooking oil.

Thank you, Tania, anyway.

If you want, come later and try it.

Tania (*off*) And how are you going to fry the plantains?

Elvira If the country isn't the same, our national dish has to adapt.

If there's no oil we'll boil the plantains!

Carolina It's healthier. Frying is the worst!

Tania (*off*) And how do we fry our fish, the *tequeños*, our arepas and *perico* . . .?

What's going to be on the menu now in this changed country?

Carolina That's why your cholesterol is so high.

Elvira You know what, Tania? Get in line and I'll meet you later.

Waiting is also on our menu now.

Carolina . . . I'm going to put you on a diet here!

Elvira There's no need. We're already on a forced diet.

Carolina I talked to Dad yesterday. He told me that he was eating oatmeal and had lost some inches off his waistline.

Elvira Yes, that's what he says.

Carolina He already spoke with *señor* Pablo in New York who invited him to play dominoes with all his *compadres*.

You see? That's looking on the bright side.

Think of it as a long vacation, Mom. That's it!

And then we'll see. It doesn't have to be a trauma. Forget the sale.

Elvira No! I really want to sell. We need more space here.

Carolina But the house is too big for the two of you.

Elvira Precisely.

Carolina Don't tell me you're going to keep renting rooms in the house?

Elvira Why not?

Carolina Oh, Mom, because it's dangerous to rent to strangers.

Besides, the way things are going, you don't know if you can make them leave later.

What does Dad say about it?

Elvira This house is too full of things to clean.

And I'm the one doing the cleaning, not your dad.

Carolina The house has always been that way

That's its charm. I don't understand why it bothers you now.

Elvira Because what's not in use should find a place elsewhere.

A new life in someone else's house.

Carolina You talk about objects as if they were people.

They're just objects, Mom.

Besides, here you'll be able to buy anything you can think of, even things you didn't know existed.

You won't need anything except . . .

Elvira . . . money to buy it, right?

And where's the money coming from?

Carolina You don't need to rent rooms to survive, Mom.

Don't you rent two studios already?

Elvira Yes, but from your room and the terrace, and the TV room, we can make another studio.

Carolina Are you going to dismantle my room?

Elvira . . . So then . . .? Who's the one who won't let go of the past?

Carolina Why don't you use Candela's bedroom for the new studio?

Elvira Candela's bedroom is full of things; it's become a storage room.

Carolina Well, those knickknacks are the first things that you have to sell!

Elvira I'm working on that, getting rid of things, little by little . . . it's been too many years forgotten inside the silence of these four walls . . . and it hurts.

Carolina Why? Haven't you had a happy life?

Elvira Precisely, it's because I've had a happy life.

Carolina I can't imagine how things must have changed.

I don't think I would be able to return.

I'd rather remember the house as it was.

All I ask is that you don't sell my books, Mom.

Elvira *hides the books she was about to put in a box, feeling guilty for having had the idea of selling them.*

Carolina (*remembers*)

Secrets of a Fisherman
Once upon a time, a fisherman, Joselo,
Had a son, Manuelo.
Who wouldn't think
That the child would go fishing like his father?

Every day at dawn,
Joselo departed with his hooks,
And always returned with fish,
To teach Manuelo what he knew.

Secrets of the craft,
It was Manuelo's turn,
To take them on.

Poor Manuelo, didn't sleep,
As dawn approached
To the sea he would not go,
Even when his father looked for him,
To journey on.

Elvira (*reads*)

To avoid going sailing,
Manuelo's excuses were unfailing:
His belly ached . . .
Or sleepwalking he did feign.
3 × 4 was 9, his math was failing . . .
Any excuse was good not to go sailing.

She takes other books from the shelf and quickly goes through their pages.

These schoolbooks only bring back bad memories; she failed math every year, never memorized the 4s table.

Carolina . . . only liked to read stories, anything that would take her away from reality.

She wanted to escape since she was little . . .

She decides to put them in a cardboard box.

These books are good for Tony . . .

She keeps the fisherman tale book and reads.

Carolina

Manuelo did not open his eyes,
Although Joselo called him,
He said he was blinded,
Dazzled by the sun

Joselo was already tired,
Of so many lies and lack of reason,
It was not a matter of choice:
Fishing was a must,
For those who lived near the sea.

Manuelo wanted to explain,
But his father turned a deaf ear:

Elvira (*reads*)

"Not another word, boy,
Tonight, you come with me."

Carolina

Manuelo cried,
He could not escape the sea.

Elvira (*reads*)

Carmen Teresa,
His beloved mother,
Wanted to comfort him,
And find out why Manuelo,
Was so afraid of the sea.
"It's better to tell the truth.
To be able to reason,"
son, she told him.

Carolina

Manuelo searched and searched,
For an answer, a lie, an excuse,
But he had run out of stories.
Then, at last, he confessed:
"I'm afraid of the sea . . .
because I want to return."

Elvira *closes the book. She thinks for a moment.*

Elvira I'm going to take this book to my grandson Santiago . . . so that he learns to speak Spanish . . . so that he learns how to return.

She talks to the laptop again.

Elvira I'm taking your grandfather's chair.

Carolina Which one? The wicker chair painted blue?

Elvira The very same!

Carolina Oh, Mom, do you know how much a wicker chair costs at IKEA?!

$25! Then you can paint it any color you want.

Elvira But the $25 IKEA chair isn't the one your grandfather used to sit on to fill out crossword puzzles and munch on nuts.

Carolina Do you know that it has been discovered that nuts are very good for you?

Elvira Your grandfather already knew it.

Carolina YES . . . COMING!

Well, Mom, when do I buy you the ticket?

Elvira I don't want to bother you.

Carolina Oh, Mom, we're not going back on that!

We discussed that already and agreed.

And for the rest, as it comes, we'll play it by ear.

Elvira Precisely, I'm trying to look ahead so see what might happen.

Do you understand?

Carolina COMING IN A SEC! I'M JUST SAYING GOOD-BYE . . .

Mom, I have to leave you, the patients are here. I'll call you later. Kisses.

She exits.

Elvira Kisses, my love . . .

Damn, always so ready to go somewhere else.

Full light on stage. We discover the typical middle-class house, full of porcelain objects, paintings of landscapes, etc. A doll house lays in the corner. In the middle there is a table full of objects. **Elvira** *sees everything with nostalgia. Suddenly she decides to unhang one of the paintings.*

Elvira It doesn't hurt me at all . . . not at all . . .

On the contrary: I'll finally be able to get rid of you!

I never liked this painting. But since Hortensia wanted to be an artist, we couldn't let her down . . .

Solidarity, bound by family ties.

And I've had to live with this painting my whole life, hovering in the background at every lunch like a critic, witnessing every breakfast . . . If those oranges could speak, they could tell the story of this family, with all its pride and indiscretions . . .

Alberta *enters.*

Alberta You've got to have great imagination to say that that mess is a plate full of oranges on a printed tablecloth.

Elvira There is something for everyone in this world.

Who knows, maybe someone will like it.

. . .

I would give it away for nothing.

But since no one appreciates giveaways . . .

Alberta Whoever buys it didn't know Hortensia, they don't have to hate the painting . . .

Elvira If they give me 300, I'll be happy . . .

Forgive me, Ramón Antonio, but I won't discuss it.

I know you loved Hortensia very much.

But I doubt there has ever been a more bitter and embittering sister-in-law than Hortensia.

Elvira *puts the painting on the table which is full of objects. She takes a little porcelain doll.*

Elvira This little porcelain doll didn't have many friends in this house, either. From the day she gave it to me . . . what was her name? Jessica . . .

Alberta . . . Elizabeth?

Elvira . . . Jacqueline . . . or any other of those strange names in American films that a husband's secretaries are called.

Candelaria, who always speaks her mind, said it was corny.

Carolina, much more practical and ready to get rid of things, suggested to gift wrap it and give it to Aunt Hortensia as a Christmas present—she would be certain to like it.

Alberta She had no shame, not even with her dad.

Elvira I did what I could, in case Stefanie showed up one day and . . .

Alberta Stefanie!

Elvira Yes, Stefanie . . .!

. . . Just in case she came to visit one day to find the porcelain doll gone.

I gave you a place all these years, but . . . I can't carry you with me to the North. I'm sorry . . . poor little thing. It saddens me, a little . . .

But you know? It gets cold up there . . .

Alberta And she doesn't speak English!

Elvira 300! But if I get 100, you're gone!

She puts the doll back on the table and takes a porcelain dog.

Elvira This dog is something else. I love it . . .

Alberta It even had a companion . . .

Elvira But it lost an ear, then the tail, a paw, and so on . . . until I had to throw it because it did not even stand up.

Alberta It survived because I put it inside the cabinet.

Elvira It was a miracle he survived your cleaning, Alberta.

Well this noble little dog, which does not bark or shit, is worth some money . . .

Alberta It is *capo del Monte*!

Elvira *Capodimonte*, Alberta!

Alberta What happens is that people nowadays are not interested in these delicacies . . .

Elvira Nobody has time to stare at a porcelain puppy, which reminds you of anybody . . .

She is about to price the little dog but she changes her mind, wraps it in newspaper and puts it in a suitcase.

Elvira Life is so unfair . . . Clemencia didn't deserve that horrible cancer.

This little dog weighs nothing, and fits anywhere.

So, I can take my friend's memory, she gave it to me with so much love and it's a way to keep her alive, may she rest in peace.

Lights turn off.

Elvira *Coño*!

Alberta The power's out again.

Elvira And Carolina says that I don't do the sale because I don't want to.

Alberta The country doesn't let us.

The sound of a music box. **Elvira** *tries to follow the sound in the darkness, until she finds the music box and opens it.*

Elvira Where did my youth go? . . .

I can still hear the sound of what's possible taking place outside the house and school, life and its mysteries, infinite, the happiness that I can still imagine as the music plays . . . what if I'd been a dancer? . . .

My mom would close the music box because there's school tomorrow and it's too late and there's no money for dancing classes.

She closes the music box.

Elvira Illusions, innocence, Prince Charming stories and boat trips, the world and its wonders . . . still here, with its music, intact.

*Suddenly, the sound of a small voice (***Alberta***).*

Porcelain Doll *Elvira . . . Elvirita . . .*

Elvira Who is it?

Alberta *takes a porcelain doll from the table and approaches* **Elvira**.

Porcelain Doll

If you leave, don't leave me behind.
What else would force you to pronounce the man's name
who gave me to you because we looked alike?
Gilberto . . . don't kill him.

Elvira *takes the doll in her hands and brings her close to her ear to hear better. Although a little bit ashamed, she confesses.*

Elvira Sometimes I go to Gilberto's brothers' bakery and buy pink and green meringues . . .

Porcelain Doll

All his meringues bear your name.
And the golfeados, the chocolate cake . . .
If you leave me, no one will know
that it was the young baker who taught you
the sweetness of love.

Alberta *exits.*

Light returns.

Elvira *is holding a porcelain doll next to her ear, talking to her. She feels kind of surprised and ashamed of herself. She looks at the doll with strangeness. The doll does not speak anymore. She returns it to the table of objects that are on sale. She thinks and decides to wrap it with a newspaper and put it into the suitcase. A remote melody is heard.* **Carolina** *enters.*

Carolina

I'm afraid of the sea . . . because I want to return.
Your dad always comes back, what makes you hesitate?
If I want to go back, why should I leave?

To bring the fish for the soup,
And a star born in the water,
The tale of the three-footed fish,

And other mermaid songs,
The secrets you'll be able to tell
To all who want to listen.

It was so that Manuelo,
Lost his fear and threw himself into the sea,
Searching for stories to tell.

He had a secret as well:
A girl, very pretty, Margarita,
Whom with these tales,
He wanted to impress.

She talks to her son.

Santiago . . . do you know where Venezuela is, my love?

It is not in the Caribbean nor in the north of South America.

That's what people believe who don't know that Venezuela is here, in the heart.

No matter where you are. You're Venezuelan, because my affections and your smiles are made of just that.

Because you fall asleep with the same story my grandmother told my mother.

She turns off a little lamp near by and exits.

Elvira *takes a photo from a frame.*

Elvira I'm going to give these photos to the girls.

Alberta *speaks from somewhere behind.*

Alberta Who else would be interested in the day she married Mister Ramon Antonio?

Elvira It was a simple ceremony . . .

Alberta . . . But heartfelt . . .

Elvira Everyone was happy, but there was no dancing . . .

Alberta Because it's bad luck . . .

Elvira Well, except for Maria Eugenia . . .

Alberta . . . The mysterious cousin.

Elvira Ramon Antonio has never wanted to tell me, but I'm sure there was something going on.

Otherwise why did she have that long face all night?

Anyway, it didn't matter, because no one said anything . . .

Alberta They all pretended . . .

Elvira . . . Because they were all in on it or because no one cared for the cousin . . .

Anyway, Ramon Antonio was so happy that his mustache curled up.

Alberta And that sign never lies.

Elvira The scratchy tickle on my lips, his sinful kisses that made me faint.

When Ramon Antonio wants, his mustache curls up.

From the day I met him at Mrs. Agustina's funeral . . . until we filled up all these rooms and walls on the land of this house . . .

Alberta . . . With such effort and love . . .

Elvira How can you ask me to leave now if Ramon Antonio's mustache still curls up?

Alberta *enters.*

Alberta Hello, hello . . . you got up early! Have you had breakfast?

What's wrong?

Elvira Nothing . . . or a lot, worth nothing.

Because when you abandon your possessions, they lose their value.

Alberta It's the trip that's making you nervous.

Elvira What happened to Tony?

Alberta Yes, they released him. But I haven't seen him yet.

He's celebrating. As soon as he gets tired he'll end up home.

I'll be waiting for him there.

Elvira As long as he doesn't insist on making bad choices . . .

Alberta Oh, you can't imagine how much I pray to God, Doña Elvira, to guide him.

We're yet to see if he's learned his lesson.

Because it was hard for him in there . . .

Is this what you're selling?

Elvira *takes another photo out of its frame.* **Alberta** *starts cleaning the objects for sale on the table.*

Elvira This was the first time I saw the snow . . .

She laughs.

Alberta She who laughs alone . . .

Elvira . . . The day I skied in the Maritime Alps.

Alberta I know that story already.

Elvira All fiction! I couldn't even stand on those skis.

Alberta Don't tell me that!

Elvira I put on the ski suit and the hat, and I posed, and took the picture, only thinking about my living room, and people asking me to tell them the story of the day I skied in the Maritime Alps.

Alberta Oh, Mrs. Elvira, what a sin!

To think that all these years I've been dusting a picture that's just a lie!

Elvira And Ramón Antonio who always listened to me as if it was the very first time. He loved to watch me trick my friends with my winter accomplishments.

Alberta At the end, you were this close to becoming an Olympic champion.

Both laugh.

Elvira Ramón Antonio was wonderful, he never said anything.

Alberta I never would have imagined Mr. Ramón as an accomplice.

Elvira He had no need to lie, because his family had money and took him to Europe when he was a child. That's why he took me to Paris on my honeymoon.

That's why he never said that the Alps story was a lie.

Alberta Everything is beautiful over there, right?

Elvira It's different.

Loud reggaeton can be heard from the street.

Alberta (*screaming at the window*) Turn that noise down . . . That's not music!

Neighbor (*off*) Come and do it yourself.

Alberta I'm going to call the police!

Neighbor (*off*) You better find a crook to defend you!

Alberta I'm sure you don't hear music this loud over there in Europe.

Music fades out slowly.

Elvira Everything is muted, people talk softly and they don't look at you . . .

As if you were invisible. So, you start feeling guilty, for being an uninvited guest.

After the dream of being in Paris is over and you're back you realize that they're the invisible ones.

Alberta But New York is different because a lot of people speak Spanish and that helps . . . and Carolina and your grandchildren live there . . .

You'll relax and forget everything.

Elvira That's what worries me! I don't want to forget.

Alberta What is it that worries you so much? We've emigrated from here anyway. Don't you realize that people no longer resemble what they were? After a lifetime of *good morning, good afternoon* . . . we don't recognize ourselves, and we're so scared that we shut ourselves up. Isn't that forgetting?

Elvira But if we all leave, who's going to tell the story?

When you belong, no matter how much changes take place, you belong, you're part of the story.

But in a different landscape with strange people, who'll remind us who we are?

Alberta Don't you want a herbal tea, instead?

Elvira *pulls out another picture.*

Elvira This was when Carolina turned six.

But the one who's looking at the camera, with that look she has when she knows perfectly well what she's doing, is Candelaria, stealing the spotlight from her sister, how sly. Such beautiful eyes filled with sparkles. She still looks like that, my Candelaria . . .

Phone rings.

Elvira ¡*Palabra cierta*! It must be Candela, nobody calls me at this time but my daughters . . . when they call me.

(*At the phone.*) Hello, sweetie . . . yes . . . Well, of course, I have *carne mechada*, I'll make some rice . . . and I've cooked some delicious black beans!

At what time are you coming?

I boiled the plantain because I didn't want to wait in line at the supermarket to get a small bottle of cooking oil.

Alberta *approves with a gesture and stays next to* **Elvira** *to better listen to the conversation.* **Alberta** *gestures according to what she hears, expressing her opinion.*

Elvira As soon as I get *apio* I'll make *buñuelos* for you, my love.

Alberta *disapproves; she is the one who makes the buñuelos.*

Elvira The sale is tomorrow and I haven't priced things yet . . .

It's not Carolina's doing . . .

I put the ad in the paper already so now I can't back down!

I can't clean so many things anymore . . .

Alberta *disaproves again; she is the one who cleans.* **Elvira** *turns and goes even further.*

Elvira Alberta is worse than ever, and you know how she is . . .

It's best if she doesn't clean.

Alberta Ok, here we go, now it's my turn!

Elvira Oh, Candela, leave me alone, we're busy here . . .

Alberta What are you saying about me, Candela?

Behave, bad girl!

. . . She's just like her mother . . . she loves fiction.

Elvira . . . So, Candela, what's that speech all about?

You can't accuse me of that . . . it's not fair.

Look, *mijita*, I was the first one to tell you about Marx, so, don't give me that catechism . . .

I know, my love, that you're struggling, and I acknowledge your work . . . Your dad too . . . don't say that.

I know, many good things have been accomplished, it's true . . .

No, it's not that. It's also so I can be with your sister and help her with the children. I hardly know Santiago!

That's her right: she wanted to leave just like you want to stay . . .

Don't talk like that about your sister!

Well, should I wait for you to have lunch or not?

Ok, if you're angry, all the worse for you.

Now you're going to have to let it go!

She hangs up the phone, upset.

Alberta Candelaria is also right: if everybody leaves, who'll be left here?

Elvira I'm not everybody, Alberta.

And I'm not leaving it's just that to see my grandchildren I need to take a plane.

Later I'll be too old to fly, and you know old parrots don't learn to speak.

Alberta *Ay*, Mrs. Elvira, but you already speak English!

Don't give me that!

Elvira I can barely read the medicine labels, that's all.

And I'm too old now to be treated like I'm worthless for speaking poorly in a foreign land.

They don't know anything about Venezuela either, only about Chavez, in favor or against; it doesn't matter . . . and about the beauty contests, because nobody comes to the beaches anymore, since it's so dangerous here . . .

Alberta One can hardly hear the Caribbean Sea anymore, with so much *bachata* and *reggaeton.*

. . .

Carolina is stubborn and after the kidnapping she's concerned, of course, she worries . . . she has her reasons.

Elvira The kidnapper also had his reasons . . . and the bankers and the ministers . . . But . . . what about my reasons?

Alberta Mr. Ramón Antonio almost died of fright.

Elvira Poor soul . . . my dear Ramon Antonio . . .

Alberta . . . And your daughters. . . and me! It was a miracle that they let you go, because Mr. Ramón Antonio had no money to pay that ransom . . .

Elvira Yes . . . it was a miracle.

Alberta I'm still paying for it.

Elvira What?!

Alberta I asked so much of the Virgencita del Carmen, that I still owe her.

Elvira What did you promise her?

Alberta That if they released you safely I wouldn't eat rice for a year.

Elvira No wonder your waistline has shrunk, Alberta!

Alberta And apparently, I'm going to end up in a beauty contest, because now I owe some more. What can one do?

If you don't pay for your miracles, your future catches up with you.

Elvira It's better to pay back your miracles than to go on useless diets.

Alberta Now that my Tony came out of jail, which is another miracle, no more rice for another year.

Elvira You said it: Tony was the miracle.

Alberta And with my taste for rice and chicken, rice pudding . . .

Elvira And you make it so well, Alberta—what a sacrifice!

Alberta For that very reason, Doña Elvira, it's best if you go to New York because it's scary going to the beach with so many hoods around here. And for you living far from the sea is worse than living without rice.

Elvira Because I'm from the Caribbean . . . That's my reason.

She pulls out another photo.

She was just a little girl when she graduated as a sociologist.

That day, Ramón Antonio told her that she had turned out a communist like her mother. But she seems to have forgotten that . . . Candelaria is such a case!

Phone rings.

Alberta There she is again!

She doesn't even stay angry for ten minutes.

Alberta *takes the phone and passes it to* **Elvira**.

Elvira (*at the phone*) Aja, what happened? Are you going to come for lunch? . . .

I'm not selling the furniture . . . No, *chica*! . . .

But Candelaria, what do you want the silver tea set for?

That's not too posh, *mija*? . . .

Yes, but your granny is also Carolina's granny . . .

And what does it matter if she drinks coffee? . . .

No. I'm not going to give it to Carolina either . . .

Let the fight with Carolina go, she hasn't asked for anything, she's happy with her IKEA stuff, she doesn't even remember the tea set . . . I'm not leaving you without memories, don't say that.

They were my memories before they became yours too, Candelaria.

Do you think it doesn't hurt? . . .

It hurts the one leaving and it hurts the one who stays, please stop messing with Carolina! . . .

Well, if you're so worried about what I'm going to sell, why don't you come, see what you want and take it? . . .

Well . . . Sure! Where will I go?

I'm going to be here all afternoon . . .

She feels tired.

. . .

For the rest of my life . . .

Alberta *Muchacha*, always spitting fire, she hasn't changed a bit.

Elvira It saved me that she's driving and there was a traffic cop so she had to hang up, because Candelaria can drive you crazy!

Alberta Well, you know she's very stubborn.

Elvira She's been a fanatic since she was a child.

If she was being Little Mermaid she wanted to sleep with her tail on; when she started reading poetry, she recited everything . . .

But not all is bad there nor is everything good here.

Alberta Well, the political situation, the insecurity . . .

I've already gone through that. I know that story too.

Elvira Emigration is erasing the past. Although in the first world, IKEA is leaving people without roots, without memories.

Alberta And what is that IKEA you talk so much about? . . .

The US emigration services?

Elvira It's a store, Alberta. That makes all households look the same . . . the same cutlery, the same trashcan, the same bathroom rug . . .

(*Screaming, urgent.*) No! Don't put that teapot on sale!

Alberta *drops the teapot. It breaks.*

Alberta *Ay*, Mrs. Elvira, what a pity, how can I repair it?

This teapot has lasted for so long . . .

Elvira Precisely, it was a miracle!

She tries to put the pieces together. **Alberta** *is ashamed.*

Alberta This time it's for sure,

I won't break anything else, I swear, Mrs. Elvira.

. . .

I'm going back to Colombia.

Elvira Oh, God, that hurts.

She starts crying, still with the teapot pieces in her hands.

Alberta Don't feel like that, please, I'll buy you another one . . . please don't cry, that makes me feel so bad . . .

Elvira No, Alberta, what are you thinking?

Ramón Antonio gave me this teapot when we went to Paris on our honeymoon.

You can't buy the memory of those days we spent together . . .

Alberta . . . Being invisible?

Both laugh, no matter the sadness.

Elvira I'm crying because you're leaving . . . because I am leaving . . . leaving, but we can't let go . . .

They embrace. They cry.

Alberta Tony needs a change.

They say things are better in Colombia than in Venezuela.

Elvira So, your mind is made up . . . Why didn't you tell me before?

Alberta For the same reason . . . because it hurts.

Alberta Maybe we can glue it with Krazy Glue, or will the water leak?

Elvira Yes, maybe, if we find all the pieces.

What can't be glued are the things that you leave behind . . .

That puzzle, your life, can never be put together again.

Every object is a piece of that puzzle.

With each piece you leave behind, a part of you stays as well.

Alberta After so much care . . . cleaning, putting everything back in the right place . . .

Elvira Imagine if the teapot, instead of breaking, ended up in the hands of strangers in exchange for some bills.

Those people would never be able to tell the story of the teas and cookies of our lives. Abandoned things become only objects, without a soul, without history. It's sad. It's better that it broke.

Alberta Because it's not the objects that matter, but the memory, right?

Elvira Yes . . . Don't you hear them crying?

Sound of distant moans. **Elvira** *looks around, listening to the lament coming from the objects.* **Alberta** *does not hear anything.*

Alberta I think it's time for a chamomile . . .

She exits but **Elvira** *doesn't notice it and keeps talking to her.*

Elvira I do hear them; it's not an invention.

There's a Nobel Prize who says that everything the potters said at the beginning of the world was engraved in the soft clay of the vessels that were molded with their hands and their conversation.

Alberta *enters with a cup of chamomile tea for* **Elvira**.

Elvira I don't want to leave.

Carolina lives far away and imagines that things are worse here than they are. In addition, Venezuelans exaggerate too much: no matter if you weigh a hundred kilos, you wear patterned leggings. Flowers, dots, or planets stretch and tremble to the rhythm of the curvy women butts that everyone turns to see.

Alberta But that's what those leggings are for, right?

So that everyone looks at you?

Elvira I doubt that in any other country leggings are as successful as they are in Venezuela.

We are passionate about everything.

I can't live without that joy.

Alberta *exists with the tea cup.*

Elvira The idea of the sale is good but: *Mami, don't you dare to sell this . . . don't sell that either, please . . .*

The room stays the same, as the song says, as if it was a museum, and I'm part of the collection.

She stays like a statue. **Alberta** *enters with a feather duster and cleans the statue which is* **Elvira**. **Elvira** *just moves her lips.*

Elvira Hello, my love, I love you and your dad loves you too, this is the house of happiness, *piñatas*, Christmas and *hallacas*, lunch on Sundays, and fights on Saturdays when the girls arrived at dawn.

Everything is intact, nothing changes, you can be sure of it . . .

She starts moving again.

Elvira Lies! Nobody is safe in their homes.

If I leave everything in its place, everything will end up covered with dust and dirt, just like the people in the houses full of absence.

Alberta *shakes the duster and exits.*

Gustavo (*off*) Alberta! . . . Alberta!

Elvira Who is it?

Gustavo (*off*) It's Gustavo, your tenant, Mrs. Elvira . . .

Elvira Oh, Gustavo, how are you?

Elvira *approaches the door to hear better. She fixes her look, flirty, although she talks through the closed door.*

Gustavo (*off*) There's no hot water, Mrs. Elvira.

I'm sorry to bother you but . . .

Elvira Don't worry; it's no bother . . .

Gustavo (*off*) Could you let me use your hot water heater so I can take a shower while the problem is solved?

Elvira Yes, of course. I'll open it for you.

Gustavo (*off*) Could you ask Mr. Martin to repair my water heater?

Elvira Alberta told him already.

But you know, Martin starts drinking on Friday what he's earned since Monday, so we have to wait till Tuesday for him to recover. But in the end, he always shows up, don't worry. I'm sorry if I don't open the door, but I'm a mess cleaning here.

Gustavo (*off*) Don't worry, Mrs. Elvira. Sorry for the interruption.

Elvira Don't worry. Come back whenever you want for a cup of herbal tea.

Gustavo (*off*) Oh, that would be nice . . .

Elvira Too much work?

Gustavo (*off*) On the contrary, too little . . .

Elvira I can hear your stress from behind the door.

Gustavo (*off*) Dollars are complicated.

Elvira Now you have to have dollars although our currency is *Bolívares*.

Gustavo (*off*) That's why now we need more than a herbal tea; we at least need Valium to keep going!

Anyway, one of these afternoons I'll visit you.

Elvira *sighs, watching her objects on sale which are placed on the table.*

Elvira How many dollars for my treasures?

Will it be enough to go a couple of times to the supermarket in New York? How many dollars for the little cups I bought on credit, one by one, until I completed the set . . . how many boxes of Corn Flakes in exchange?

Pause.

Elvira But if my grandchildren continue to grow far away, they'll never love me . . . Also, I'm forgetting everything lately . . . how do you say grandmother in English?

(*Calling.*) Alberta . . . Alberta . . .!

Let the hot water through for Gustavo to take a shower!

Alberta (*off*) Coming . . .

Candela *enters from behind. She is bringing flowers.*

Candela (*mischievous*) Who's Gustavo?

Elvira The new tenant.

Candelaria And why is it your problem whether Gustavo takes a shower or not?

Elvira What if he were my lover?

Candela Oh, Mom! You love to talk nonsense!

Candelaria *looks for a vase for the flowers, in the middle of the chaos of objects.*

Elvira Do you know why Gustavo is renting here?

Because your dad didn't see how good-looking he is.

Otherwise he would have looked for another tenant.

With all the years we've been married and how old I've become.

Candela He always finds you beautiful, Mom.

Elvira Because I take care of myself!

Ramón Antonio Quintero has never seen me in a mess!

Love is a matter of two, *mija*. You can't blame men for everything.

Candela Well, today you don't look very well put together, I would say.

Do you really think that if I'd looked good all day, Carlos would have stopped drinking?

Elvira Ramón Antonio left early this morning to get his visa and this sale is driving me crazy.

Carolina calls, the neighbor knocks on the door, the cooking oil's arrived, and the tenant claims he doesn't have any hot water . . .

Candelaria *notices that the doll house is empty. All its furniture lay in a box next to it.*

She starts to put everything inside the doll house.

Candela That's because you decided to rent out part of the house.

I don't understand why you insist on hiring Martin if you know he's not reliable.

Why don't you hire one of these plumbing companies?

Elvira They are too expensive and they are not reliable either.

Luckily, I have Martin to solve any problem with this house!

This morning the water company came to remove the water meters from all the houses.

You know why? Because they're stealing the meters that are made of bronze to do business.

The government's going to replace them with some Chinese plastic meters.

When? Nobody knows. Certainly, they won't be enough . . . for sure the Chinese won't be bringing new plastic meters until the government pays what it owes.

So, those bronze meters that are still functioning are going to be stolen, probably sold back to the Chinese.

In the meantime, water is being wasted, falling . . . through the hands of the government, the Chinese, the thieves or the people? Answer that!

You know so much about politics!

Candela Now I understand the cement in the main entrance.

Martin is very careless.

Elvira Hidrocapital left a hole and Martin fixed it.

If it wasn't for Martin this house would have fallen to pieces, because you know that your father isn't very talented with a hammer or saw.

Candela Now that he's retired, Dad could entertain himself helping around the house.

Elvira And who are you to decide what entertains your father?

He likes to play dominoes and watch Animal Channel.

Candela That's because you never wanted to have pets.

Elvira I had enough with you two and your father to look for more pets to take care of.

Candela I have an idea! I'm going to give dad a dog on Father's Day.

Elvira Is that what you came for? To pick a fight with me?

Candela Mom, I don't think you're allergic to dogs.

No one is allergic to dogs. A cat, then . . . what about a canary?

Elvira What part of "we are going to New York" didn't you understand, Candela?

Uncomfortable silence. With sadness, **Candela** *looks at the priced objects exposed on the table.*

Candela Are these the things you plan to sell?

Elvira Yes.

Candela Are you going to sell the silver jug with the family monogram, mom?

Elvira Do you want it? Take it.

Candela Aunt Hortensia's painting! Don't you care?

Elvira Oh, yes, I care. . . finally, I'm free from it!

Both laugh.

Candela *takes another object.*

Candela Oh, Mom, this is your wedding picture frame . . .

Where is the photo?

Elvira I kept it . . . to give it to you . . . after I die.

For now, I need it to remember . . . just the photo.

I don't need the frame.

Candela Do you really think you could move to New York?

You're not going to stand it, Mom, Carolina either.

Elvira Don't start. I don't want you to talk about your sister.

Candela How do you want me to say nothing?

Carolina left to go live the American dream, but from being a dentist she ended up serving drunks in a bar, walking dogs, and babysitting!

Elvira You should acknowledge her merits of finally becoming a dentist assistant instead.

Candela After six years of suffering! Did you know that she used to go to the department store with the children and told them they could put everything they wanted in the cart, made them imagine that they used all those things until they went bad . . . Then she would leave the cart in the store, went back home empty handed?

With just the feeling of having bought something . . . because in the North, if you don't buy you don't exist.

Elvira Poor thing . . . she didn't say anything to anyone . . .

She's like me. She doesn't like anyone to give her anything.

I found out that she was getting a divorce, when Fermin's mother told me. Carolina has never been much of a talker. She's like her father.

Candela It's not Carolina. No one tells the truth when they leave.

Everyone is doing great: those who deliver pizzas on a bike say they bought a pizzeria; the dog walkers say they're veterinarians . . .

I don't know how Venezuelans, who are so pretentious, have ended up being such conformists. Cowards!

If you think that the country is in need of honest, hard-working people, why don't you stay and help, then?

They prefer to go to Miami and spit out their demons talking badly about the government on Facebook. Pathetic!

Elvira I don't want to talk about politics.

We've never talked politics in this house.

Not even when your dad was a democrat and I was from the Communist Party.

Candela You started it. And I don't talk about it; I work hard, every day, to make this country a fairer place, with equal opportunities for all.

You are aware of the social debt here, mother.

But it's as if you forgot . . .

Elvira Let's go one step at the time, I really don't know if it's Marx, Carolina, the tenants or Father's Day. To begin with, the tenants keep us company, fill the house with noise, and keep it alive. Because the house, which was big to begin with, became huge when you left. As for the pets, do you know how much a bag of canary food costs?

Not to mention dogs or cats! At least we have a TV set.

Since we can't go out, at least we can watch the soap operas and as for pets, you just switch to Animal Channel.

Because you coming twice a month for lunch, isn't enough.

Is that all?

Candela I don't say you shouldn't go out; just that you have to be careful. You're arbitrary, Mom.

Elvira Arbitrary, no! When the refrigerator no longer makes ice, you have to buy everything the same day because do you know what a new refrigerator costs, *mija*?

Candela So, what . . . in USA they give them away for free, the refrigerators?

Elvira Don't be cynical or superficial, Candela.

Show me some respect; I'm your mom till the day I die.

Candela Carolina blackmailed you with your grandchildren.

Do you know what happened to Juliana when she arrived in Canada? It wasn't a modeling agency at all, it was a brothel!

Elvira I know the story; you don't need to scare me with it.

I know that the so-called equality of opportunity is nothing more than the standardization that annihilates the will of individuals, and thus control any possibility of social cohesion and free will . . .

Candela Wow . . .

Elvira *sits. She does'nt feel well. She uses a piece of newspaper as fan.*

Elvira This is an endless story . . . the end will be when I die, *mijita.*

Candela *worries.*

Candela No, Mom, you still have much love to give us.

Alberta *enters bringing a tray with a bottle of scotch and two glasses.*

Candela Let's have a drink to lower our blood pressure.

Elvira Stopping the fighting lowers blood pressure as well.

It's too early to drink.

Alberta *exits.*

Candela It's late enough.

Elvira Oh, don't say it's late if you want my blood pressure to come down.

Candela I mean, it's already 11, so we can have a drink.

Elvira 11:00 already?

Oh, my God, your dad is going to come and see the state I'm in! Where did I leave the brush?

Elvira *searches with urgency.*

Candela *finds the brush. She combs her mother's hair.*

Candela What I don't want is for you to have a bad time there.

Carolina's very selfish, as a good capitalist should be.

She wants you to be her babysitter, now that her husband left her.

Elvira *stops* **Candela**, *with love.*

Elvira Why are you so angry with your sister, Candela? That's bad.

That poisons your blood, which is the same as hers, *hija.*

Candela Maybe it's because you have always preferred her?

"Candela is strong; she knows how to defend herself.

The one that needs support is Carolina . . ."

So now Carolina is going to take my mom and dad away.

Elvira It's only a vacation.

Candela Haven't you thought that the ones that act stronger are weaker, more sensitive? That it's a defense mechanism, used by those weaker inside, afraid of anyone harming them. You've never thought about that?

Elvira I love you both the same. Carolina has been away for almost eight years now, we hardly see them once a year for few days.

Spending time with them is a joy.

Candela Some joys are sad.

Elvira You could also take a vacation.

Candela In that case, I'd go to China or Egypt, Mom, not New York.

And how long is that vacation of yours?

I know she wants you to stay for good.

Elvira Carolina never asks for anything, she doesn't complain.

Candela So, you're considering it?

Elvira They're my grandchildren.

They deserve the opportunity of a better life, with more security. And Carolina needs help.

Candela So, you're considering it!

To go live as an undocumented migrant, taking care of little children . . .

Elvira My grandchildren!

Candela You've already raised your daughters!

Now it's your turn to enjoy life, Mom.

Elvira Precisely, spending time with my grandchildren.

Because if I wait for you to have kids . . .

Candela Let me tell you that I'm dating a Cuban I met at the congress . . .

Elvira Oh, what good news that he's Cuban!

Candela I don't understand.

Elvira Well, because as soon as he can, he'll escape to Miami and then we'll all be in the same country!

Candela I won't fall for your provocations.

Tell me once and for all: are you planning to move to New York?

Elvira I already told you: no!

Candela But you don't sell everything to go on vacation or to grandchildren. I can't believe Dad agrees. Or do I have to ask Carolina? Because she's the one behind all this, isn't she?

Making the decisions . . . Where is the tea set?

Elvira I'm going to give it to Alberta; she's the one who has kept it polished all these years . . . so she can pay for her trip to Colombia.

Candela But, Mom, Alberta died years ago!

Elvira *feels very confused.*

They both start searching for the silver tea set.

Elvira Could it be that someone stole it?

Candela When was the last time you saw it?

Elvira Since when, I don't remember. Your dad says that tea keeps him awake, and chamomile tastes like medicine.

So, I just drink chamomile in my cup, we haven't use the tea set in a long time. The British are the ones who drink tea.

Candela That tea set belonged to the poet Ramos Sucre, your great-uncle, Mom! Where could it be?

What you inherit isn't stolen.

Elvira *thinks for a moment.*

Elvira That is not the meaning of that saying. Although said like that, changes it. You turn everything around at your convenience, with such intelligence!

She notices that the doll house is full of its furniture again. She starts pulling out the little furniture, putting it inside a cardboard box.

Candela It's true; I inherited it from you.

Elvira You can't say I'm a liar. Nor a cheater!

Candela And how are you going to get a resident visa if it is not cheating?

They don't want more Latinos in the USA, much less old ones.

Elvira Leave the USA where it is, Candela.

We're fine right here, enjoying the fresh afternoon, the breeze that comes down from the Avila . . .

Candela Tell me, what are you willing to do to get a visa?

You could divorce and remarry . . . as more than 40 percent of immigrants do . . . who get the visa by spreading their legs.

Elvira *throws whatever she is holding, with violence, into the box.*

Painful silence.

Candela Forgive me, mother.

Elvira You talk too much bullshit, Candela.

Candela I don't want you to leave.

She cries. They hug each other.

A Skype call sounds. **Elvira** *gets nervous, looks to* **Candela** *as warning her not to fight with her sister.*

Elvira *answers the call on the laptop.*

Carolina *enters.*

Carolina Hi, Mom. I couldn't call you before because we had one patient after another.

Tell me, is the sale ready to go?

Doorbell rings.

Carolina What's that? The door?

Don't open it without asking who it is . . . it could be a thief.

Candela *passes by the laptop camera. She goes to open the door.*

Seller (*off*) Cheese! . . . Fresh cheese!

Elvira Oh, it's the cheese seller, it doesn't matter, I still have some left. Leave it, Candela. He knows that if I don't open the door it is because I still have some.

Seller (*off*) Buy it now; it won't last till tomorrow . . . Cheese!

I have cheese!

Candela *comes back.*

Carolina Hi, Candy, Candy!

Candela Don't call me like that, fuck!

Elvira *sighs, disillusioned.*

Carolina Well, you always say what's on your mind, no matter how it affects others.

Candela That's what's happening? So, let me ask you something that I've been wondering about: why the United States has one of the highest number of prisoners per capita in the world? Seven times more than in Venezuela!

Carolina Because here you pay for what you do.

It's a non-impunity system. If you don't break the law, you live in peace. Not like in Venezuela where criminals are free while honest people live locked up in fear.

Candela You call white people honest people, I suppose.

Since the majority of prisoners are black and Latino.

What a coincidence! That's proof that whites are better, right?

Carolina I won't argue with you.

Candela What I'm saying is: what is the point of leaving Maracaibo to keep praying to La Chinita with a bunch of *maracuchos* in Texas?

Carolina Because it's not the same sleeping over at a friend's house, after a party, so they don't fine you for driving drunk back to your house, than to have to stay over until dawn to avoid getting killed. You choose, being fined or murdered . . .

Candela Oh, Carolina, you're watching too much CNN.

It's much more complicated than that.

Carolina *Mama*! . . . Enjoy Candelaria's visit, since she doesn't visit frequently . . . I'll call you tomorrow morning, okay? *Besitos*.

She exits.

Elvira (*to the laptop screen*) Goodbye, my love, see you tomorrow . . .

Candela There're not 25,000 deaths per year; lies of the opposition.

Elvira 11,000 are not just a few either, truths of the government.

Candela Did you know what happened to Margarita Cardenas?

Elvira Her mom told me she was doing great.

She already has a good full-time job, a home . . .

Well, I know Carmencita exaggerates a lot, and Margarita is a spoiled brat but . . .

Candela Margarita works reading the tarot; she doesn't even have a tourist visa. It turns out that she had a client who didn't like the future she predicted for him in one of her readings, and he beat her to death, he almost killed her, she ended up in a hospital. That's how it is in the North.

Do you know what they have a lot of out there?

Crazy people! Enough to give away!

She takes a couple of candlesticks from the table.

But, Mom, are you going to sell the silver candlesticks?

To buy what: a peanut butter jar, a bottle of apple juice, a box of Corn Flakes, skim milk for breakfast and a few Milky Ways for your grandchildren?

Candelaria *discovers a little box among the things on sale on the table. She takes it with great care. She opens it with parsimony, and begins to play with colorful candy wrappers that were carefully kept in that little box. She remembers.*

Candela

But, Mommy, after eating the chocolate,
I can't throw this beautiful paper in the trash.
I can't be so unfair. The chocolate came wrapped.
I can't be so ungrateful after eating it.

She puts back the colorful wrappers in the box. **Elvira** *takes the box and puts it back on the table.*

Elvira Ramón Antonio is right: Candela was born worried.

Always aware of others, she never liked being alone.

While Carolina was so self-absorbed, dreaming of living a different life, like a princess or a mermaid in another world with other people . . . What was it that she didn't like about her real life?

That took her far away. Although Candela is also gone, living a better future that doesn't exist.

Candela *exits.*

Elvira *looks tired and sad.*

Nevertheless, she tries and takes her robe off, fixes her hair . . . **Alberta** *enters.*

They start taking objects from the table.

They talk to the public, offering the different objects on sale.

Alberta It's not expensive, look underneath, it's signed!

This porcelain doll is so beautiful . . . Authentic Lladró . . .

Elvira 300 is OK, take it . . .

Yes, it's big, and it became bigger after the children left . . .

I have two, one is out of the country, and the other works here . . . two grandchildren, one of twelve and one of four . . .

Alberta *offers the robe* **Elvira** *was wearing until now.*

Alberta That's 100 percent silk, Chinese, ancient, Chinese, authentic, almost new, nobody has ever used it . . . How much? . . . Nooooo, 100 is too little . . .

Elvira This frame is perfect for a wedding photo, or a graduation photo . . . It's pure silver . . .

Alberta Don't you see the oranges?

Elvira It's true, it's a bit abstract, but here's the plate, you see?

Alberta And this is a printed tablecloth, like an Indian print . . .

Elvira She's not famous but you know, you never know, art sometimes gets revalued and surprises you . . .

Alberta Give me 50 then, I'm not going to argue.

Elvira Hello, Carmencita, what's up? Have you heard about Margarita?

. . . I'm glad . . . Yes, of course we'll call her . . .

No, it's only for a few months, to give it a try, you know . . .

Oh, I still have too much stuff . . .

The silver tea set? Oh, I'm sorry, I already offered it . . .

Don't you like the tureen . . . or the candlesticks?

Alberta *exits.*

Elvira *sits in a chair, exhausted; she is feeling "sold out."*

She counts the money from the sale, and put it into her shoe.

She falls asleep.

Down the lights; it is early evening.

Alberta *comes with the silver teapot, and places it on the side. She exits.*

A masked man comes in. He goes directly to remove the shoe to get the money inside. **Elvira** *wakes up.*

Elvira Hey . . . what's the matter . . . Tony?!

Tony *pulls out a gun.*

Tony Shhhhh . . . Don't make noise, old lady, you're already gone.

Whoever leaves town, I forget, I don't know you.

Elvira But I've known you since you were a child.

Tony Stop recognizing and give me the money, you're not going to do anything with those *Bolívares* in the US.

Elvira Tony . . . I know you took part in the kidnapping . . .

Tony *gets closer to* **Elvira**, *threatening.*

Tony I didn't, don't make it up.

Go on your trip and nothing's happened here.

Give me the money!

Elvira *pulls out the money from her shoe and hands it to* **Tony**.

Elvira I know you were in the kidnapping. It was your voice . . .

Tony Oh yeah? And why didn't you say anything, then?

Elvira Because I love Alberta.

Tony That's paid for. Why do you think they let you go?

You are so stupid.

Elvira They let me go, but you're going to kill your mother.

Tony Shut up!

He hits **Elvira** *in the head; she faints.*

Tony *runs out; on his way out he takes the silver teapot. A little piece of paper drops from it.*

He exits.

Lights fades in slowly.

Elvira *wakes up, very confussed. She feels pain in her head.*

She looks around; everything looks the same, but for a little piece of paper, carefully folded on the floor. She takes it and unfolds it. She reads it. It is cut from an old newspaper.

Elvira Mrs. Alberta Suarez has passed away.

Her son Tony Suárez, Elvira Gutiérrez de Quintero, and her daughters Carolina and Candelaria . . .

She cries silently.

Your family, Alberta . . . We are your family, Tony . . . wherever you are.

Sounds of honking.

She reacts, coming back from her memories.

She saves the obituary inside her cleavage.

Quickly, she repairs her appearance.

Honking again.

Come on, what an annoying taxi . . .

Hurry up, Ramon Antonio, the airport taxi is here!

She takes the suitcase she was filling with special objects.

Alberta *waits for her at the door.*

They stare at each other for a moment. **Elvira** *exits.* **Alberta** *exits after her.*

Elvira *enters again, in a rush.*

She talks to the objects she is leaving behind.

I'm going to come back . . . don't worry . . .

If you're nothing without me, I'm no one without you.

I'll be back. The center of my world is still in Caracas.

I can't change that. I'm leaving because I'll return.

I'm the country and it's right here, even if I leave . . .

I am a fish of this sea, even if the coastguards want me picked up.

She exits.

The end.

Questions of Home

Doreen Baingana

Doreen Baingana is a Ugandan writer and arts manager. Her story collection *Tropical Fish: Stories out of Entebbe* won the Grace Paley Prize for Short Fiction in 2003 and the Commonwealth Prize for Best First Book, Africa Region in 2006. Two stories in the collection were finalists for the Caine Prize. The title story *Tropical Fish,* was performed in 2016 at the Writivism Festival and the Kampala International Theatre Festival and in 2017 at the AfriCologne Theatre Festival. Baingana's awards include a Bread Loaf Conference Fellowship (2005), a Miles Morland Scholarship for African Writers (2014), a Rockefeller Bellagio Residency (2017), and a Tebere Arts Foundation Residency (2020). She has published two children's books and fiction and essays in numerous international journals. She has a law degree from Makerere University in Kampala and an MFA in creative writing from the University of Maryland, College Park. She has been a chairperson of FEMRITE, the Uganda Women Writers' Association, and a managing editor of Storymoja, a Kenyan publisher. Baingana co-founded and is the director of the Mawazo Africa Writing Institute in Entebbe that trains creative writers and other professionals from across Africa.

Baingana has adapted this performance piece from a short story of the same name published in her collection *Tropical Fish.*

Setting

After eight years in the United States, a Ugandan woman returns home. Having adjusted mentally and emotionally to life in the US, she is now faced with the challenging task of readjusting to her country of birth and navigating her fluid identities.

Production History

Adapted from the short story "Questions of Home" published in *Tropical Fish: Stories out of Entebbe* by Doreen Baingana, University of Massachusetts Press, Amherst, February 2005.

Aah! I feared the plane was just about to land into Lake Victoria, but had just missed it by one quick swoop to the left. Whew! Looking down at Uganda's international airport, I could tell the lake was down below because there were no lights at all, just a blank indigo mass. Entebbe International Airport shone dimly in one tiny area. The town's lights were scattered and weak; Entebbe was asleep. How different it was from the spread of strong lights that was Washington, DC, where I had departed. There, the night is never dark, but rather a hazy yellow. Bright orbs illuminate the memorials and monuments, giving passengers a film version of the city as planes circle up and away. I was glad to leave Washington, and only keep a few choice images of it in my mind. I was back home for good after eight years away.

Back on earth, we passengers clapped, most of us Ugandans happy to be back home and glad for a safe landing. Camaraderie had blossomed after sitting so close together for over fifteen hours, through all the take-offs and landings of the Ethiopian Airlines plane in New York, Rome, Addis Ababa, Nairobi, and finally Entebbe. We'd shared the cramped seats, the safety instructions repeated monotonously in English, French, and Amharic, the tiny toilets and scary blue water, the cramps, indigestion, cold dry stale air. and dull Muzak. The pretty Ethiopian air hostesses had become as familiar as maids and the long hours had merged into one endless drone of a moment. Arriving was such a relief.

On the ground, the crew, looking flustered, talked to each other in Amharic, and then one of them announced that we were asked to stay seated. No explanation was given. Peering through the cabin windows, I could see we had stopped far from the main airport building. After an uncomfortable, weary half hour, the pilot explained: the plane was stuck in mud. It was the rainy season, mud washed over the runway even after repeated clearings. I couldn't stop myself smiling at the news, my amusement compounded by the groans of frustration around me. How perfectly third world, I thought. This was the kind of thing I vehemently denied happening when talking to my American friends. The stereotypes of 'Africa' filled me with self-righteous anger. Well, here I was then, about to wrangle with the reality itself.

Finally, the plane doors were opened, letting in a dark warm lake breeze. At last, we would be free from the cabin's cramped prison. The fish smell and heat hit as I stepped out of the plane and walked to the bus that would take us to the terminal.

Surprise: the airport, which I remembered as an imposing building of towering cement columns and huge glass windows, now looked more like an abandoned barn than anything else. Was I going to experience expatriate clichés at every turn? This was home; I wasn't here to make comparisons at every turn. All I wanted was for my memories to become solid again, to become real physical things after living for eight years in my head.

Immigration and customs were easy, but my body tightened with excitement, or was it anxiety at the thought of meeting my mother and Patti, my sister, after eight whole years away. There they were! Maama seemed to have shrunk – she was not as comfortably plump as she used to be and looked shorter. Oh, but the sweetness of familiar faces, bodies, gestures, hugs.

"*Kurikayo,*" Maama said.

She spoke to us in Runyankore, her husband's language, not her mother tongue. We had grown up answering back in English, but this now seemed wrong, so I answered in Runyankore too but with my clumsy accent, embarrassed, "*Narugayo.*"

Patti laughed at me as she gave me a hug. She used Luganda instead, "*Kulika, bambi,*" which we used at school once outside class.

My mind was crawling behind my body to get here, and the jet lag wasn't helping. It would take a while to catch up with what my eyes saw, ears heard, and skin felt. Here was Maama, right here, no longer only a thought, but resurrected into warm flesh. I had dwelt on certain physical details all these years, such as her brown toes with curved pink and white nails. I had imagined Maama's warm slightly tangy bodily scent was a private message to me alone, but then I caught whiffs of it on the metro in D.C., in class, from one or two women I passed by on sidewalks. I would turn around quickly in surprise, not even fully conscious that I was looking for someone thousands of miles away. Now here we were, in the same room.

Was I ready? I felt like a cardboard copy of myself. Strangely enough, this was exactly how, in certain flash moments of awareness, I had felt in America. Like an African doll. An actress dressed up for the part. A mechanism that could be wound up and then let go and watched. This feeling of not being quite real, the absurdity of it, became normal. Thank God all that was now over.

Patti was all practical help, ushering us forward, collecting my three matching sets of green suitcases. The rest of my belongings were coming by cargo. Since I was home for good, I had brought as much as I could, including all I thought I couldn't get in Uganda.

"All these suitcases, *bannange*! As if you haven't lived here before with what we have here," Patti scoffed gently.

Maama took my side. "Let her have her extra, until she gets used."

"Until you settle *down.* When your American shoes and suits are worn out." We laughed.

I knew all this, but still had bought lots of organic decaffeinated coffee, apricot and peach bubble-bath, pink women's razors with aloe and vitamin E, and enough lubricated, ultra-sensitive, extra-strong, non-expiring latex condoms to last anywhere from two to six years, depending on male availability. That was wishful thinking, of course, but I bought them anyway. I smiled now as I remembered the drug store clerk in D.C. counting the packets, her eyes bulging with shock.

"For a school," I murmured. Luckily, I was too dark to blush.

Outside the airport building, the warm indigo air was a light embrace. "Oh, how dark the sky is." I leaned back to take it all in. The sky was spread open like an endless scroll, the stars mysterious yet meaningful writing. "Just look at all those stars! You can actually see the stars!"

Maama and Patti looked at each other. "*Ahaa, nga* you're romantic these days," Patti said.

But I couldn't help myself. "And that . . . oh, I remember that perfumy smell . . . what is that?"

"Maybe those flowers over there, the pale blue ones, lilacs?" Patti pointed to a large bush whose delicate flowers glowed faintly in the dark. Their sweet smell wafted by again with a change of wind.

"I hadn't even noticed," Maama said. "Yes, they do smell nice."

"Nice? Not *nice*." Some other *new* word, I thought to myself.

The road from the airport had only one army checkpoint, which was quick and business-like. Patti said there were now almost no demands for *chai*, no threats to dodge by secretly slipping money into soldiers' fists. The roadblocks weren't even permanent like they used to be. I couldn't imagine not being scared. No starving-thin, red-eyed, angry-looking soldiers with harsh voices? No more repetitive, insistent interrogations meant to intimidate rather than to get information?

I held my breath out of old habit but was pleasantly surprised by the friendliness of the soldiers, the casual way they swung their guns. They greeted Maama respectfully, and then actually *told* us that they were checking for drugs or other smuggled goods, and apologized for the inconvenience!

The road from the airport passed along the lakeshore for about a mile. The air was cool and fresh as it rushed across my face. All I could see was a dark expanse in place of the lake. How calming. Physical things remained the same, or at least it seemed so. I couldn't wait to walk along the thin strip of beach at Lido; the lake was Entebbe, its waves would always slap against its shores. I sighed deeply, enjoying the car's hum. Here I was, together with my mother and my sister. I was home.

* * *

I planned to live with my mother for a few months while settling in. I had left Uganda soon after graduating from Makerere University. I could not turn down the coincidental approval of my application for an American visa just then, when I hadn't got a job yet. My plan was to do a Masters in Public Administration then come back, but I had stayed on and on in Washington, D.C. Maama, especially, had not been happy with my 'delay' as I called it. I wouldn't admit that America had begun to seem like home, albeit a strange one. I could not dare say I might want to stay in America for good. African immigrants, especially, didn't do this. I didn't even admit it to myself, as though it was a betrayal of some kind. It was easier to postpone the decision.

What changed? The painful end of yet another relationship made me feel I would never belong. Everyone who truly loved me was backing home. And then came Ugandan President Munino's speech to the Association of Ugandans in America, calling on all of us 'brain-drain' Ugandans to go back home and help re-build the country. The speech made me feel so good, so necessary, heroic even. Before this, I had scorned any kind of nationalistic fervor; if I felt any allegiance at all, it was to my ethnic group, the Banyakore. That was who I was. But the president's speech, listened to as a foreigner in America, turned me religiously into a Ugandan.

I applied for an administrative position with the Uganda Human Rights Commission, and got it. And so, here I was.

* * *

A week later, I started work. I took a minibus, what everyone called a *matatu*, from Entebbe to Kampala. The early morning ride on my first day, through fresh new air, thrilled me. My fellow travelers were shiny with Vaseline and hair oil. Their shoes were so highly polished you'd think they would never be defeated by the dust. The women wore dresses of a metallic sheen that apparently was still in fashion after almost a decade. The *matatus* were no longer squashed to the breaking point with passengers like they used to be. Now they sat only three to a row, with enough maneuvering space. Back then, the whole length of their bodies intimately touched and slid across total strangers as they were bumped and shaken all the way to the capital. This intimacy, which had been natural to me, was something I now dreaded. I had learnt in America to cringe at the touch of strangers. Now that more *matatus* meant more space for everyone, the ride back home at least would be bearable, when I would be sweaty, tired, and longing for privacy.

The taxi-ride gave me half an hour to look ahead at the day calmly, make plans, and think nice little expectant thoughts. I would not worry. My new boss, Mr. Musozi, had been very helpful, if rather scatter-brained, by phone and fax. I was sure I would do a good job. By the time the *matatu* got to Kampala, the sun was completely awake and flexing its muscles.

At the ministry building, a rusty brown gate was wide open next to a wooden box large enough for only one person, marked SECURICO. It was empty. That perhaps was a good sign. The office building was beautiful: old and broad, with thick cement walls, and a veranda all around divided by tall, solid columns. It was the kind built in the colonial days, when the British could get all the materials and land they demanded, once they ordered the local people to move away. There were huge windows all along the walls of the wide, one-level building to let in cooling air. The walls were painted gray to about hip-level and white above.

I walked around the building looking for an entrance. I found a doorway at one corner. In I went and immediately found myself outside again in a courtyard: a large square piece of grass with small flowers, sunlight, and more office windows and doors facing onto it. How nice. My workmate in D.C., Tamika, in her windowless office on the eighth floor of a building in the gray downtown, would envy me now. I peered into a window. Because of the blinding sunlight, I could only make out space, lots of it, and large wooden heavy-looking furniture. Then I saw a young woman, pregnant, or merely fat and ripe looking, sitting behind a huge counter. Her shiny red dress was stretched tight across her breasts and stomach. She was bent over a green piece of cloth she was embroidering.

"Good morning," I said. No reaction. I cleared my throat and raised my voice, "Good morning."

The woman looked up startled, and then frowned. She turned back to finish a stitch, and asked without looking up, "Can I help you?"

"I'd like to see Mr. Musozi."

The receptionist gave me a look that seemed to say, don't you know anything? "Mr. Musozi?" she asked.

Didn't she know who he was, for God's sake? "Yes, the Director of—"

"I know that. I work here." A pause. Two more stitches.

What to do? Should I have addressed the receptionist as 'auntie' like the market women did? This was an office! "Well, can you direct me to his office?"

"Does he know you were coming?"

"Yes." I felt more pricks of annoyance. But the less said, the better. Back in the States, I had gotten used to nonsensical roadblocks like this set up by receptionists, clerks, police, and sales-people who assumed I didn't know what I wanted, who I was asking for, where I was or was supposed to be, and of course that I couldn't read a map. Not to mention those who couldn't or wouldn't understand my accent. So, I had learnt to speak slowly and loudly, assuming it was my fault I wasn't understood. But speaking more clearly meant hitting the consonants harder, which actually was less American and therefore less clear to Americans. After about two years I learnt to slur a little, and then did so unconsciously after that. Now back here, at the airport for example, I had slipped into my American accent, and stopped talking abruptly, mid-sentence, feeling foolish. Maama and Patti laughed, but the baggage clerk gave me a disparaging look, as if to say, *you poor lost wanna-be-white.*

Anyway, who was this fat receptionist to interrogate me? I had admired her womanly pregnant softness, but now wondered how someone so feminine could be so hostile. Moreover, to a "sister," as was said back in the States, except that here the two of us were not sisters since almost everyone was black.

Finally, the receptionist said, "Mr. Musozi went to bury in the village. I don't think he will be here today." She smiled a trite maliciously at me.

Well, I hadn't been a 'sistah' for nothing. "Miss, you *think*, or don't you know? Would it be too much to ask you to find out?" I put as much sarcasm as I could in my voice, and gestured toward a huge dusty black phone sitting on the counter like a gigantic dead beetle. It looked like a remnant from the colonial days that hadn't been used or dusted since then.

The receptionist ignored the phone. "Did he know his relative would die?"

"Don't ask me! Look, this shouldn't be so difficult—"

"—Even if he was coming today, he wouldn't be here at this time. It's only nine o'clock. First, he has to take his children to school and his wife to work."

"Listen," I put both my hands on the counter firmly. "I am the new Executive Assistant to the Director of the Human Rights Commission. Mr. Musozi specifically asked me to come here today." I took a deep breath and then said slowly, "Now, is there someone who can direct me to my office? Besides you, of course." I stepped back and waited.

Incredibly, the receptionist broke into a huge smile, put her sewing to the side, and stood up, straightening her tight dress over her bulging breasts and belly. "Eeeeh, why didn't you tell me? Christine Mugisha, yes? You are very, *very* welcome. My name is Peninah. Oo-oh, you are the lady Mister Musozi has been praising. Okaaay. *Bambi*, how are you?" She held out both hands warmly, and I, confused, placed both of mine in them. She laughed, showing two neat rows of tiny white teeth and larger purple-pink gums.

"I'm fine, thanks," I answered, not smiling. I took back my hands and crossed my arms in front of my chest.

"So, how was America?" Peninah asked enthusiastically, as if we were long lost friends. "My uncle's wife, the second one, when he died, took off to America with his two children. Stole them, basically. It's been what—ten years now, can you imagine? And you know, she said she would help me go there to study catering, but have I heard anything?"

"Oh," I said and shrugged. What did she want me to do with all this personal information? I looked at my watch pointedly. It was already after nine.

"*Bambi*, you got tired of the *bazungu*? Or weren't the dollars enough?" Peninah laughed at her own joke, her breast shaking. She covered her mouth with fat brown fingers, each with startling white half-moon tips. She was beautiful, I had to admit grudgingly. She had large eyes with heavy 'bedroom' eyelids, but almost no eyelashes or eyebrows. Pregnancy gave women such lush skin, as though they were now *really* women. Not like me, with my stick figure, no hips or breasts to speak of, which had not been a problem in the States. But here, as my mother had reminded my already, as she heaped more *matooke* onto my plate, it was not appreciated. Thin people had problems; one had best keep away, Maama said. Especially now with HIV/AIDS, better known as "slim."

Peninah came out from behind the counter. "Let me take you to Mister Oduro. He works with Mr. Musozi on the Commission. Oh, there he is. Georgi!" She shouted at a tall thin very black man walking rapidly down the corridor. He stopped, turned, and stood stock still, looking down as he waited. Peninah continued, "He is always the first one here. He eats and sleeps work."

A real officer at last, I sighed with relief as we approached him. I reached out my hand. He shook it with a quick jerk then dropped it without a smile, without any expression at all. He glanced at me then away, like a bird. "I'm, Mugisha, the new assis—"

"Yes, yes, I know. Mister Musozi had a death in the family. He will be here tomorrow. I'll show you your office. Thanks, Peninah." He turned like a stiff soldier and walked swiftly down the corridor. I followed at a trot as Peninah's languid laughter faded behind us.

Oduro stopped and pointed: "Enter. It leads into Mister Musozi's office. He likes to talk when he works." Oduro turned on his heel and walked away.

The room was huge, with a bare table, chair, file cabinet, and bookshelf. There was the same kind of old-fashioned phone that the receptionist had. I wanted to ask if it worked but dared not. Mr. Oduro came back in with a large pile of dusty files and plumped then on my desk. I sneezed.

"You're allergic? Use Piriton. Every day. I don't even wash my shirts. They just get dirty again."

I stared at him in surprise, then noticed his tight smile and laughed in relief.

"Read these. Applications under the Human Rights Act. Mr. Musozi will explain. Ask Peninah for stationery. Call me Oduro." And off he marched.

My eyes followed him. How odd. Well, he could make a joke, at least. Thank goodness, Mr. Musozi had sounded congenial over the phone. And there was always Peninah for company. Oh, no! I smiled to myself.

I turned to the heap of files. The sun made a big hot square of light right in the middle of my desk. Curtains, anyone? Hallo? But, I didn't want to face Peninah again just yet. I should enjoy the sun after all those miserable winters dreaming about it. Dust danced in the light as I flicked through the files. I wanted to be ready and make clever observations to Mr. Musozi tomorrow. I had no distractions anyway; no e-mail or Internet. By the way, how on earth was I going to work without a computer? A sneeze punctuated my every thought. I should make a list of things I needed, including a writing pad and pen to make the list with!

I walked into Mr. Musozi's office to search for paper and pen. He had more furniture than I had: a worn carpet, more cabinets, and bookshelves overflowing with volumes of statutes, law journals, and more dusty files. His desk was strewn with paper that covered his computer too. He had a picture of President Munino on the wall. A much younger, thinner Munino, just out of the 'bush,' when he had just taken power. The only other wall hanging was a government calendar with Munino's face again, more wealthy-looking now, less gaunt, more self-satisfied. Eight years later, eight years fatter, and he was still president. But, he was better than anyone they had in the past: Idi Amin, Obote, and so on. A stable government and security in most of the country was a relief. People could breathe again. I hoped Munino wouldn't get a heart attack and die, what with all that weight. That would plunge Uganda back into chaos. Enough already.

I tore a piece of paper from a pad on Mr. Musozi's desk, and found a pen underneath a pile of papers. Back in my office I wrote the list. I would give it to Peninah in the afternoon, not right now. I couldn't face her again just yet.

* * *

The sun was so brilliant the next morning, I wondered how I had woken up for eight years without it. I got myself chock-full of antihistamines and coffee to ward off the accompanying sleepiness. Maama said my skirt was too short; I was taking too much medicine and too much coffee and I was going to be late. The traffic on the Entebbe–Kampala road was a mess these days. And, by the way, did I have taxi fare? I should pack some lunch—

"Maama, stop! In case you've forgotten, I'm twenty-seven and have been living on my own—"

"I'm just warning you. Don't waste time; you better go now."

I sighed with exasperation and walked out. I would deal with Maama later; there was a job to be done. How on earth did Patti manage Maama?

At eight-thirty the next morning when I got in, Oduro was already at his desk. My hallo was answered with a curt nod. Feeling dismissed, I went back to my office. Well, I was ready for Mr. Musozi, having written down questions for him and organized the applications by date and category of request, valiantly ignoring the dust. I waited nervously, skimming through the files again. At about ten-thirty, I heard Peninah loudly welcome Mr. Musozi from across the courtyard. They talked for about twenty minutes. I checked my watch and wondered whether I should go up and join them. Would that be rude or the polite thing to do? I hadn't had a real job as an adult in Uganda, so was unsure about office etiquette here. Mr. Musozi had been nice on the phone, but still, he *was* the Director of the Human Rights Commission.

Mr. Musozi came in at last, bustling like a bumblebee. I was surprised to see that he was such a small man, but with a round ball of a belly sitting on top of his small frame. He looked pregnant. His gray suit was old, frayed, and out of shape, his glasses thick, old-fashioned large squares of brown plastic. If he hadn't a bald crown with short white fuzz around it, he could have been mistaken for a boy.

I nervously stood up to greet him. Mr. Musozi rushed over and grabbed my hand. "Hallo, hallo, hallo, welcome, Miss Mugisha, is it? Yes, yes, how are you? Good, good. I see you've settled in, straight to the paperwork, good, good."

He rushed behind his table and sat down. His stream of words and energy swept through the air. "So, yes, yes, sorry about yesterday, had to go bury my *senga*, you know how people die. Every three months it seems I make the trip to Mubende, you have to, you know, or they will talk, and your wife will stop talking to you, and so on, and who will attend yours, you know? Yes, yes, our wonderful traditions, oh yes. Let's see, here we are, this is the Committee." He spread his short arms wide, showing me the room. "The Uganda Human Rights Committee set up by an Act of Parliament. Ha! Not what you were expecting, no?" He laughed cheekily, as if he had played a clever trick on me. I sat back down, stunned.

"Now, now, where are we? What do you need to know? Let me bring you up to date. Our problem is money. Not surprised, eh? No, no, me neither." As he talked, he stood up, walked around his desk, drew out of his trouser pocket a large, startlingly white handkerchief, cleaned his glasses, folded the hanky in half, wiped his face, walked back to his seat, sat down, got back up again. I just sat there, mentally open-mouthed.

Mr. Musozi stopped when Oduro walked in and shook hands with him. "Sorry about the loss."

"Yes, yes, these things happen. My mother's younger sister, you know? Well, she's gone, she's gone. And how is Karamoja? How is the project going?"

"Slow. I'm still trying to get the funds from Accounts to travel there. I can't do anything until I have been to the area and talked to the chiefs themselves."

"Yes, yes, the fight with Accounts, those thieves. Always the first step. Can't they at least give you half? Let them steal the rest." They both laughed shortly. Mr. Musozi turned to me, "I hope you took this course back in America, 'How to Fight for Your Money.' It's required. Absolutely mandatory. You didn't? Well, that's the main thing we do here. Yes, yes." The two men laughed again. "Luckily, you came with your own money. Very wise. Very wise indeed."

"Accounts won't like that." Oduro noted dryly, and they laughed again.

I didn't think it was so funny. This was exactly the kind of thing that made the well-planned projects fail, the lack of money to implement them. If the money was allotted for the project, how dare the Accounts Department not release it? All of it? Not to mention the wasted time and energy begging. Such major setbacks should be dealt with, not laughed at! I couldn't stop myself: "Sir, why hasn't the Accounts Department been held—"

"Oh, no, no, my dear, do not call me sir, no, no, no. Just Musozi, okay?"

Before I could go on, an officer came in, then another and another, all to offer their condolences to Mr. Musozi. I went back to my desk after a few minutes, since it was clear his colleagues had settled down for a good talk. But I couldn't do very much before conferring with Mr. Musozi. The other officers passed back and forth by my desk, and my boss's high-pitched voice and squeal of laughter carried.

Was it the coffee that was making me tremble or was it my frustration? Was I this nervous? Meanwhile, there was a party in full swing next door! Right away a major issue had cropped up: Accounts. How would I deal with that? I wanted to leave, to step out for some fresh air, but what would Musozi think? Should I tell him? I sensed something . . . sharp underneath his cheeky laughter. I ran my hands over my bare desk. They came off grimy. Another item for Peninah. My boss must be very popular, or was it normal to spend half the morning chatting? I had forgotten how important, and to my mind silly, not to mention inefficient, courtesy was. God forbid the bereaved person thinking you had a malicious reason for not expressing your sympathy! And a phrase or two wasn't enough; you had to listen to the story of the death and how the burial went while murmuring condolences: "*Nga kitalo, bambi*," and, "We'll pray for you." I sat there looking out of my curtain-less window blankly, then aimlessly flicked through the files. I'd been through them already. How helpless I felt, how useless. Out of place.

By the time Musozi's visitors left, more than half the morning was gone. Musozi called me back into his office. At the same time an older woman in a faded *busuti* of cream and blue flowers came in with a tray and two cups of tea. She placed the tea on Musozi's desk, then knelt down and greeted him in the lengthy Luganda way, with lots of questions, pauses, and sighs. She asked after his wife, the children, the other relatives, the farm, cows, and groundnuts. And then, of course, came the condolences. I wondered why Musozi let the old woman kneel through all that. In the office! Her hair was cut very short on the head and shone with oil. He called her Nnalongo—the mother of twins. She was too humble for my taste. This wasn't the village! By the time they got to the tea it was lukewarm. Nnalongo had already put in the sugar. It was so sickeningly sweet; I could not take more than two sips. Nnalongo then asked what we would have for lunch. Musozi repeated the question in English.

"I didn't know we got lunch here. And by the way, I know Luganda." I smiled to soften my rebuke.

"Some people forget, or try to. You people who go abroad, you come back with all sorts of airs. My nephews too!" He laughed. "Nnalongo makes lunch and sells it here. She's a good cook. Isn't it true, *Nyabo*?"

"I try." Nnalongo smiled self-effacingly.

"I'll have *matooke* and meat. You should have the same. It's good."

"I don't eat meat."

Musozi stopped fidgeting with the papers on the desk and looked at me in astonishment. So did Nnalongo from her position on the floor. Then he said, "Oh, you're allergic? That's too bad."

"No."

"It's not Lent, is it? I can't keep up with these religious dates. Anyway, nothing can make me give up meat!" he patted his belly and laughed.

"It's for ethical reasons." I felt I should explain, in case he thought I had simply rejected his offer.

He stopped mid-face-wipe. "What?"

"Well, um, cows and other animals are living beings who . . . who love their lives, and . . ." Musozi's incredulous expression deepened. He took off his glasses and peered more closely at me as he cleaned them, as if the answer were in my face. ". . . and the animals are killed in such inhumane ways . . ."

"Inhumane?" He burst out laughing, and then turned to Nnalongo, "You heard what she said?" He translated, "She said animals are not killed the way people are." He whipped out his handkerchief and wiped his face as if to control his laughter. "Let's not talk about how *people* are killed!" He laughed harder.

Nnalongo laughed softly behind her hand, then asked, "And goats? Sheep? Fish too?"

"Well, actually I eat fish, because, because . . ." How could I explain this? Where should I start?

Nnalongo said, slowly and emphatically, as if to an idiot child, "Animals are not people."

"I *know*, but . . . but—"

Musozi swept away my attempt with a wave of his handkerchief. "Give her beans, like a commoner. Maybe she ate enough meat in America. Yes, yes, that must be it."

I knew he didn't mean to insult me, but I felt insulted all the same, and annoyed at not being able to explain the obvious. Annoyed at looking like a fool from the very start. Annoyed at everybody's constant laughter. Nnalongo got up from the floor and left, still smiling.

Musozi asked, "How long were you in the States?"

"Eight years."

"Too long, too long. That's why. You'll settle in soon, don't worry. Yes, yes. You'll like meat again. When you feel lucky to get it."

The standard vegetarian speech was silly in response to that. Or was it silly, period? Was it just a matter of time before I would cave in, settle down, or become myself again, as Musozi would call it? Whatever that self was. My American voice, disgusted, silently replied, whatever.

* * *

I was so glad to leave work that day. Nothing much was accomplished that afternoon either, because Mr. Musozi was called to an urgent meeting. As he rushed out, he slammed another bulging file onto my desk, saying, "Here you go: some more meat to chew on." He chuckled. "The best way is to dive right in. Get involved. Let's talk tomorrow," and he swept out, wiping his face and smiling largely.

At the taxi park, the jostling hawkers, babies' cries, and jangling music mirrored the turmoil in my mind. I wasn't able to read during the *matatu* ride back home to Entebbe. There was a lot to untangle, to make sense of, including why on earth I was so troubled. I was home, right? I felt like I had to make some sort of a decision, but about what? I couldn't turn around and leave, just like that. Go back to the States with my tail between my legs. Then, what? This was ridiculous, I didn't have to leave. I pressed my eyes closed to keep the tears back.

The taxi's tumble and drone calmed me down somewhat. I looked forward to peaceful tea with Maama and Patti. My sister Patti worked as an administrator for a Christian organization for the disabled, also in Kampala. I wondered why Patti had not left home and moved to Kampala, but was also glad she hadn't. Almost all of Maama's letters praised Patti for one thing or another. At least Patti is here keeping me company, she wrote. You know I'm growing old. Patti reminds me to take my insulin; she drives me to Kampala and the village now that my eyesight is going. I'm so glad she's here. *Come back*, was what I heard.

I was free to live wherever I wanted to, of course. But, repeating this to myself didn't relieve the weight of guilt. A dutiful daughter should be at her old parents' side, just like how Maama had looked after her own mother and Taata's mother too, before they passed away. Well, here I was, back home again, wasn't I? Moreover, I found Maama just as strong and resolute as ever; she wasn't an invalid at all.

The taxi reached Entebbe's fresh, lake-filled air as the evening mellowed with the sun's last rays that seemed to mark the end of that day's possibilities. I could not help noticing, again, what had been so ordinary before. For example, there were no bus stops; passengers called out to the driver, "*Awo, Ssebo, kutaala.*" "Right there, sir, at the light," or "by the big mango tree," or "*Ku Leeke,*" meaning Lake Victoria Hotel, which was opposite the golf course, or what was now a cows' grazing field. The taxi got lighter and more jumpy as passengers scrambled off one by one. I hadn't realized that I had stored the sensations deep inside, these small details that made up the theater of the everyday. The memories now rose up and resonated with the reality around me. The sound of the *matatu* door heaving open and clanging shut repeatedly. Yes, that was exactly how the heavy creaking doors sounded back then. That was the true sound of home. Or was it? What about the changes that did not match my memories?

My stop was at Queens Road. I raised my voice, *"Awo, ku Queenzi."* I forced myself to pronounce 'Queens' in what I and my sisters had called a *maalo* village-ish way back when we were kids. But it wasn't merely a different pronunciation: it had become a Kiganda word, just like how 'cent' had become 'esente' meaning money. If I pronounced 'Queens' properly, the driver would refuse to respond to what sounded like an affected way of speaking. The accents and new words were the sounds of home; they made sense to me.

I walked for about ten minutes down Queens Road to my mother's house. The residential area had been built for colonial administrators around the 1940s. 'Entebbe' actually meant 'chair' in Luganda; but not because the town had been the seat of the colonial government, but because of the many shrines along the lake shore of Mugula, who had been a powerful chief long before the colonial era. When the capital moved to Kampala at independence, Entebbe remained a small intimate town with a few ministries left, an international airport and half-empty National Zoo, and the surrounding lakeside villages of fishermen. The former colonial houses were now occupied by civil servants like my mother had been. I was so glad Maama had remained in town instead of retiring to the village, Bushenyi, in western Uganda. That was considered her *real* home because it was where my father was born and raised, but his family had migrated from the further west, somewhere in or near Congo, long before the present borders existed. Maama was a Munyoro from Masindi. The question rose up and faced me again: where was home then, really, after all these multiple transplants?

The walk through the long evening shadows calmed me down. Surely, I would adjust to the workplace, sooner or later. Would I have to become more like them, or they more like me? I sighed. At least the dusty road beneath my feet, still not repaired since I had left, was familiar, with its pot-holed patterns.

At home, Maama was having tea in the living room and reading the day's newspapers. She had her glasses on, which had been another surprise. It was a mark of time passing, and of Maama's coming frailty, however strong she was now. The glasses were perched low on Maama's wide nose, the same nose I saw in my own mirror every morning. Just like how my own toes and fingers were Patti's too. Perhaps we were simply different copies of each other. Looking at my mother, so at home in the familiar room, I wanted to kiss her in greeting, but they didn't do that. It was too *zungu.*

Maama looked up. "You're back. How was it?"

"Okay, I guess."

Maama lifted her glasses off her eyes and tilted her head in question. I sat down hard on the sofa and sighed heavily. "Frankly, work was a mess. We did absolutely *nothing* today."

"It's only the second day—"

"—I know, but I thought at least they would be ready for me, you know, at least have a computer on my desk, for Christ's sake."

"This isn't America." Maama smiled.

I gave her an irritated look, but went on, "And then there's this receptionist, Peninah, who's going to give me trouble, I just know it."

Maama smiled sympathetically and took a sip from her flowered China teacup. "Be patient. You're always so quick to judge."

"Oh yes, blame me."

Maama shrugged and put back her glasses.

"We've been planning your arrival for months!"

"You know how it is here."

My mother paused, as if silence would ease my exasperation, and then offered in a softer voice, "Tea?"

Maama's sympathy irritated me even more. "Yeah, tea will solve all our problems." I noisily turned my teacup over, banged it down onto its saucer, filled it with steaming tea, and placed the pot back onto the tray as hard as I could. Maama looked at me for a long moment, and then turned back to the paper. I sipped my tea, fuming. How did Maama do it? She turned me into a silly petulant child all over again.

As I poured myself another cup, Maama exclaimed, "Oh, look, Lisa's wedding announcement! Your friend Lisa Atwoki from your Gayaza days, remember?"

"Of course. Who's she marrying?"

"Dr. Leopold Musiime. He must be the Musiime who heads Nsambya Hospital."

"Isn't he a little old?"

"Not for your age. Lisa is also almost thirty, isn't she? People have been getting married right and left. You've missed. And they all have asked about you."

"About what? Whether I'm married or not, right? When I was coming back."

Maama gave me a long questioning look, and then turned her eyes back to the paper. Her body was still, alert. "Is that a bad question to ask?"

"Prying into my business," I muttered. Why was I acting so defensive? I should just shut up. Be nice. I drank the rest of my tea in silence.

Maama turned a page of her paper, and as she scanned it, murmured, "I had been wondering about that."

"What?"

"Calm down. I have just been wondering, that's all – whenever people ask."

"If you want to ask me, ask." I gave a sharp laugh of annoyance.

"You get angry for no good reason. A normal person would want to get married, have kids; it's not such a strange question."

My scalp began to itch. I scratched it fiercely.

"Don't scratch your head like that; you'll go bald. Maybe if you were with someone you'd be happier."

I shot up off the sofa. "What do you mean *happier*? Were you happy?" I stomped out of the room, ignoring my mother's shocked call.

I hurried outside, out of Maama's reach and expectations. Happier? Okay then, I was abnormal. I had come back, hadn't I? What more did Maama want? I was only twenty-seven! What my mother didn't know was that I was forced to begin my life all over again when I arrived in America. I had to learn everything anew; even roads were crossed differently over there. No wonder I had felt young, foolish even, for years. Now, back here, I was instantly an old maid! It was ludicrous. I laughed angrily and kicked at the road's loose stones.

All the same, I shouldn't have answered Maama like that. I never would have before, of course. I had forgotten how strong and indirect and persistent Maama was. A bully, really. No, that wasn't fair. How on earth had I thought I could live at home with Maama? Back in the States, after a hard day of fake smiles and isolation, alone in my apartment at night, I had imagined the three of us, with Patti, as close companions growing older together; serenely sipping tea or shelling a large basket of fresh peas, smiling. The proverbial strong African family. I laughed out loud again in the fading light. That dream *was* home. And what was this? Home was supposed to be a permanent solid fact. A created one was fake, wasn't it?

I walked around the house to the back, where I found Patti working in the vegetable garden shaded by the huge green leaves of the banana trees. Patti was bent over, picking yellowish-red tomatoes off the low plants. Her open basket was almost full. She turned and squinted through the evening light sensing someone behind her

"Hard at work, as usual."

"I had to get to these before the insects did. They're ready." Patti continued plucking the tomatoes and throwing them into her basket. I stood apart, careful not to soil my shoes, as I watched my sister's rhythmic movements.

Patti stopped and turned. "What's wrong? I know you didn't come to help me." She smiled. She knew me too well.

I sighed and looked away. "It's Maama. She's been harassing me with marriage again."

Patti grinned as she continued working. "Well, you know, she wants us to be settled. To be happy."

"Please! I've come back here; isn't that enough for my? I'm sick of being told—"

"—you know you can do what you want." Patti straightened up and sighed. "Anyway, what you want and what Maama wants aren't so different. In fact, if anything, you've become more like her. I live with her, I know—"

"—I really don't know how you manage it, Patti, really."

"It's my home." She wiped small beads of sweat off her forehead with one hand and waved at the garden with the other. "Work on this hard soil for a few years and you'll know what I mean." I half-laughed.

I shrugged, but was reminded of what Mr. Musozi said as he gave me another file this afternoon. Dive in. Get involved.

Patti looked at me sympathetically for a long quiet moment. "It'll be alright, it really will." She sighed. "I'm kind of tired. I'm going in."

"Okay. Me too. Soon," I answered.

Left alone, I walked up to the highest point of Queens Road and turned back west. The sun had disappeared, but the sky still glowed red, pink, and purple. The lake far away gleamed flat and placid. Most of the compounds now had less lawn and more vegetable gardens. The extravagant leaves and vines became huge dark shapes in the dimming light. I had to admit I loved these disorganized gardens where life unleashed itself every which way. They were the exact opposite of the tiny rectangular patches of immaculate green lawns back in the US that had to be watered, fertilized, fenced off, teased, and begged to grow. One day, all this vibrancy, this living chaos, would be normal again. One day. But this meant I wouldn't notice it anymore.

The dark was closing in. I could hardly see anything anymore as the last blood-red streaks across the sky turned indigo. I breathed in deeply. Patti and my boss were right. I should dig my fingers deep into the mud until I couldn't remove it from my fingernails anymore. Merge with it, like how day had smoothly become its opposite, night. I sat on a huge stone between the road and a garden. The words I had heard the whole day were like that too: *Queenzi*, *Leeke*, *esente*, and so on. A new language formed by old ones running underneath and over each other. An ever-changing in-between. I could accept this fluidity as I now accepted the night creeping up over me, this blanket of warm dusk. And not just because it was inevitable, but because it was different every night: a performance, an adventure. I would have to learn all over again how to live in this new old place called home. The sky was now completely black. And somewhere far away, right now, it was dawn.

On the Last Day of Spring

Fidaa Zidan

Translated into English by Amir Nizar Zuabi
Editors: Samer Al-Saber, Anna Jayne Kimmel, Alexandra Aron

Fidaa Zidan is an actress, writer, and director. Born in Palestine, she received a BA in social theater from Haifa University and an MFA in acting from Tel Aviv University. She wrote and performed the Arabic version of *On the Last Day of Spring* (2018) throughout Palestine and at the 2019 Kampala International Theatre Festival. In 2019 she translated the play into Hebrew, where it was presented as part of her MFA final project at Tel Aviv University. In 2019 she performed in Amir Nizar Zuabi's play *Grey Rock* at La MaMa Theater in New York and then toured the US. She has also worked with Zuabi in *Against a Hard Surface* with YSDT (2017) and other productions. Zidan's films include *Polygraph* (2019) and *Another Point of View* (2018). Her children's theater projects include *The Dragon of Beit Bethlehem* by Hoda Shawa, edited by Fidaa Zidan and composed by Faraj Sulaiman, *GarGar the Kangaroo,* and *Naqtota*, which she edited and performed. Zidan participates in social theater programs for disadvantaged communities and various educational projects. She is editing a children's story for theater, writing her first short movie script and spoken word poetry, and working on a project with Remote Theater Project in New York.

Setting

This theatrical monodrama is partially based on the autobiography of a Palestinian woman from a Druze village in the Upper Galilee. In this story, the protagonist's encounter with a tragic loss leads to an unexpected path in her attempt to reclaim her Arab identity.

Production History

Produced by the A.M. Qattan Foundation in Ramallah, the Mossawa Center in Haifa, and Al-Hakawati Theatre in Jerusalem.

Palestine, November 2018

Cast and Crew

Writer and Actor	Fidaa Zidan
Director	Siwar Awad
Translator	Amir Nizar Zuabi
Dramaturgy	Alaa Hlehel
Artistic Consultant	Khalifah Natour
Music	Habib Shehadeh Hanna
Lighting	Moaz Ju'beh
Sinography	Majdala Khoury
Production Assistant	Gina Asfour

Scene One: The Forum

Stage left, there is a chair that faces center stage. Upstage/left, there are four buckets of soil side by side. Between them is a notebook. The actress stands upstage/right, walks in silhouette to the other side of the stage, then looks over to the audience. Takes two steps forward, then speaks.

My parents were one of the first to join the bereaved families' forum. Back then I was seven years old.

The forum is a meeting place for bereaved Palestinian and Israeli families. I was the only one that spoke Hebrew among the Palestinians, and the only one that could speak Arabic among the Israelis.

The forum would organize gatherings where we could discuss where we came from, what we liked, what we didn't, and what is common. It would organize lectures, demonstrations, women's meetings, summer camps. Some of the summer camps were abroad: Spain, Germany, Italy twice, Ireland, Japan. Sometimes I wouldn't want to go to the summer camps, but my dad would always convince me, and my mom would always prepare flatbread with sour cheese, olive oil, Za'tar,[1] and a jar full of olives.

I was always assisting the guides; they always chose me. I would do the rounds to the rooms, banging on the doors:

"Everyone is up? Hat? Snack? We will meet momentarily in the courtyard. We can play with a ball before we start our day."

Our motto was peace. We just didn't want anyone else to join. Sometimes when they would divide us, they would say:

"You come from there, you come from here."

I wouldn't know who I belonged to. When everyone would sit together, I was usually the translator from Arabic to Hebrew and vice versa.

Abir is a girl from Halhul, a village close to Hebron. I know her from the day she first started attending the forum meetings. She always asked me the same questions:

"You speak Arabic?"
"You speak Hebrew?"
"Your parents speak Arabic?"
"And at school you learn in Arabic?"

Arabic, we learn in Arabic, Hebrew, in Hebrew; then other subjects, some in Arabic, some in Hebrew. Except English. English we learn in . . . well, English.

When I grew up I started attending the meetings where we had to talk about the people we lost.

"Hello, my name is Fidaa. I like to watch martial arts. Bruce Lee, Kerry von Erich, and I really, really hate parsley."

[1] Thyme. Palestinians mix thyme with sumaq and sesame to make Za'tar.

Scene Two: Karate

Heads to the center of the stage in the first move of the classic ballet.

All the girls in my class went to ballet, so I did too. When the ballet class was over, they would go home and I would sneak into the grocery, buy a piece of bubblegum, chew it while counting to 100, then turn back to the gym because I knew that's when karate class started. And I would join the other kids, faces glued to the window to watch the karate lesson:

"Iche, Ni, San . . . straighten your legs, stretch your arms, exhale"

When the instructor would see us, he would shout *Iche* in our direction and we would all run away. It happened until I understood I wanted to learn karate, just like my brother did.

From the first lesson, the instructor would walk around his students and correct their postures. When he got to me, I had already straightened my legs, stretched my arms, and exhaled. Once he looked at me and he said:

"I know these hands. I trained your brother."

While I was on my way back home, a kid named Hussain, always with a ball underneath his arm, followed me and started asking questions all the way home:

"Why do you want to learn karate? You are a girl! And why doesn't your brother train you? Is he still planning to go to Japan to learn martial arts? Does he still train the neighborhood kids at home?"

"Yes, he does. If you come and put one shekel in the tin box, you can come in and he will teach you Mae Geri, Mawashi Geri, and low kicks. Come if you want."

I left Hussain and went home. I found my brother hanging posters of Bruce Lee, Kerri von Erich, and Muhammad Ali. I started giving him tape. My favorite poster was from the movie *Enter the Dragon*, when Bruce Lee fights Han who has metal in his hand and splits Bruce Lee open. We suddenly heard a megaphone sound in the village:

"Oh good folks of the village, the legendary wrestlers Kevin and Kerry Von Erich are coming to Acre. Anyone that wants to see the match should be on the bus that leaves from the entrance of the village tomorrow at 11 in the morning."

My brother heard that and went crazy. He didn't sleep all night, as we only see them on TV. The next morning, he went to school. In the second recess, he went straight to the head principal to get a one-time permission to miss class and go see the wrestling match. The principal declined his request:

"If you leave the school now, you won't be allowed to come back to school again."

"So I won't," my brother replied.

He went running from school to the village entrance, hopped the bus, and went to see the match. When he returned, he was so happy telling us how Kevin, how he is always barefoot, how he eyes his opponent and when his rival comes close, he jumps on the ring ropes and leaps on him, legs forward, flooring his opponent instantly.

The next day my brother refused to go to school. My father and mother sat there patiently trying to convince him:

"You have one year left; go back and finish your studies."

But he would have none of it. And when eventually they managed to convince him to return, the head principal didn't want him back.

He spent his days barefoot on the tractor. He would fill the tractor cart with vegetables and drive around the village selling them. That's when my parents started organizing the lower floor of the house, which is how it became a gym for my brother to teach his martial arts there instead of selling vegetables.

In that period, I remember, we started getting official mail. After a while, I remember, my mom was packing my brother's duffel bag, but I didn't understand where he was off to. The day he travelled my mom stayed standing in the doorway long after he disappeared.

He left. Whenever he did come back to visit, he would bring me small presents: pencils, a notebook, a t-shirt with Bruce Lee's face on it, stickers, a Barbie doll house, and music tapes. My mom would wash his clothes and I would help her hang them: a buttoned-up olive green shirt, olive green trousers with pockets, a white t-shirt, a Bruce Lee printed t-shirt, another buttoned-up olive green shirt, and another olive-green trousers with pockets. The clothes would dry, then would be folded and packed in the duffle bag. He would leave for longer and longer stretches. I would ask my mother:

"When will he be back?"

And she would bite her lip and say:

"In God's will, next week in God's will . . ."

When will my brother come back? Next week, in God's will . . . in God's will, next week.

Scene Three: The Land

One day I was in my brother's room looking at the posters when my mom called:

"Look who came! Come fast!"

My brother had returned. Everyone was excited. My father started preparing the equipment and the tools for the ploughing. We were going to my grandfather's lands. My mom prepared sandwiches, Labaneh sour cheese and olive oil and Za'tar and a box full of the most bitter olives.

(*Aside.*) I help my mom pack everything.

My father shouts from outside:

"Come on! Come on!"

Our tractor, an 80-model blue Fiat, is humming outside. My brother helped my father load. He also took the martial arts training gear, an empty canvas bag, boxing gloves, the weights, the skip rope, and the nunchaku. I leave my mom behind and run to help my brother with his most exciting load.

"I am on the tractor!" I declared.

My brother hoisted me up in one swift move onto the seat behind him. I grabbed the metal bars and leaned back. My head touched his back, and we hit the road. Our house is in the centre of the village. My brother greets people:

"Good day, neighbor! Hope you have a good one, aunty! How are you, Uncle Abdullah?"

Every time we cross a speed bump, I see the flowers on the balcony, pots, and fresh laundry everywhere. Everywhere a flower pot, a buttoned-up olive green shirt, a black skirt. A buttoned-up olive green shirt, olive green trousers with big pockets, a white shirt, a buttoned-up olive green shirt. The whole village has the same clothes, the same uniform. They all bring it back home from somewhere.

"Why were you late? Why did you not return? Three weeks with no sign of life. Why were you late?"

"Look! Look how the village seems small from here. Can you see the lake, the lake of Galilee and that hill? There is the hill of Hattin (where Salah Al-Din fought the lionheart).

I asked, "Why were you late? Why did it take you so much time to come home this time?"

"That is Nazareth, and there is the Mediterranean Sea and Haifa, and further down that's Acre . . ."

We got to the dirt road that took us to the land, our land, the Khait plots.[2] These lands were confiscated by the state, but they were ours and we kept going to cultivate them, even if they took them. My father always told the same story, how my grandfather used to walk for four hours to get to the plots, and how my grandfather, even in his old age, would insist on visiting the land.

From the distance, we saw our parents moving around strangely, like they were arguing about something. When we got there, my brother took me off the tractor and we went to see what my parents were up to. Apparently, by the time we got there my father had already cleared a six by six meter stretch in the middle of our plot. This would be the family burial ground. My mom wants my father to move the designated place a few meters to the left. My father insists that this is the perfect location. My brother starts to laugh:

[2] These lands are called the Khait plots and they are in the north-east of Palestine.

> *"You want to stay together even after you die? And what about us? Can we be buried beside you, or do you want to stay alone so you can be intimate?"*

He grabbed the boxing gloves and the sack from the tractor:

"Let's see what you learned in your karate lessons!"

"I know four movements. 1, 2, 3, 4."

"If you make these movements yours, next week when I come back home, I will take you to the sea."

My brother left that day, and a week passed.

"Mom, why is it taking him so long?"

"Next week, in God's will."

"Mom, he promised to take me to the sea."

"Next week, in God's will."

"Mom, the kids came to practice with him. Mom, when will my brother return?"

"Next week, in God's will, in God's will, next week."

Scene Four: Since You Left

I came back home from my karate lesson. I found my father standing, looking at the window that faces the main street. He was restless, pacing from side to side. He went and turned off the lights in the house, then returned and planted himself in front of the window facing the main street. Then he came to me and said:

"Go, sweetheart, go wait at Uncle Abdallah's house until your mom is back. Now go, darling; now go, darling."

I changed my practice clothes and left the house. I saw people in olive green clothes gathering in the neighborhood. I went to my uncle's house. I played with my cousins. We played tag for a long time. I wanted to go back home, but my uncle said no. I tried to leave but they wouldn't let me. My oldest cousin ran after me and dragged me back inside.

Then Hussain came. I don't know how he knew I was there. He said that there are a lot of people gathered by our house and lots of cars. I tried sneaking out and, as I opened the door, my uncle returned and stood there, his eyes were red and he was wearing a white head scarf.

"Uncle, can I go home now?"

He started crying.

Since you left, everything that belonged to you has been put in a box: your boxing gloves, your training gear, your clothes, and the presents you brought me. Everything was put in a box and stored on top of the big closet. The walls were now covered with pictures of you, pictures with a black ribbon, in the living room, in the kitchen, in the hallway, in the bedrooms, on the balcony, walls of your pictures with a black ribbon. My mom's closet was now all black garments, and my dad would dream and mumble to me:

"Ravens, my darling, I can see black ravens."

It's been a long time since you are gone. Father and Mother stopped arguing about the best locations of the burial grounds. My father still says he wants to be buried there in the Khait lands, but now my mother doesn't want that. She wants to be buried close to you.

And I? I just want us to be together.

Scene Five: The Forum Again/A Question of Belonging

When they would split us into two groups, as per usual "these people are from here and these people are from there," I would become very uncomfortable. There is something in me that resembles this group, but I came with that group. This group was always careful not to upset that group, and that group was always careful not to upset this group, but when I would speak both groups would stare at me. None of them could place me.

It was clear to what group I should officially belong, but that was uncomfortable for me because of everything: the way I looked, my language, my feelings, the way I moved, my parents. So, slowly, I stopped participating in the talks and instead started to translate.

"My name is Mohamad. I come from Bethlehem. My father was ill. We were having lunch. My father started to twitch in pain; he asked me to get a car to take him to hospital. I brought my cousin's car. When we got to the road exiting the village, there was a checkpoint. I told the soldiers my father was ill and needed to get to hospital fast. They said wait. I tried to explain. I tried to argue, to shout. Then I heard that one of them was speaking in Arabic."

I interrupt him: "Sorry, Mohamad, who was speaking in Arabic?"

"The soldier. So I went to him, begging, please, please let us pass. My father's head was leaning on the passenger window. They let us through after that. When I got to the hospital, they told me, "Your father is dead. He has been dead for half an hour."

Ceremonial military music.

Scene Six: The First Last Day of Spring

In this scene, she moves in military style.

On the last day of spring, my parents and I went out of the house and into the car. We stopped near the flower shop. No one wanted to be the one who went to get the flowers.

I got out of the car. There was a long queue inside. But the moment I stepped in, the queue of people parted in half. I went to the shopkeeper and took three bouquets.

We walked between two lines of drummers. I am not sure who was by my side. My head was buried in someone's arm, not sure if it was my father or my mother. The drums were very loud.

We got to the square. Someone handed us small water bottles and stickers with a remembrance poppy. We sat on squeaking plastic chairs under a stretched blue tarp. A guard shouted:

"Ready, front. Ready, front."

Everyone was asked to stand still for two minutes. Everyone got up.

"Port, arms. Port, arms."

Now they asked everyone to sit. Everyone sat down. The Sheikh was invited to read Al-Fatiha.[3] He did and returned to sit. The representative of the government spoke next:

"We have gathered on such a sad day in remembrance of our fallen ones, our heroes who fell in the line of duty while protecting the homeland against our ruthless terroristic enemy. In 1956 and with great joy we have started this alliance, an alliance marked by blood between your community and the state, and this has become a symbol of the life of our two faiths together. Today we put aside our doubts and differences and we stand united. United by our common values, we stand united, one hand firmly positioned on the gun, the other hand stretched out eagerly seeking peace."

"Port, arms. Port, arms."

"Aim, ready, unlock. Fire! Fire! Fire!"

"Port, arms. Port, arms."

She stands at her brother's grave. Talks to him.

"Every year on the last day of spring, it is the same. We walk up the stairs, Mom on my left, Father on my right. We lay flowers, stand up. I hold her hand so she doesn't fall. We get home. Father sits opposite Mother and says:

'On our land.'

And she says:

'We will be far from him.'

My father locks himself in his room. My mother gets busy in the kitchen. And I go to your room. I count to three. I hear a gasp of muffled pain, and for the rest of the day the house is full of silence and the smells of buret cooking. I say:

[3] The opening verse in the Quran.

"Why won't we all be together?

If we want that, we have two choices. We either come to where you are, but that is impossible as you lay in a military cemetery, or you come to us to the old lands!

And you can't come alone, can you? It means someone needs to take you."

She picks up a bucket of soil and empties it onto the stage in a line from upstage left to upstage right.

Scene Seven: Hussain

When I was in the eleventh grade, I was going home one day, and a big tractor passed me. It was Hussain, but this time he had no ball under his arm. I knew they had lands in the Al-Zaboud plots, but I didn't know they had a tractor or that Hussain had become so handsome. He turned his head. Our eyes met. He started passing with his tractor every day when school ended. Our eyes would meet. Every day, I would imagine myself sitting on the tractor beside him on the way to the plots.

When I would be at home doing something and I would hear a hum of a tractor, I would leave everything and go to the grocery to buy something we didn't need, or run to hang the laundry on the cord on the balcony. One time I smiled at him. He didn't flinch, but he did smile back. The next day his young sister approached me at school.

"Hussain says that he will be here when school ends. If you want to talk with him, you can."

That day I went home walking. I left school and walked to the edge of the street, where you could see if someone was coming.

At the sound of the tractor from far away, my heart started dancing. The tractor got closer, and I didn't know: should I stay or not? Should I? Shouldn't I? And the tractor was getting closer. To stay or to go? Then the tractor passed me. He turned the tractor around and stopped it. He jumped down, his boots covered in mud. He had a white shirt on. He was holding twigs of Za'tar in his hand:

"These are from our lands."

But he didn't give them to me or look into my eyes. His eyes were dark; his brows were thick and his hands were rough. And behind him parked the tractor.

Before long, Hussain and his parents came to our house. Then he got the conscription letter. He was about to go. I told him not to.

Scene Eight: Black Ravens

(*She remembers.*) Black ravens, my darling, black ravens!

It's dusk time and I am standing on a boulder in the middle of our lands wearing the black shirt that hadn't left my body since the beginning of the mourning.

Drowning in my heart's blood.

My right shoulder is heavy.

My legs feel as if they are about to fall off.

I turned my head and saw it: a black raven fixed on my shoulder. I got cold.

I looked at my arm.

It was missing, cut just above the elbow. The raven looked at me and threatened:

"I swear on the soil of this land, you will not have any hands left as long as these clothes remain."

Scene Nine: Forum—How Could He Raise a Gun?

It was an evening meeting—only women. Abir was there and other women I didn't know. New women who had stories I still hadn't yet heard, but Abir's story I knew. When she was young, soldiers came into their house to make a search. They wanted to enter the girls' room. Her brother tried to stop them. The soldiers hit him on his head. They hit again and again until he was blue, and cold, and dead.

"Yes, Yael?"

Yael asked for me to translate her words to Arabic.

It was ten years ago. Yotam left home. I gave him a sandwich, some cookies, and a kiss. The next day, we received a call from the hospital. Yotam was in critical condition. By the time my husband and I got there, he was already gone. I didn't want to go in and see him dead. I preferred to remember him alive.

Abir raised her hand to ask a question.

"Yes, Abir?

"How come?" she asks.

"Sorry, Abir?

"I mean you know . . . it's easier to see an occupying Israeli soldier speaking Hebrew in uniform and killing us than to see an occupying soldier that speaks Arabic in uniform and is killing us. I don't know how your brother could raise a gun and shoot at his brothers, Arabs just like him."

Ceremonial military music.

Scene Ten: Another Last Day of Spring: Transfer Plan

Like every year on the last day of spring, my mother woke up at six and immediately started cooking—stuffed vine leaves, roasted chicken, vegetables, rice, salad—because on this day, friends and family started coming to our house to visit.

"But why do you need the parsley in there, Mom?"

My father wakes up early, I buy the flowers, and we go to the cemetery. Someone hands us small water bottles, stickers with a remembrance poppy. The guard says "Port, arms. Port, arms." Everyone stands. The guard says, "Aim, ready, unlock." Everyone sits.

The Fatiha, the minister's speech. We walk up the stairs, my mom on my left, my father on my right. We lay flowers.

Speaking to her brother.

"Don't tell me you are comfortable here. It's crowded here.

About the transfer, I checked the law. According to the Law of Military Burial 1950 Article 6:

'For a transfer of a corpse from a military cemetery to a different grave, one needs to attain three signatures: The Minister of Defense, the religious figure, and our father.' I tried to talk with Dad about it. It wasn't easy.

Abir said you are a murderer. I couldn't explain how come a young man can be the guy who spends his time barefoot on a tractor, and goes to his grandfather's plot of land regularly, then becomes the same soldier who arrives home late. When you were late, I couldn't explain why, and I asked you why. You said: 'I saw a girl with hair like yours. So I refused to go into that house to search it. Because I refused a direct order, I got slammed.'

I know what that means. It means you wouldn't do as they told you, and that they put you in jail for three weeks with no visiting rights, but I couldn't explain it to Abir. I froze.

Now we get home. Father sits opposite mother and says:

'On our land.'

Mom: 'We will be far from him.'

Father locks himself in his room. Mother gets busy in the kitchen and I go to your room. I count to three and I hear a gasp of muffled pain. For the rest of the day, the house is full of silence and the smells of burnt cooking."

She picks up a bucket of soil and empties it onto the stage in a line from downstage right to upstage right.

Scene Eleven: A Womb of Soldiers

Hussain parked his tractor in front of our house. He stayed until nightfall. He had dinner with us. We had coffee. My mom served fruits for dessert, and we were staring at each other. He stood up to leave.

"Don't go."

"I have to. Two years. I have two years left. If I don't go, I will be jailed as a defector. Tomorrow, before I leave, I will pass and we will talk."

"Even so, if you leave how do I know I will ever see you again? What do you think is going to happen? In the morning, your mom will stand above you as you sleep, and will agonize: 'Should I wake him? Should I let him be?'

But she will wake you so that you are not sent to jail. When you get out of the house, she will rush down the stairs with a box of pastries, so you are not hungry when you are deployed. And she will say:

'God keep you safe. And if you pass by Damascus Gate in Jerusalem, buy some wild spinach. It's the best there. If they deploy you in Nablus, get some wild chicory; it's the best there.'

Then you will board the bus and get off at some checkpoint. You will stand with your rifle, pointing it at young girls like me and saying in Hebrew:

'You can pass; you can't pass.'

'Stop or I shoot you.'

In a perfect Israeli accent. Leaving your Arabic behind. You will become Mista'arev—an Israeli with Arab skin.[4]

Then one night, when the wind is howling, they will come to knock at your parents' door to inform them what has happened.

Don't pass in the morning. I'd rather remember you in this white shirt and not in any other color. Every time you say: I am coming back next week, I am coming back soon.

My womb clenches around the small soldiers that will grow in there.

Go, Hussain, I would rather you go now than to lose you after we are married and have children who will become soldiers that come into people's houses to wreak havoc and then don't return home alive."

Scene Twelve: The Last Day of Spring: Signatures

Like every day at the end of spring, my mother wakes up and starts to prepare food. Why the parsley? Why? My father wakes up early. Flowers. We get there. I don't want water, thank you. We stand up, we sit down. The Fatah. The Minister of Defense's speech. We walk up the stairs. We lay the flowers. We walk down the stairs. Mom, be careful not to fall.

When we got to the car, I told my parents: "Go ahead, I want to walk home." I left my parents and sneaked to see the Sheikh.

"Sheikh. Sheikh, greetings. God give you blessings."

[4] Mista'arvim is an Israeli military unit in which soldiers can appear and pass for Arabs.

The Sheikh stood up.

"God have mercy on your brother's soul."

"God save your loved ones. By your leave, may I ask you a question, Sheikh?"

"We are here to serve, dear. Please ask."

"God bless you, Sheikh. We have a problem at home. My mother and father wanted to be buried in the land (al-khait), but now my mother has changed her mind and refuses. Now she wants to be buried next to my brother. But we are not in Canada. In Canada, a loved one can be buried in a military cemetery but, as you know, we are not in Canada. So my mom wants to be buried in the general cemetery that is just next to the military one. But if that happens, we will be separated. I don't want my parents to separate, and I too want to be with them, buried with them. So I thought of a solution: I will take my brother from the military cemetery and transfer him to a new burial on our land. That way we will all be together."

The Sheikh was confused. Under his breath, he mumbled a quick "God be our guidance" then he cleared his throat and said:

"This is a complicated matter, my child. It has many details."

"So it's possible."

"Such things have happened before, with dignitaries or transferring people into the military burial grounds."

"So it's possible."

"Possible, but not preferable. The military cemetery is something the state introduced. It wasn't our choice. In any case, does your father know?"

I flinched.

"Bring your father's signature and then I will give you mine."

I thanked the Sheikh and rushed to see the state representative of the Ministry of Defense.

Me (*in Hebrew*):

"Excuse me, sir. May I have a word? I am a bereaved sister and we have a problem at home. My mother and father wanted to be buried in the khait lands that you people confiscated. But now my mother has changed her mind and refuses. So now she wants to be buried next to my brother, but we are not in Canada, sir. In Canada, a loved one can be buried in a military cemetery, but as you know we are not in Canada, so my mom wants to be buried in the general cemetery that is just next to the military one. But if that happens, we will be separated and I don't want my parents to separate, and I too want to be with them, buried with them. So I thought of a solution: I will take my brother from the military cemetery and transfer him to a new burial on our land. That way we will all be together. For that I need your signature."

He looked at me, pulled out a pen, clicked the pen shut on his thigh, and said:

"Well, you will need more signature, so good luck."

And he signed.

She picks up the third bucket of soil and empties it onto the stage in a line from downstage left to upstage left. The soil lines now form three sides of a square, with the fourth still missing.

Scene Thirteen: Alternative

It's been a while since we all went to our fields. We filled an ice box with food, took some picnic blankets, and headed to the Khait field. Naturally, we forgot the coal for the barbeque. Uncle Abdallah and his gang followed and brought the coal. We lit the barbeque and roasted the first round of meat. Uncle Abdallah started to sing.

"With your permission, Uncle, today is my turn."

I ran to the car and played the song I love. I turned the volume all the way up. Everyone was looking at me. I was only looking at my parents, straight ahead.

She dances on stage in a martial arts style, using the moves of Bruce Lee, Kevin, Kerry, and Rocky.

She stops and speaks to her family.

"This is what the last day of spring should be like on our land.

Every year it's a memorial day and a memorial night, and the week before is a memorial, too. Another picture of a young dead man, another black ribbon, and a bouquet of odourless flowers.

What is this day for? For whom?

Every time we participate in it, everything is strange. Everything is alien. The flowers and the people seem fake. Sit! and we sit; Stand! and we stand. the Fatah is said on command. Even the water in the small plastic bottles doesn't taste like water. It tastes like checkpoints and burning tires.

On this day, my brother drifts further away from us. They took him alive and returned him dead. And between us and him are the battalions of an entire army.

If we want us all to be together, we need to transfer my brother."

I looked at my father's upper lip that was shaking. He was on the verge of tears. My mother was also surprised and had a look of "enough is enough." We packed our things and drove home. A long silent drive all the way to our house. No one dared utter a word.

Scene Fourteen: The Last Day of Spring: The Accused

Like every day on the last day of spring, my mother wakes up and starts to prepare food. Why the parsley? Why? My father wakes up early. Flowers. We get there. I don't want water, thank you. We stand up, we sit down. The Fatah. The representative of the government has a speech. And this year I had a speech.

She picks up the notebook, opens it, and reads to the audience.

From my brother's ninth-grade notebook, "I am the accused":

"Monday the 19th of February 1984

I am innocent. I swear to God, I am innocent of this crime

I am incapable of trampling a flower or the smile of a child

I am innocent. Innocent, and can only be accused of innocence

They have ripped hope from my clinched fingers and scattered the tune that gives me pride

Believe me when I say I did not assault your dreams

Notice my character—free of victors, cruelty, and arrogance

Believe me or do not believe me, now it matters not

But I leave it for your conscience and your judgment

Teacher's note: I truly hope that this is your own composition. Grade 16 /20"

We got home. My father went into his room.

Scene Fifteen: Just Say Yes

She takes the last bucket to the direction of her father's room, stage left. She speaks to her father.

"We don't have another solution except moving my brother. Or we will stay like this, you in pain and my mom in sorrow. It's your right to be on our ancestral land, and if my mom agrees to be with you there, we will be far, and if my brother stays in the military burial grounds, he will be far. Me and Mom and my brother want to be near you. You are not alone, Father.

I know how you feel when you wake up every morning. By six you are tossing and turning in bed and not able to sleep. And you only fling into action if there is another bereaved family that needs your help in getting their stipend from the state because of their dead son. Or if a widowed wife, who is not much older than me, wants your help with her parents-in-law because she wants to continue her life. You are good at these things because you care. You just agree, just say yes.

From a legal point of view it is possible. We fear the power of the state because we see everything from under its boot. The state took its toll from us. We owe it nothing. Now the state owes us. No one can return my brother, but no one can convince me that my brother is in the right place.

I want my brother, my dead brother. I never asked you why he died. Why did my brother die?

Let's bring him to our land. We will all be in the land.

It would take my grandfather four hours of walking to go to the lands. And there, he would search for the water of the spring, the spring they drained in order to fill the water in small plastic bottles that they sell to us along with the buttoned olive-green shirts that they forced on us. My grandfather would scoop up the soil in the dried spring and drink it. The land of my grandfather that they took from us, exactly like they took my brother. And you and my mother will be taken away from me when we die.

Just say yes, Dad. I'll take care of everything.

We will put a headstone, and we will write on it whatever we choose. Every year, on the last day of spring, I will help you carry the ploughing tools. Me, you, and Mom will go to our land, invite my brother's friends, have a dinner, play the music he loved, hang the punching bag, and I will wear Bruce Lee's shirt.

Just say yes, Dad!"

Silence.

She places the last bucket at center stage, returns to her slow karate movements, heading back to the spot where the play began.

I'm leaving the house, walking alone in the village.

It's dark outside. I'm carrying a hoe over my shoulder. Silence!

I'm walking and walking, till I reach the military cemetery. I walk up the stairs. I reach the graves.

The moonlight disappears. Where is my brother's grave? I don't want to dig up someone else's grave. I dig and dig.

And black ravens, Dad. I can see black ravens.

I catch something, and start to pull.

It is heavy. So heavy . . .

End of play.

Letting Go and Moving On: Two Monologues on Losing and Finding Home

Louella Dizon San Juan

Louella Dizon San Juan is a playwright, author, illustrator, technologist, and businesswoman. Her children's fantasy series *The Crowded Kingdom* is about a tiny kingdom in New York City, the two little girls who discover it, and the fragile balance between the human world and the fairy world. The series features three books: the title volume, *The Crowded Kingdom*; the dark sequel, *The Underground Labyrinth*; and the exciting final installment, *The Elemental Battle*. San Juan's staged and published dramatic work under the name Louella Dizon includes New York productions of *The Color Yellow: Memoirs of an Asian American* performed at La MaMa ETC, *The Sweet Sound of Inner Light* at The Public Theater, *Till Voices Wake Us* at the Soho Repertory Theater, and the Echo Theater in Texas. Her work is featured in *Contemporary Plays by Women of Color*, edited by Kathy A. Perkins and Roberta Uno and archived at the University of Massachusetts, Amherst in the Roberta Uno Asian American Women Playwrights Scripts Collection, 1924–2002. San Juan is an active advocate for girls and women in math and science. She holds a bachelor's in English from Princeton University and a master's in computer science from New York University.

Setting

In this monologue, San Juan reflects on the real life experience of losing a home and the subsequent journey of finding a way to make a home in the aftermath of Hurricane Sandy in 2012.

Part One: Letting Go

Today we went to visit our home—to take pictures of the things we lost, and to say goodbye.

Our building sits on a cobblestone street that opens into an embrace of a park—gently sloping into the East River. Cool breezes blow off the water in the summer; the city of Manhattan glints, statuesque, on the other side. It is where the children play; where the street fairs gather; where weddings of all sizes take pictures by the golden light which always shifts and changes by the rocks, by the water.

It is why we live where we live. And why we chose to stay when the news said that Hurricane Sandy was coming.

Hurricane Irene had come last year, and we had cheated Fate—seeing the river's waters rise only as far as the street corner before seeping back to its bed. Irene had been hyped, and concerns of sandbags and go-bags circulated in the building for days beforehand, so that when the actual storm came—and then passed like an angry rain—we breathed a sigh of relief and moved on.

We expected the same this time around, although some of us expected much worse, and so therefore, at some point, my husband and I turned to each other and asked, "How much shall we do?" We brought upstairs as much as we could carry—electronics; files; favorite toys; photos. My girls brought up their books, but I looked at years of old friends accumulated on the shelves—Homer; Faulkner; Allende; Will (Shakespeare) and I had incomplete conversations with myself: "Which do I choose? I can always download. But not these books. Electronic is easier. But what about *these* books?" And round and round.

"There comes a point of diminishing returns," I said to my husband at some point in the night.

We had brought upstairs many things, and left behind, with eyes open, many others.

While we somberly ate dinner by the drone of the nightly news, the wind rose with a voice of banshees outside, and we heard the thump and bustle outside of people in the hallway.

I opened our door. "They are bringing things to a higher floor," I said aloud. After watching nervously, we finally ran outside, and we saw the water rising—creeping stone by stone up the block with dark certainty. More of us spilled outside; we realized we needed to stop it, and we started to throw sandbags in front of it; plastic construction barriers; garbage bags—anything to keep it from coming in.

It rose to our waists. It spilled over the barriers. It rushed into our lobby, past rolled-up rugs, plywood barriers, while we yelled to close the elevator doors, stop it from spreading, leaking into everything.

"It's broken through the windows!" someone shouted. My daughters and I ran—downstairs to seal our doors and put towels in the cracks. Surely we could stop it, I thought, and they came with me to help. We were grabbing linens, stuffing trash bags with filler, and were just about to form a wall when the lights went out and the world was pitch black.

"Mommy?"

That's when we heard the roar of water—water rushing into the outside hallway and through the cracks in the door, in the pitch black, toward us.

We ran upstairs, and the girls started to cry. People were screaming while I searched for the flashlights, listening for the water as it came up the stairs.

* * *

Rushing the girls to safety.

Finding my husband.

Finding our escape bags.

Finding the cat.

Dark everywhere.

What do we do.

It was all over in an hour, and by 9 p.m., we were huddled, all clumps of people—in hallways and apartments, doors gaping open, hoping for high tide to pass and for the water to go far, far away.

* * *

Today we came back to the apartment we call home. Upstairs was a mausoleum full of too many things; no hum of electricity to shatter the silence or shed light.

And downstairs? Past strange fibrous debris and standing water, upturned boxes and broken shelves—our downstairs door sagged open, bent back from its steel hinges onto a blasted wall from some unbelievable, aqueous force. Something like Spanish moss—but dirtier—hung from the ceilings and walls. Under foot lay things hard to see and harder to love: a sodden mattress; broken bowls; a huge wardrobe felled. A sofa wrinkled beyond repair. Book spines melted to sludge. I saw forlorn stuffed animals buried under furniture, and a happy photo from 1998 too gray for me to want to touch. It was all so broken and unrecognizable, we took pictures of it all and said aloud, "It's time to go."

It was easy to shrug, in that musty, ugly room, because it bore no resemblance to the warm laughter and bright colors we remembered. But coming back, and hours later, we fell silent, thinking about it. And when I finally was forced to say aloud, "Today we went back to our place to say goodbye . . ." I found myself—for the first time in all these days—filling up with tears, and I realized that it was time to let myself go.

Part Two: Moving On

On a crisp Sunday afternoon, the air full of damp and melancholy, we loaded our car with suitcases and bags to go back home.

* * *

We had learned through Hurricane Sandy what it was like to have lost, and in the *letting go*, realized some of what we had really saved.

Our resolve. We experienced extraordinary generosity from ordinary people: friends; colleagues; people whom we previously knew from waving on the street or at church.

To be reminded that one could give without having an agenda, without expecting anything back, was humbling, and made us want to give back more—to those in Red Hook, and Sandy Hook, and those less fortunate but more brave. We, in turn, felt our loss become resolve, to build back what was once ours, and to help others do so too.

Our perspective. In the days after Sandy, we recovered very few things. My younger daughter's baptismal album, her newborn picture still gazing with wonder through a grimy cover. The girls' scooters, that, with a little cleaning and shining up, looked ready to ride again.

And a vase. Next to smashed bowls and wrecked furniture, I found lying gently on the chaotic floor an ivory Lenox vase. "Brave little vase," I said aloud in amazement. Why didn't it break? The water must have surged in, opening the cabinet doors and carrying out all that was inside, lifting everything to the ceiling. The vase must have floated along, and despite the big objects and the structure breaking down violently around it, it came to rest gently on the floor, waiting to be found. It now stands clean and unique on a shelf, so delicate. Yet it didn't break.

And we? Thank God that our lives were spared, our livelihood intact. The girls were our light—children, I realized, adapt to change because every day is a day of change: each hour, they are that much taller, wiser, older.

But there were days when the adults, he and I, foundered, because it was a test: this trying to rebuild while New York continued to be difficult; while work kept demanding; while we kept "discovering" more of what we no longer had.

We were so busy, we were robotic.

We were so sad, we couldn't admit it.

We were so tired and flawed and wanting, that on our worst day we were screaming at each other, at the top of our lungs, rock bottom, raw—about something so stupid I don't even remember. We were at the end of a very long stretch.

But we didn't break.

For just as, at the end of a long stretch, you cry aloud, out of relief that you have finished and could somehow look back with some distance, so did we finally step back and realize that after twenty-two years of being together, we could still redefine what we wanted from each other, and from ourselves. It was as though something snapped and woke up, and at some point—I can't place my finger on when—we became different people, looking at things from a great distance, in a much grander scheme, unafraid of possibilities, unencumbered by what had been swept away.

I remember finding, in one of the boxes we saved, all my colored pencils and sketch pads, my drawings for my children's book, still waiting to be finished.

"What am I waiting for?" I thought. I better get this book out there.

It was freeing, to have this "What do I have to lose?" courage. Loss can do that to you, in an ironic, empowering way.

* * *

In our poorly lit apartment, from a mound of boxes and clothes hastily thrown together, we set about reclaiming our space. One light didn't work; we moved a lamp from another room. We made room for toys and packed up summer clothes for storage. Bit by bit, a home emerged, if not a gracious home, at least one that we recognized, where the cat could ceremoniously walk to all corners and confirm, as cats do, that it was "good enough."

"It's as though nothing had ever happened," said my little daughter. I smiled at the simplicity of the very young.

And so, we moved on.

There is probably another time when I will write about "coming home," because the home part may happen later, when it hits you that you have reclaimed that sense of comfort, security . . . your own space. We're not there yet.

But we came out fighters. A runner, a reader, an experimentalist, a *writer*—each one of us having gleaned a little bit from each other, a whole much greater than the sum of its parts.

Much greater.

Antimemories of an Interrupted Trip

Aldri Anunciação

Translated by Viviane Juguero

Aldri Anunciação is a playwright, screenwriter, actor, and television host. His plays include *The Battlefield: The Fantastic History of Interrupting a Successful War*, *Immediate Shipment*, *The Construction*, *The Woman from the Bottom of the Sea*, *Gusmão Inventory: Chronicles of an Imagined Biography*, *Antimemories of an Interrupted Trip*, and *Black Skin, White Masks: How We Forget What We Are*, inspired by psychiatrist Frantz Fanon. In 2013 he received the Jabuti Literature Prize for his children's play *Namíbia, não!* At the Indie Memphis Film Festival in 2020, Anunciação was part of the screenwriting team that won Best Screenplay for *Medida Provisória*, and he has written for the television programs *Conexão Bahia* and *Black Chat*. He acted in the feature films *Café com Canela* and *Ilha*, which earned him the Candango Award for Best Actor at the 2018 Brasília Film Festival. He also received the Cultural Merit Commendation in 2014 for his contributions to the conceptualization and realization of the Melanina Dramaturgy Festival and the Digital Melanina online platform that catalogs and studies black dramaturgies. Anunciação has a BA in theater theories from UniRio in Brazil and is a PhD student in performing arts at the Federal University of Bahia.

Setting

In transit to Brazil aboard a slave ship in the 1800s, an enslaved African woman is thrown overboard into the Atlantic Ocean. Living now at the bottom of the sea, she articulates thoughts about contemporary life while reconstructing her memories through objects that constantly fall from the ships that cross the ocean above.

Production History

Dramatic reading at Goethe Institut Theatre of Salvador/Bahia in Brazil, September 15, 2018.

Cast and Crew

Woman	Tatiana Tibúrcio
Director	Fernanda Júlia Onisajé
Production Coordinator	Leonel Henckes
Executive Producer	Giro Productions
Assistant Director	Fabíula Nansurê
Music	Fabíula Nansurê
Light Designer	Luiz Ailton (Caboclo de Cobre)

Synopsis

In *Antimemories of an Interrupted Trip*, the reader-spectator is faced with the solitary confinement of an enslaved African woman of the nineteenth century who, in transit to Brazil aboard a slave ship from which she was thrown into the Atlantic Ocean, fantastically comes to live on the bottom of the seas. From these depths, she articulates thoughts about contemporaneity (from the audience), while reconstructing her memories through objects that fall from the ships that cross the ocean throughout the narrative.

Scenario

The scenario consists of an utterly aged home office oxidized by salinity and irregularly stuck in a thick layer of a white salt that fills the entire floor-board. The home office is surrounded by tapered walls as if to indicate the end of a large sewer. On the rusty desk in the home office, it is possible to see an old microphone resting on an aged table pedestal. Coming from the ceiling are rusty tubes that provide memory objects that come from the surface of the seas.

the generalized use of biometric data as a source of identification [. . .] will aim to build new population species with a predisposition for [. . .] confinement. [. . .] The contemporary world is profoundly shaped and conditioned by these forms [. . .] which are the cloister, the fence, the wall [. . .], and ultimately, the border.

– Achille Mbembe, *Critique of Black Reason*

Scene One

In a tiny, cut-out spotlight, we notice a completely naked woman. Her hair is wet, and drops of water slowly slide across her black skin. She remains silent for a few moments, facing an audience seated in the secret darkness of the theater. She then starts light, disinterested steps on the white salt that covers the entire floor of the stage. A strange and watery sound takes over the environment.

Woman at the Sea Bottom As if trying to understand where I come from, I feel vibrations in my skin. A hint of heat coming from a central region that pulsates and pumps a red juice that feeds my most vital organs! I see signs of recognition and history in the surrounding waters . . . on the surface. (*Looks at the sky-sea.*) A surface that breathes and is unaware of my millennial existence. The waters tell stories. When they rub against the skin, wherever they go, they try to explain the natural strength of things not said, but known to everyone! Everyone knows their story, even if they don't recognize it. And those who know about their history will surely know about mine! The proof of this is the feeling that you feel when you see me here . . . in the space surrounded by abyssal waters. Those waters that at the same time keep me alive with their concentrated amount of vital salt, also keep me static in time . . . and in the arrogant space of all official stories preserved in the words of Western languages. My story, being unconsciously known, says a lot about everyone! Because we all have to recognize that the stories at the bottom are part of a whole . . . driven by ourselves. Whether through small daily activities carried out since our dawn, until our disturbing contempt for what happened to the other. Believe me . . . for sure . . . maybe everyone knows more about me than I do about myself! Deep down here, try to perceive the waters like a mirror in a blind spot on the wall. That point does not seem to mirror who is in front. But deep down . . . deep down, we know that this is a reflected reality. This mirror reflects a past that also belongs to everybody. A past that we will build together here and now! Me in my abyssal solitude . . . and you on the solid ground of convictions. But remember: the mainland may become less firm because of the ocean that surrounds me! Believe me! Ah . . . as you are not here at the bottom of the sea . . . I will refer to you as stones! (*Laughs.*) Here and now, you will be rocks! (*Laughs.*) Stones at the bottom of the sea. Stones! (*Laughs.*)

Whistling sounds from old ships invade the environment. The **Woman at the Sea Bottom** *performs a choreography based on the underwater harmonic sound. In this choreography, the character will adjust and organize the space, as if formatting a ruined-rusty home office, with several old books scattered on the white salt floor. Through rusty aerial tubes, four memory-objects fall in different sizes on the trail scene. The character does not react to these objects. In a light choreography, she approaches a rusty microphone attached to a small table pedestal on the old desk.*

Scene Two

Still dancing the choreography, the character starts to dress old and worn pieces of clothing scattered on the stage and the salt layers of the floor. Sitting at the rusty desk,

Woman at the Sea Bottom *adjusts the old microphone to her mouth, as if preparing for a lecture.*

Woman at the Sea Bottom I am . . .

A memory-object falls through the rusty tube, interrupting her speech. The woman gets up, takes the object, analyzes it, and puts it in the chest-wall.

I am at the bottom . . .

Another memory-object falls through the rusty tube, interrupting her speech again. The woman gets up, takes the object, analyzes it, and puts it in the chest-wall.

I am at the bottom of the sea . . .

Another memory-object falls through the rusty tube, interrupting once more what was going to be said. The woman gets up, takes the object, analyzes it, and puts it in the chest-wall.

I'm at the bottom of the sea! That simple! It makes no noise here! No . . . I didn't come on my own. (*To herself*.) Or did I come? (*Pause*.) I don't remember exactly. I'm here! And that is what matters. Fish . . . many fish pass through here day and night! Actually, days and nights are something far from me. I can see a point up there: when it's clear . . . day! When nothing . . . night! Sometimes I have memories! I live when I remember. And when I remember in a flux . . . wow ! It's a lot of people . . .

Another memory-object falls through the rusty tube, interrupting again what was going to be said. The woman gets up, takes the object, analyzes it, and puts it in the chest-wall.

It's a lot of people! Incredibly crowded with people! (*To herself*.) Guys. Yes, I remember people. People most often move me! It really moves me . . . from the heart! People look at you and say, "Hello!" Funny! Hello comes from "Look over there . . .", the greeting itself orders you not to look at us. But look over there! And so we go in that subliminal order of separation!

Another memory-object falls through the rusty tube, interrupting her speech. The woman gets up, takes the object, analyzes it, and sets it in the chest-wall.

Hello! So I remember people, yes! Just as I remember the surface! The firm ground of convictions. The stones may be asking how I got here! It does not matter! I'm here. Under the sea! Where there is no meeting. Did I follow the maximum order of "Hello," huh ?! (Brief pause.) We still don't know for sure . . . or at least we even haven't built up the reason I'm here. Fact is . . . here I am! And here, I go from here to there . . . from there to here . . . and ready! Ah . . . before we skip this point, it may seem crazy, but I'm alive, right?!

Another memory-object falls through the rusty tube on the Scene-Trail, interrupting the speech. The woman gets up, takes the object, analyzes it, and puts it in the chest-wall.

Here in this aquatic, soft, blue place, where the sound is something that is transmitted by molecules of water in continuous flow penetrating my body, maybe I am even more alive than up there! (*Points to audience.*) Do you know that this flow of water produces sensations? Many sensations! Sensations that remind me of an era. (*For herself.*) Era? From an era! Ready! Era! Now the story begins! The era was mentioned. Thus, we can start.

She gets up from the rusty table and goes in front of the table to speak more lightly and academically.

There was a time when I didn't have that immensity! In fact, I had a lot, yes! And the immensity I had didn't belong to me, you know? But it didn't belong to me because I didn't want to! Everything was less real. Everything was fleeting! Everything was a lie. Nothing you think was created was actually created! Everything was a sweet pictorial illusion. The senses created by those who breathe on dry land were just neurological paths deviated! (*Laughing.*) Small and induced neurological disorders. Deviated from on the Scene-Trail emotional coherence! The emotions left those who breathe on the firm ground of convictions . . . and were lost in time and space!

Another memory-object falls through the rusty tube, interrupting her speech. The woman gets up, takes the object, analyzes it, and sets it in the chest-wall.

They let them out and never found them again! They lived the second sweet illusion that such emotional elements would return one day! They never came back! (*Brief laugh.*) The emotions stayed there! It is not known where! That's why I came here . . . (*For herself.*) Did I come?

A sudden figural sonority of a ship shows the silence of the environment. The **Woman at the Sea Bottom** *interrupts her lecture, puts her ears against the funnel wall, identifying through the sounds which objects are about to arrive through the rusty tubes.*

Scene Three

The **Woman at the Sea Bottom** *sits beside the chest-wall, waiting for the memory-objects that are about to fall into her confined home office. Then another memory-object falls on the salt floor, interrupting her speech. She gets up, takes the object, analyzes it, and places it on the rusty table.*

Woman at the Sea Bottom Well . . . as far as I can remember, I came here to the bottom of my own free will. (*To herself.*) My willingness?

Another memory-object falls into her home office, interrupting her speech. The woman gets up, takes the object, analyzes it, and places it on the rusty table.

But I may be wrong! The fact is that here I find the lost emotions of the firm ground of convictions! Those emotions!

Another memory-object falls on the scene, interrupting her speech. The woman gets up, takes the object, analyzes it, and places it on the rusty table.

The possibilities of finding them are endless! I can find them inside one of these oysters . . . tormented and invaded by small grains of sand! Our hearts would never allow these invasions. This is very crazy, right? That is why I say: you need to know how to deal with your own lucidity . . . how to deal with your own intelligence . . . so that it does not swallow you, and takes you to strange and uneven paths of breathing. Intelligence sometimes wants to fill everything! Even that time between inhaling . . . and exhaling.

Another memory-object falls to the salt floor, interrupting her speech. The woman gets up, takes the object, analyzes it, and places it on the rusty table.

This space must remain empty. It is a vacancy that determines the pace of something that we don't know what it is. And no understanding should fill it. Some say that there is a lifetime within this breathing interval! And that being so, we are made up of several small lives. Every breath . . . a life that is complete. If in one minute you breathe fifty times . . . then you lived fifty times in one minute. (*Smile.*) As simple as that! Now I ask: do those who breathe know this?

Another memory-object falls to the salt floor, interrupting her speech. The woman gets up, takes the object, analyzes it, and places it on the rusty table.

(*Irritated.*) Time is a sacred thing that needs to be respected! And everything has its time. So, everything is sacred!

Another memory-object falls to the white salt floor.

For example, right now, we are exchanging our times.

Another memory-object falls to the white salt floor.

You are giving me yours, and I am giving you my . . . time.

Another memory-object falls to the white salt floor.

Thus, a sacred exchange! If I consecrate mine to you, you offer me yours.

Another memory-object falls to the white salt floor.

And then justice is done! That simple! We adjust our times. Our times are intertwined, and right now, we are just one time!

Another memory-object falls to the white salt floor. The woman feels tired and leans on the pile of objects that are on the rusty table, and remains static in her thought-flux that continues to flow toward the audience.

Indeed, my time is here at the bottom of the sea . . . separated from the mainland of convictions! Some people say that times happen at the same time. That there is no past, present, and future. These three instances happen at the same time . . . at the same time! It means that the past is not as static as we think, and the future is not as malleable as we want.

She takes a memory-object from the table. A beam of light cuts out the object in her hand.

I read in one of those books that the retina of our eyes captures the image with a certain time difference. Between the moment the light illuminates the object . . . and the moment the information is sent to the brain, there is a delay! A moment! In other words, everything we see now at this instant, actually, is already past!

At this moment, she hears a kind of ship siren on the high seas that "crosses" the sound of the environment. She observes different sides of the space as if unbalanced with the insistent call of the ship that crosses the seas on the surface.

Scene Four

Suddenly, the **Woman at the Sea Bottom** *heads for a small, rusty three-step staircase that is embedded in the layers of white salt on the seafloor. When standing at the top of the small and rusty staircase, in a sharp light effect, we are sent to another atmosphere. We no longer notice the ruined home office that receives memory-objects that continuously fall from the surface of the seas. A kind of spotlight cuts out the woman's eyes, and another one suggests a backlight. Dark atmosphere. She now takes on another diction (I), as if she transforms herself into another person in an instant corresponding to the change in the ambient lighting. Her voice is now projected by a rusty microphone that reverberates resized throughout the room. In the background (in the whole scenario), piercing images are projected and locate parts and pieces of memories that go back to shattered figures, thematically related to the times of floating slave ships. The woman digs up a silver ribbon from the sand and ties it to her left forearm. Her voice is microphoned. Attention to the fact that the phrases uttered in Yoruba mean exactly the previous sentence spoke in Portuguese [English].*

Woman at the Sea Bottom (*diction I*) (*soft shout*) No . . . I don't want to go! You think and believe that the best for me is to enter! But something tells me that this vessel will not take me where you are planning! And what plans are these? The route may not correspond to the facts! *Awọn gigun le ko baamu awọn mon!* I know that history will not register this fragment of time, where I stand at the entrance of a large and imposing ship that wishes to be bigger than the gods! I reiterate and implore that if you put me on this ship . . . internal storms will happen, tearing hearts from both sides! Immeasurable consequences will spread across the planet . . . spreading hatred and sadness . . . I repeat, for both sides! Distant souls will cry out for comfort and the return of comfortable maternal laps! *Awọn ọkàn ti o ni ẹkun n kigbe fun itunu ati ipadabọ awọn ọfin ti iyara.* And even the forged and apparent comfort will appear fleetingly, I insist, for both sides! Mutual disgust and hysterical attacks against immaterial designs of faith will occur, I repeat, for both sides! Desires for revenge and refinements of rejoicing in sovereignty. Excessive work, paradoxically combined with the lack of results, will be established, I predict, for both sides! Forgetfulness of identity, allied to the search for it, as well as the undue and illegitimate appropriation of ancestral cultures, I reinforce . . . for both sides! *Agbegbe ti idanimọ, ti o darapọ* *pẹlu wiwa fun rẹ, bakanna pẹlu aiṣedeede ati aibikita ti awọn aṣa idile, iranlọwọ . . . fun awọn mejeji!* Small boats in vain will try to recover rescues of material and immaterial fortunes across the seas as if to settle accounts . . . and that will affect both sides! Citizens will sink in blue seas . . . and the moment they feel the salt of ocean waters in their skins, they will no longer know where they came from and where they would go. And we will only know that this dive will vibrate safely in the conscious and unconscious of . . . both sides! Both sides! Both! Both! Sides! And both sides! This moment of mine . . . when I am static in front of the ship's entrance, generously alerting all this vision that passes through me . . . this fragment of history will never be narrated! This fragment of history will not be considered in the official records! I complain to the weather to register what happened in the wind. And that each ear that the same wind caresses, this fact is magically told . . . and narrated! Spiked! Narrated! Sent! Announced! Spoken! Stated! The wind and the fact . . . narrated! *Ti sọ! Gbe si! Tẹ Tu! Loro! Awọn afẹfẹ ati otitọ . . . sọ!*

A loud and continuous sound of the ship's siren corrupts the environment. In a light effect, we are sent back to the atmosphere of the ruined home office of the **Woman at the Sea Bottom***'s memory-objects. Sudden silence.*

Scene Five

A figurative sound of a ship echoes a little far. It is not known for sure whether the sound comes from the top of the surface of the seas or the corners of the **Woman at the Sea Bottom***'s memory . . . or even from behind the audience. She descends the small rusty three-step staircase and sits on the same staircase. She appreciates and enjoys the sound of the ship crossing the surface. She stares at the sea-sky.*

Woman at the Sea Bottom (*looking up*) Ah . . . another one is crossing the immense ocean, cutting the green-blue waters of the seas. From here, I can feel the vibrations of the mechanism that mobilizes the waters, creating invisible waves that come to caress my skin! (*She looks at the skin behind the palms of her hands. She stranges something about her skin, but soon the flow of thought follows.*) How many people are on that ship? (*To herself.*) Or vessel? Or boat? Where do they think they are going? What is the purpose of each of them? How many are currently looking deeply into these waters . . . to them mysterious and uninhabitable? (*Laughs a lot.*) Poor people! They don't know the impossible . . . the possible! They don't know that they can come here too! Just throwing themselves . . . throw themselves into the space between the sea and them. And so dive deep! And come off there. Over there? I don't know what is there anymore. Here, I let go of something that imprisoned me. But at the same time, it fed me. Desires for displacement . . . or even involuntary displacements resulting from the firm convictions of those who breathe always propel us to utopian lands. Land that has perfection only in our imagination. (*Slight laughter.*) So whenever I can, I retreat to these wonderful utopian imageries of the mind! Where no shark can attack me! Where no firm ground conviction can lead to uncertain paths! Did the cause of my abyssal existence in this ocean come from there?! (*She looks at the sky-sea.*) They cross the seas, but they don't know where they are going!

Scene Six

Suddenly, loud and strange sounds seem to come from inside the rusty tubes, cheering the lonely **Woman at the Sea Bottom** *in expectation.*

Woman at the Sea Bottom Here comes something else!

She goes to the yellow tubes. She is disappointed to realize that nothing comes from there.

Nothing? It seems like they know I'm here. Often, they guess my thoughts!

Following the sound again, she goes to the chest-wall, which is in the opposite direction of the rusty table. Suddenly, from the top of the sea-sky, a can of peas falls directly on her rusty table, slightly surprising her.

Sealed . . . and it's valid! Look that! (*She sits down at the rusty table.*) I can't believe anyone has given up this can of peas! If someone throws it down, it did it with the full awareness that someone would get it here. Was it a religious offering? Once they threw a book that talked about offers to the seas. I kept that book . . . it's in the closet! If this pea was offered to any goddess, may she forgive me and lend me this food!

She goes to the accordion-chest and keeps looking for something while following her thought flow.

Images of people throwing things overboard often come to my mind! I don't know if they are my memories . . . or some photo I saw! But they are beautiful images of cheerful people . . . vibrant . . . as if that act made them more satisfied. (*She finds a can opener in the accordion-chest.*) Satisfaction is what I feel now . . . here . . . about to eat these peas! (*She goes towards the rusty table and starts to open the can of peas.*) I think the act of giving should be praised! We may even question that whoever receives should fight for its things. But we don't always have that possibility. Like me, for example, here at the bottom of this ocean. What am I going to work for? For who? Why? At least I could fish . . . fish for fish . . . my neighbors down here. (*She finishes opening the can of peas and speaks into the rusty microphone.*) But at the same time, I find it very uninteresting and not very pleasant for you to kill your neighbors. They respect me too. For example, one of these times, they would be here already bothering me because of these peas. But not! They respect me. Don't invade my space! (*She picks up a plate that comes out of the accordion-chest and returns to the rusty table, sitting down.*) Good appetite for myself! Hmm . . . what a delight! They came at the right time! As things are, isn't it? These thinking things here work very well! I once thought: "I need something to help me sleep at night." Because some fish roam here in the wee hours, which is hell! So I thought, "It would be great if something falls from the surface that could help me against these nocturnal fish." Ready! I thought, and this object soon descended here . . .

She suddenly gets up anxious to show the object, an old rusty fan that has been in the corner of her tapered home office all the time. She turns on the fan. The woman activates the device at the base of the old fan that starts to work . . . spin. Its rotation draws small swirls in the waters that go towards the table with a plate of peas.

I turn on, and this thing spins! And it keeps frightening the disturbed night fish! Nice invention! Those who breathe invented it up there! (*She finishes taking the last bite of the peas.*) Once they threw that device here! (*She goes to the book-chest and takes out a small, old smartphone.*) That's when I met Pedro! Ah . . . you still don't know Pedro?! (*She sits down on the rusty chair.*) Pedro is a buddy who lives inside. He does not speak. He's static. And I determine his emotions. (*She shows a picture of Pedro.*) Look at Pedro here, happy, look! (*Pedro's photo changes on the smartphone. Projection on the wall of Pedro's images, resizing our character's action.*) Here, he's more distressed . . . sad! Inside here, Pedro does lots of things. Sometimes, I put him like this on my side . . . (*She puts the smartphone-Pedro on the rusty table.*) And I spend hours talking with Pedro. What a partner! I just don't understand why he doesn't come out of there. He arrived in that box . . . and there he stayed. But anyway . . . each in their way! Here at Pedro's house, there is such an exciting thing! A sound that when it works is really fun!

The woman triggers a song on the rusty smartphone, and a fantastically loud sound starts to play unrecognizable music—something like rusty music. A soundtrack of what would be Western music. The woman turns down the volume on the rusty smartphone.

I once read one of those spontaneous articles that suddenly fall from the seas, which explained that Pedro's house caused a hell of a revolution over there! People were talking through Pedro's house. They could be close, but each one maintains connected to its own little Pedro's house! They just talked like that. Until one day, they failed to recognize their voices. (*To herself.*) I imagine it must be crazy when you lose track of what things really are. Then there was only the inner voice! The inner voice! But . . . what about this one? Was it possible to be heard?

She raises the back of her hand to her ears in an attempt to hear her inner voice.

I can't hear anything more.

Scene Seven

Whale sounds invade the environment. The **Woman at the Sea Bottom** *tries to understand where they come from. She recognizes that they come from the left of the home office, and reacts as if she understands the whales. She looks at her right arm and removes a piece of her old clothes, leaving her forearm exposed, in which we see tied a silver ribbon similar to the one found in the sand of Scene-Trail 04.*

Woman at the Sea Bottom The whales are very friendly! Whenever they come by, they never fail to greet me. And they always send cryptic messages. Right now, they asked me to expose my right forearm. (*She surprises herself.*) I haven't noticed my right forearm in a long time. It's just that here I don't need to take my clothes off to take a shower. I'm always fresh and washed! The sea currents ever caress me, so I never need to take off my clothes . . . someone threw them up there a long time ago. I don't even remember when it was anymore. I think this outfit is beautiful! It fits my body well and makes me ready for any eventuality. If someone suddenly shows up here . . . to have a bottle of wine! (*She rushes to the revolving chest and takes out a rusty bottle of wine. Puts it on the rusty table.*) Look how beautiful! It fell from up there . . . like that! Full! But I always have a glass. (*She takes two rusty cups from the chest-drawer.*) I always put that other bowl here. As if someone would show up to drink with me. I know the possibilities are minimal here . . . at the bottom of this ocean. But there is always a possibility for everything, right? It is mathematic. And we must always be prepared for the possibilities! The possibilities are something created by those from up there! Those who breathe on the firm ground of convictions! But, actually, it was the nature that created the possibilities. Nature created the possibilities so pertinently that those up there think they created them. (*Laughing.*) And they are so happy! This feeling is important.

Scene Eight

Suddenly sounds of desperate crowd invade the aquatic environment. Through a light effect, we are sent to another atmosphere. We no longer notice the **Woman at the Sea Bottom***'s ruined and old home office at the sea bottom, with white salt flooring. A spotlight makes the image of the woman backlit. Dark atmosphere. The character now takes on another diction (II), as if she were transformed into another person, in an instant corresponding to the illumination change. In the background, projections that subliminally go back to distorted images of spaces, of ruined forests and large vessels of possible slave ships. The voice of the woman is now microphoned, along with the annoying sounds of crowd in despair.*

Woman at the Sea Bottom (*diction II*) (*moderate shout*) I have children, and my children have a mother! I don't know what this journey is about! *Emi ko mọ ohun ti irin-ajo yii jẹ gbogbo!* If you don't leave me alone, for the breast milk that has been sucked for all the citizens of the earth by feeding power to those who have turned against their own mother, I swear that the once vital milk will turn into deadly poison within your guts, and the crossing will not take place! I have children, and my children have a mother! *Mo ni awọn ọmọ wẹwẹ ati awọn ọmọ wẹwẹ mi ni Mama!* You can't leave me in a state of inverted paradise! Get off me . . . *Gba mi kuro!* The milk has dried! And do you still insist on me . . . dry and malnourished from my own vital nutrients, made food for your greed and brutality? Get off me . . .*Gba mi kuro!* I need to breathe! I can't move! Where are you sailing to? And why so much party in such a troubled crossing? Get off me . . . *Gba mi kuro!* This home does not belong to them! Don't put your strength inside me! Stop it! I will not stay! Please don't make me part of that distant and unknown universe that for now is unique! I am not part of this ritual! My milk is drying! Painful manipulations will not work . . . My milk has dried up! Get off me! *Gba mi kuro!* The waters below are not happy! Who said you couldn't see with your hands? Who said you could only see with your eyes? The waters scream . . . I have children, and my children have a mother! *Mo ni awọn ọmọ wẹwẹ ati awọn ọmọ wẹwẹ mi ni Mama!* Give me life as I gave you one day, and throw me into the endless seas of return. I didn't go. . . but I already want to come back! *Mo fẹ pada sẹhin!* Don't squeeze me! Don't touch me! My waters are screaming! My waters are drying up. Navigation is not adjusted! Get off me . . . I have children, and my children have a mother! *Mo ni awọn ọmọ wẹwẹ ati awọn ọmọ wẹwẹ mi ni Mama!*

The woman falls exhausted to the white salt floor as if drained of energy. In a light effect, we are sent back to the atmosphere of the home office of the lonely **Woman at the Sea Bottom**.

Scene Nine

Suddenly, metallic sounds of a current sea echo, scaring the **Woman at the Sea Bottom**. *She is attentive and looks expectantly to the sides and through the rusty aerial pipes. Suddenly, the sounds are interrupted, giving way to silence.*

Woman at the Sea Bottom For a moment, I thought I would finally pour someone a glass of wine! But it's good as it is! I drink in both glasses . . . and so I drink more. (*Smile.*)

At this moment, the flow of her thought is interrupted by the same metallic sounds of a current sea. It is identical to those of the previous Scene-Trail but much stronger. This current' sea brings a memory-object that we soon perceive to be a large mirror that has been thrown from some ship that was crossing the sea surface at that moment. Contemplative silence in front of the new object, now embedded in the white salt layers of the home office. The woman takes the big memory-object (mirror) and observes it. When she turns the object over and sees herself in the mirror, she gets scared and throws the mirror to the white salt floor. She silently contemplates, for the first time, her image reflected in the large mirror set in the white salt sand. Upon seeing the mirror, the woman faces her own reflection as if it were another being, another person with whom she is now sharing the abyssal space of the ocean floor. The woman then begins to dialogue with her image.

Who is there?

She is completely surprised at the possibility that someone is inside something so thin. She understands the mirror as a kind of transparent box. She circles the mirror, trying to unravel the mystery.

(*Stunned.*) How can you stay inside this box?

Quickly she takes a rusty measuring tape from the rotating chest and begins to measure the thickness and height of the mirror.

How is it possible? Looking at you like that from the front, I would say that you are even full-bodied . . . (*Embarrassed.*) Can you get out of there? Don't you feel confined? I have enough space for the two of us out here. Come! Here are me and some fish. You may come! (*Waiting for a reaction from the woman in the mirror.*) Ok! You don't want to come! (*Walks to her rusty table.*) I can suppose a reason for your fear! I really don't have the best equipment in modern life here! All that you see are objects that came from up there! From the surface of the seas! But I don't mind! All of these things still work really well! I have repeated things . . . like Pedro's house, for example . . . I can give you one! (*Goes to the revolving chest.*) Hey! You also have one of these little houses! (*Smiling.*) I see that we have a lot in common! And I like your clothes! I really like it! Same as mine! (*Looks at the dress itself.*) I was lucky that the cut fits my body perfectly! There are times when I think that . . . although it suits me well, I could try other things! My memory sometimes betrays me . . . and I can't remember what I wore before. You don't understand, do you? So, when that outfit fell here, I was wearing something else that "I don't remember exactly what it was." And at the same time that I miss this "something else, I don't remember what it was," this outfit is already part of me. I mean . . . I was inserted in it! It's mine now, you know? At least I think it belongs to me. It does! I must not dispense it! But at the same time . . . pay attention . . . at the same time I feel that I must remember my old "something else that I don't remember what it was." A certainty that I feel, that the "other thing I don't remember what it was" was essential to me, and guided my soul in some very fundamental sense. But my memory, invaded by these salt waters, does not allow me to have access to this data! So I no longer have access to that "other thing that I don't remember what it was." But let's not get stuck on this subject! Let's entertain a little! I have some drinks here, and we can choose something to drink! What do you like in terms of drinking? We have . . . let me see . . . white wine . . . beers . . . soft drinks . . . canned juices and some drinks! What would you prefer? Don't you know what you want? Well . . . so let's go with white wine. (*Laughs.*) Let's get distracted because one of the beliefs up there is that life is something that passes . . . and fast!

The woman triggers a song on the Pedro-smartphone with an instrumental predominance of balafons, djambês, and traditional kora. The music totally invades the environment, and she dances an unusual choreography with the mirror woman. Suddenly tired, she finishes the musical number quite happily and sits down on the rusty table.

Come on! Having fun also tires! I discovered this song on a pen drive. Probably whoever threw the pen drive in the sea should be sick of hearing it. But not everything disgusting and repetitive for someone is so for everyone else! I hear this song every day as if it were a prayer or a mantra! It makes me feel good! (*She smiles.*) You in there, tell me about yourself! Where are you from? How far do you want to go? Your food preferences? Do you like to travel? What do you work with? And when you have time off, what do you like to do most? Hobbies? Do you have any? Children? Woman? Partner? Sexual preferences? Gay? Hetero? Bi? Pan? Trans? Cis? Dating? Occasional relations? Or are you married? And politically? Is it from the left? Right? Center? Extremes? Do you have a bank account? Which one? Because it makes all the difference! Where do you apply for your money? Properties? Handbag? Savings? Have you fixed income funds? And own home? Already has? Or are you paying financed parcels? Because if you still pay the financing, the property is still not yours! It seems to be . . . but it isn't! Car? Do you have any? (*Getting angry.*) Do you have a car, woman? Answer me? (*Getting even more irritated.*) Won't you say anything? Ah . . . that's it, right?! You're nothing! You are just the mirror resident . . . who does nothing . . . does nothing . . . communicates nothing! Nothing! Nothing! Nothing! And you don't give me any chance to know you. Not even your voice? The inner voice, I understand . . . it's tough to hear! But your metallic voice . . . where is it? Sound your metallic voice! Mechanically rub these two vocal muscles and introduce yourself, woman! You turn things hard, you know?! So, there is no conflict! Give me back my wine . . . you didn't even drink it! (*The woman at the sea bottom takes the wine and drinks.*) If you don't drink, I drink! Do you know why? Because I don't need you! I've been here for some time, and I'm fine! I don't need any charity . . . any companion! Now you, with that strange look of yours. . . that ridiculous outfit of yours, that undefined face of yours, doesn't convince anyone! It is evident that this outfit does not belong to you . . . that you do not remember what it was! You must be asking yourself, "Why is she treating me like this? What did I do to her? I didn't even talk to her!" That's precisely what is puzzling me, young lady! You don't say anything! You don't help me at all! What kind of matter am I made of? Where do I go? And how far am I going? Yes . . . because it may seem absurd, but all of this does not belong to me! I know . . . I admit it! They came from the top . . . (*Pushes a rusty chair irritably to the white salt floor.*) I am fully aware of that! They fit my body, fit well in my living room . . . (*Throws the plate of peas on the white salt floor.*) But in fact, I don't remember . . . I don't remember . . . I don't remember!

At that moment, several memory-objects start to fall continuously from the rusty overhead tubes in an amount that gradually increases. They fall non-stop throughout the scene, but, unlike other times, the woman doesn't pay any attention, as she is stressed with the mirror woman.

I don't remember . . . or they stuck in the sanctuary of my memory! That's it; I need someone to help me access this sanctuary! These books here (*Opens the chest of books, throwing several on the floor in irritation.*) tell me nothing about this issue! Nothing! I've read everything . . . and nothing! I have the slightest feeling that they stole me! It looks like they erased me. They hid the woman I really am . . . (*Pushes the other chair to the floor.*) You came from above . . . from the firm ground of convictions! I saw! No one spoke to me, no! I saw you coming down from above, ok?! So I feel that you are my only hope! At least something makes me feel calm and relieved! Do you know what it is? To know that I am not like you! Strange . . . disgusting! Dressed in a suit that doesn't suit you well . . . by the way, there shouldn't even be something that suits you! Look at that hair! That skin! That eyes! I'd rather not know who I am than be like you! (*Screams.*) You are very ugly! Ugly! Ugly! (*Pushes the table, turning over all the objects that mix with the white salt floor.*)

Suddenly, followed by a loud sound, an unexpected and tremendous sea storm begins at the bottom of the ocean. The woman is startled by the sound of what would be a sea tornado. She recognizes the severity of sea storms. Things move as if they were going to split in half. The mirror starts to spin very fast, driven by the currents of the marine storm. She realizes that the mirror can break at any moment, or even be carried away by the marine storm currents. She tries to contain her objects in places but is very attentive to the mirror so that it does not break. She holds it for a while, but the storm is strong enough to get her out of the mirror, which starts to spin even harder. The mirror spins at speed and vanishes into the vast ocean, amid scared shoals. The woman screams to the mirror, but it has gone.

(*Shouting.*) Woman, don't go! Wait! Do not go! Don't leave me here alone! Come back!

The memory-objects suddenly stop falling from the rusty tubes. The sea storm is also calming down, and we can see the woman in her home office wholly messed up by the storm. But now, it is calm and silent. She is sad that she was unable to hold the mirror-woman, who left with the sea storm. Silence is definitely installed in the abyssal environment.

(*Sadly.*) She's gone! The mirror woman is gone!

Scene Ten

The **Woman at the Sea Bottom** *begins to straighten the rusty table and the two chairs that fell at the floor on the white salt sand. She tries to fix the disorder caused by the sea storm. She is exhausted and overwhelmed by an atmosphere of bad luck . . . and by the failure of not being able to prevent the mirror-woman from leaving with the sea storm at the bottom of the sea.*

Woman at the Sea Bottom What a beast I was! That woman seemed to be a good person! But I couldn't help myself! I was tired of just fighting with the fish! But just like the fish, she didn't react! (*Admiring.*) She didn't react! And what clothes were those? She definitely had no good taste! Her appearance was also not the best! A worn-out skin! A color that wasn't ugly, but it also didn't attract my attention! (*Contemplative.*) Yes, that skin didn't attract my attention. The skin!

The woman looks and analyzes the skin on the back and palms of her own hands.

My skin looks just like hers! (*Slight pause.*) Where's my melanin? Where did my melanin go? The salt! The white salt made my skin vulnerable! My skin!

She quickly begins to undress, in a kind of selfish despair. When she is naked again, she observes her hands spread and wonders.

Who stole my skin?

She takes a few of salt and rubs it on her skin.

Scene Eleven

Tired, naked, and laid on the white salt floor, the **Woman at the Sea Bottom** *recovers energy. She opens the chest of books. The woman takes a rusty book out of the chest. A strange underwater sound invades the environment and intensifies gradually. She opens the rusty book and begins to read.*

Woman at the Sea Bottom I once met a girl on the street . . . at that moment she was selling candy . . . she must have been four or five years old. However, her face was like that of an older woman. It was an old girl. That face conveyed to me such great wisdom, that before she tried to sell me those sweets, I asked her to sit down and say something to me. She asked me, "What do you mean something?" I said, "Anything." Then she said: "Anything or something? (*Brief pause.*) Do you want to buy candy? They are as sweet as honey!" It was then that I thought, "Sure! I had not realized that the candy copies the effect of honey." And even though honey is something from nature and therefore free. I was preferring to buy the candy, which would be a copy of the copy of the honey . . . and it wasn't even natural! Why was I looking to buy the copy when I could have the original for free?

Besides the woman still holding the rusty book open in her hands, we realized that the projection of the woman's image reading the rusty book unfolded on the stage as if the book were a webcam that captures the image of its reader and projects it across the underwater scene. Afterward, we see projections of several black bodies floating on the seabed. Faceless bodies. Men, women, and children. Floating bodies in projection. The woman then perceives the floating bodies in projection and risks a slight smile, perhaps due to the possible non-loneliness, even with dead bodies.

Woman at the Sea Bottom (*diction III*) *Okun na ṣi wa . . . ati awọn okun ti o wa niwaju mi ni ailopin.* The ship was traveling . . . and the seas in front of me were endless. The reasons that pushed me away were the same reasons that made me want to stay. *Okun na ṣi wa . . . ati awọn okun ti o wa niwaju mi ni ailopin.* But we were all on that vessel. The holds of the ships made us invisible! Only the cracks of light that came from the ship's floor streaked our skins! Yes . . . the floor was our roof. But, even though streaked by the cracks of light, we were invisible there. The desire for invisibility did not correspond with the mirrored relationship of female vanity. But still, I'll never recognize myself in a mirror. I no longer know my face streaked with light. I don't know my body anymore! I wonder: when do you want to be invisible? The basement seemed to protect us from those seas. We went on aimlessly! That simple! People, most of the time, move me . . . they really move me . . . from the heart. *Awọn eniyan julọ ti akoko gbe mi . . . gan fi ọwọ kan mi . . . lati inu.* Our tight bodies forced us to imagine a crowd! A small crowd of fifty people! I have children . . . and my children have a mother. From the empty traces of the floor-to-ceiling came invasive drops of seawater . . . And our bodies, hot and wet from the invasive waters, clung to each other . . . and at that moment I felt safer! I could hear the sails insisting . . . trapped sails were insisting on flying by the force of the winds . . . the winds . . . were those that record everything! But my hands rested on the bottom hull of that ship! The desire for invisibility was the source of our strength! The waves moved on the contrary direction as if insisting on a possible unwanted return by some and desired by many! We were of different desires . . . Different gods . . . although equal! Different voices, albeit the same! Different languages, but unified and matched by the pieces of wood loose from that bottom ship hull! The hull! My hands on the hooves. By placing my ears on the hulls, I could hear the heartbeat of the seas! (*Imitates the sound of a heartbeat.*) The seas live! The seas pulsate! And those fifty lives! Fifty lives! I repeat those lives that breathed according to the heartbeat of the seas . . . Yes, we breathed together as if we were one! With each breath, a life that was completed . . . And the space between inspiration and expiration was filled by our expectations there! And for the previewed missing of here! At sea, the air from our chest started to escape, joining the winds . . . our air at the winds! *Afẹfẹ wa si awọn afẹfẹ*!

The sound of a maritime storm invades the environment.

With the air of the chest turned into the wind . . . our weights exceeded! They crossed the control line! An excess of weight and hope that condemned my body to the bottom of the seas. *Opo ti iwuwo ati ireti ti o da ara mi lẹbi isalẹ awọn okun.* My children, who have a mother, were chosen to the martyrdom of being launched into the sea . . . as if in sacrifice to the seas. My children . . . chosen by those who stepped in our sky full of lights! That's when I shouted: "*iye owo ti awọn ọmọde kekere mẹta . . . jẹ dọgba pẹlu iwuwo ti iya!*", "The sum of the weight of three young children . . . is equal to the weight of their mother!" Nobody heard me . . . but I repeated: "the sum of the weight of three young children . . . is equal to the weight of their mother!", "*iye owo ti awọn ọmọde kekere mẹta . . . jẹ dọgba pẹlu iwuwo ti iya!*" Yes, I went up to the skies from that ship's floor. And finally, I found the source of the drops of the seas that refreshed us. My arms then became huge . . . and long . . . and so, I hugged the seas! I embraced the immense sea with my long, enormous arms!

At that moment, we finally noticed the cooling of an aqueous atmosphere in the scene. Bubbling images of blue waters take over the environment, and an aquatic sound is amplified where we perceive the sound impact of oxygen molecules with the molecules of sea waters. Among confused images of blue waters, there are stretches of silver robes. The woman is confused by these projected images, which suddenly disappear, leaving only a precise and soft light on the face of the woman who, with a slight smile, still says:

People, most of the time, move me . . . really move me! From my heart! *Awọn eniyan julọ ti akoko gbe mi . . . gan fi ọwọ kan mi . . . lati inu.*

The projected image of the **Woman at the Sea Bottom**, *now with immense and giant arms, slowly dissolves at the bottom of the ocean waters.*

The end.

So Goes We

Jacqueline E. Lawton

Jacqueline E. Lawton is a playwright, dramaturg, producer, and advocate for access, equity, diversity, and inclusion in the American theater. Her produced plays include *Blood-bound and Tongue-tied*, Deep Belly Beautiful, Edges of Time, *The Hampton Years*, *Intelligence*, *Mad Breed*, and *The Wonderful Wizard of Oz*. Her work has been developed and presented at the following venues: Classical Theater of Harlem, Folger Shakespeare Library, The Kennedy Center, Pasadena Playhouse, Rep Stage, Rorschach Theater Company, PlayMakers Repertory Company, Round House Theatre, Theater J, and Woolly Mammoth Theater Company. Lawton has received commissions from Arena Stage, Adventure Theatre & ATMTC Academy, National New Play Network, National Portrait Gallery, National Museum of American History, Round House Theatre, Tantrum Theater, and Theater J. She received her MFA in playwriting from the University of Texas at Austin. She is a 2012 TCG Young Leaders of Color award recipient and an alum of the National New Play Network, Arena Stage's Playwrights' Arena, and Center Stage's Playwrights Collective. Lawton is an associate professor in the Department of Dramatic Art and co-director of Southern Futures at the University of North Carolina at Chapel Hill. She is a dramaturg for PlayMakers Repertory Company and a proud member of the Dramatist Guild.

Setting

This socio-political performance piece is presented as a choral drama. The story follows the fraught and intersecting journeys of asylum seekers and their legal advocates in post-2016 America as the country draws shut its proverbial "golden door."

Production History

New Play Development Workshop at the University of North Carolina at Chapel Hill Department of Dramatic Art, December 2019.

Cast

Kervens Jean-Baptiste	Thaddaeus Edwards
Dominique Jean-Baptiste	Rasool Jahan
Josie Lamont-Patterson	Tia James
Kazima Lamont-Patterson	Monèt Marshall
Sarita de la Cruz Snyder	Sarita Ocón

Production Team

Director	JaMeeka Holloway-Burrell
Dramaturg	Jules Odendahl-James
Stage Directions	Takhona Hlatshwako
Stage Manager	Erin Bell

Characters

Josie Lamont-Patterson (*black woman, forties*), *an immigration lawyer.*
Kazima Lamont-Patterson (*black woman, forties*), *Josie's wife, geneticist, community-based activist and organizer.*
Dominique Jean-Baptiste (*black woman, thirties*), *ethics professor, political activist, refugee seeking political asylum.*
Sarita de la Cruz Snyder (*Latinx woman, forties*), *Josie's best friend, immigration lawyer.*
Kervens Jean-Baptiste (*black man, forties*), *Dominique's husband, economics professor.*

Cast Breakdown

Four women, one man.

Time and Place

July 2018 to May 2019.
Various.

Production Notes

- There are five chairs. By each chair, there are water bottles for the actors.
- There are also various props that will be used throughout the play.
- Larger items, such as a table and sofa, are off to the side. These larger items should have casters on them for ease of mobility.

Notes

- (—) dashes at the end of a sentence are cut-offs by the following line.
- (—) dashes within a sentence are a self-cut-offs, an acceleration into the next thought.
- (. . .) ellipses at the end of a sentence indicate a character unsure of what to say or how to say what comes next.
- (Pause) is a shared moment of silence.
- (Beat) is a longer pause in which a shift has occurred, this could be an intention or a discovery.
- (Silence) is a much longer moment, no words are spoken, but a deep understanding is felt. The characters remain connected to one another. Even if that connection is a growing distance.

There is really nothing more to say—except why.
But since why is difficult to handle, one must take refuge in how.

– Toni Morrison, *The Bluest Eye*

Prologue

Now.

Lights up on a mostly empty stage.

In the center of the stage, there is a glowing bowl.

The glow is orange and radiant like fire.

The cast enters from multiple directions.

They each carry a chair and wear a backpack.

They set the chairs down in unison.

The chairs are in a semi-circle that faces the audience.

The cast is lined up from left to right as follows: **Sarita**, **Kazima**, **Josie**, **Dominique**, *and* **Kervens**.

They take a collective breath. Darkness.

Voiceover Are you a citizen of the United States?

Dominique, **Josie**, **Kazima**, **Sarita**, *and* **Kervens** *stomp their feet once in unison.*

Voiceover How did you enter the US?

Dominique, **Josie**, **Kazima**, **Sarita**, *and* **Kervens** *stomp their feet twice in unison.*

Voiceover How long have you been here?

Dominique, **Josie**, **Kazima**, **Sarita**, *and* **Kervens** *stomp their feet three times in unison.*

Lights return.

They each remove a scroll from their backpacks and set their backpacks down.

One at a time, the cast steps forward and read from the scroll.

When they read together, it is in unison . . . as one voice.

Dominique
Not like the brazen giant of Greek fame,
With conquering limbs astride from land to land;

Dominique/Josie
Here at our sea-washed, sunset gates shall stand
A mighty woman with a torch, whose flame
Is the imprisoned lightning, and her name
Mother of Exiles.

Dominique/Josie/Sarita
From her beacon-hand
Glows world-wide welcome; her mild eyes command
The air-bridged harbor that twin cities frame.

Dominique/Josie/Sarita/Kervens
“Keep, ancient lands, your storied pomp!” cries she
With silent lips. “Give me your tired, your poor,
Your huddled masses yearning to breathe free,

Dominique/Josie/Sarita/Kervens/Kazima
The wretched refuse of your teeming shore.
Send these, the homeless, tempest-tost to me,
I lift my lamp beside the golden door!”

One at time, on their line, they crumple the scrolls and toss them into the bowl.

Josie (*crumpling and tossing the scroll into the bowl.*) So it goes.

Sarita (*crumpling and tossing the scroll into the bowl.*) So it goes.

Kazima (*crumpling and tossing the scroll into the bowl.*) So it goes.

Dominique (*crumpling and tossing the scroll into the bowl.*) So it goes.

Kervens (*crumpling and tossing the scroll into the bowl.*) So it goes.

As the scrolls burn, they look to one another.

All So goes we.

They begin walk in a circle at first and then cross and interact with each other.

There is a cacophony of their voices.

Josie Immigrants are overrunning our country, and most are here illegally.

All So it goes.

Dominique Immigrants bring crime and violence to our cities and towns.

All So it goes.

Sarita Immigrants take our jobs and use our services. And they don’t pay taxes.

All So it goes.

Kazima Immigrants are coming to the US to obtain welfare and other benefits.

All So it goes.

Kervens Immigrants are coming to the US with the express purpose of having babies here.

All So it goes.

Josie Immigrants are bringing diseases into the US.

All So it goes.

Dominique Terrorists are infiltrating the US by coming across the border from Mexico.

All So it goes.

Sarita All undocumented immigrants sneak across the Mexican border.

All So it goes.

Kazima We can stop undocumented immigrants coming to the US by building a wall along the border of Mexico.

All So it goes.

They walk in a circle at first and then cross each other.

They repeat the following lines, overlapping with each other.

This is repeated three times.

There is a cacophony of their voices.

In the midst of this, the bowl is picked up, passed around, and then removed.

Josie So it goes.

Sarita So it goes.

Kazima So it goes.

Dominique So it goes.

Kervens So it goes.

Josie So it goes.

All So goes we.

They stand in front of their chairs.

There is a collective breath.

Sarita It is night.

Josie It is night. There is only the moon.

Kazima It is night. There is only the moon. A strawberry full moon.

Sarita A night filled with promise. A moon for wishing. And night animals all around.

All Their sounds permeate the air.

The sound of night animals (owls, crickets, frogs, and cicadas).

Josie There is the moon, night animals, and a pool of water.

Sarita Two lovers speak across a great distance.

As **Dominique** *crosses to center with a backpack,* **Kervens** *collects his backpack and crosses to the tables.*

Dominique *removes a letter from the backpack.*

Kazima She is tired and worn from her travels.

Sarita Where has she been?

Josie Far away from here.

Sarita How can you tell?

Josie Her smell.

Kazima She smells of fear.

Josie Her eyes.

Kazima They are distant. Alert. Unsettled.

Josie The clench of her fist held in anger.

Sarita Yes, if this were home—

Josie If this were home, she'd smell of peace, her eyes would be soft with love, and her hands would be open.

Josie/Kazima/Sarita Unless—

Kazima Unless home was as dangerous as the journey it took to get here.

Dominique *removes a plastic bag from her backpack.*

Simultaneously, **Kervens** *removes a pen and piece of paper from his backpack.*

Dominique *removes an envelope from the plastic bag.*

She removes the letter from the plastic and kisses the letter.

Josie There will never be another moment like this.
She knows this and savors it.
She feels time slipping away.
She feels herself slipping away.
There is nothing she can do to stop any of it.
So, she inhales all that surrounds her.
She inhales it all in order to mark the time and place.
She inhales the full knowledge of herself and all that will never be.

She opens the letter.

Kervens *writes a letter to* **Dominique**.

As he speaks, he writes.

Kervens/Dominique My dearest Dominique . . .

As he continues to speak and write, **Dominique** *sets the letter down.*

She undresses and steps into the water.

The sound of water rippling gently is heard.

Kervens The journey you have ahead of you is a challenging one, more challenging that anything you have ever faced. But know that you have what it takes to overcome any adversity that stands in your way. Time and time again, you have shown this to me. Your courage and strength, your kindness and beauty, your brilliant mind and passionate heart have been an inspiration to me and so many others. Please know that with each step you take, I am with you. It has been an honor to stand by your stand, to love and be loved by you, to learn and grow with you. So, when you read this letter, my love, please know how much I do love you, how much I believe in you, and how much I long to be with you again. Yours, Kervens.

Josie, **Sarita**, *and* **Kazima** *surround* **Dominique** *and help her to undress.*

The women sit cross-legged and stretch out their arms to each other.

They become the pool of water.

Dominique *steps into the water.*

She bristles at the coolness of the water.

She settles into the water.

She cleans her face and body.

As **Kervens** *finishes the letter,* **Dominique** *steps out of the water and dresses.*

He folds the letter and places it inside of an envelope.

He places the envelope inside of a plastic bag.

Dominique *takes a deep breath and looks to the moon.*

Josie, **Kazima**, *and* **Sarita** *return to their chairs.*

Josie, **Kazima**, **Sarita**, *and* **Kervens** *stomp their feet three times in unison.*

There is a collective breath.

Scene One

Kervens July 2018. Three months ago.

Josie July 2018. Three months ago. Haiti.

Kazima July 2018. Three months ago. Port-au-Prince, Haiti.

Sarita After the earthquake.

Kervens After the earthquake, after Hurricane Matthew.

Josie After the earthquake, after Hurricane Matthew, in the midst of the revolution.

Sarita On the streets of Port-au-Prince.

All A protest.

Kazima Hundreds of people fill the streets.

Kervens Hundreds more follow after them.

Sarita Hundreds more will come tomorrow and tomorrow and tomorrow.

Dominique *stands.*

Josie, **Sarita**, **Kazima**, *and* **Kervens** *act as a crowd of protestors.*

Dominique *Viv Lib ou Mouri!*

Josie/Sarita/Kazima/Kervens Live Free or Die!

Dominique *Viv Lib ou Mouri!*

Josie/Sarita/Kazima/Kervens Live Free or Die!

Dominique *Viv Lib ou Mouri!*

Josie/Sarita/Kazima/Kervens Live Free or Die!

Dominique We are here to fight for equality and a better education.

Josie, **Sarita**, **Kazima**, *and* **Kervens** *cheer.*

Dominique For the right to clean water and quality healthcare.

Josie, **Sarita**, **Kazima**, *and* **Kervens** *cheer.*

Dominique For the right to feed ourselves and our children.

Josie, **Sarita**, **Kazima**, *and* **Kervens** *cheer.*

Dominique We are facing food and energy shortages unlike anything we have ever seen. We are facing price gauging and inflation. This is an unprecedented humanitarian crisis. And our government is too corrupt to care.

Dominique We're going to keep showing up here until the administration is held accountable for the wrongs they have committed in our names.

Josie, **Sarita**, **Kazima**, *and* **Kervens** *cheer.*

Dominique *Viv Lib ou Mouri!*

Josie/Sarita/Kazima/Kervens Live Free or Die!

Dominique *Viv Lib ou Mouri!*

Josie/Sarita/Kazima/Kervens Live Free or Die!

Dominique *Viv Lib ou Mouri!*

Josie/Sarita/Kazima/Kervens Live Free or Die!

Sounds of chaos are heard: glass bottles breaking, an angry crowd, police sirens, etc.

Josie *and* **Kazima** *enter as Haitian police.*

They grab **Dominique** *and wrestle her to the ground.*

Dominique *calls out in defiance.*

Dominique *Viv Lib ou Mouri!*

Josie *raises her arm to strike her.*

Sarita *and* **Kervens** *stomp their feet three times in unison.*

Josie, **Kazima**, *and* **Dominique** *freeze.*

Sarita *and* **Kervens** *take a collective breath.*

Scene Two

Sarita One month later.

Kazima One month later. The home of Dominique and Kervens.

Sarita One month later. The home of Dominique and Kervens. They are in their dining room.

Josie Dominique has decided to leave.

Kazima She's decided to seek asylum in the United States.

Sarita She will travel with her five-year-old daughter.

Josie A daughter, who she has raised from infancy.

Kazima A daughter, who has known no other mother, but Dominique; no other father, but Kervens.

Sarita A daughter named Grace, after her birth mother, Dominique's sister, who died in childbirth.

Josie Once in the United States, Dominique will send for Kervens.

Kazima But first, there is news.

Sarita *and* **Kazima** *move a table to the center.*

Dominique *and* **Kervens** *bring their chairs to the table.*

On the table is a pile of clothes for a child and an adult.

Josie *hands* **Dominique** *two empty backpacks and returns to her seat.*

Kervens *sits at the table and reads an email on his phone.*

Dominique *folds the clothes.*

Kervens "This letter is to inform you that your employment at the university will end effective immediately."

Dominique They can't do that.

Kervens Obviously, they can. I'm reading it right here.

Dominique Kervens, they can't just fire you.

Kervens They can do whatever they want.

Dominique No, there has to be a reason. There has to be just cause. What reason do they give?

Kervens (*reading*) As discussed—

Dominique "As discussed"?

She looks at his phone.

Kervens We had a meeting last month.

Dominique You didn't say anything about a meeting.

Kervens With everything you had going on—

Dominique Oh, I was busy. That's no excuse.

Kervens Dominique, you were receiving death threats.

Dominique Not for the first time.

Kervens You were detained—

Dominique Yes. It's the same after every speech.

Kervens This time was far worse.

Dominique Kervens, after every protest, I'm arrested, detained, and questioned—

Kervens Only this time, you were beaten.

Dominique *returns to folding clothes.*

Dominique Still.

Kervens You were hospitalized with a concussion, two broken ribs, and a fractured pelvis.

Dominique I was still capable of having a conversation.

Kervens I did what I thought was best.

Dominique You were trying to protect me. How noble. You shouldn't keep something like this from me!

Kervens I'm telling you about it now.

Dominique There's nothing we can do about it now.

Kervens If the roles were reversed, you would've done the same. I'm not going to be made to feel guilty.

Dominique I'm not trying to make you feel guilty.

Kervens Good. Because I also had Grace to worry about. She was not eating. She barely slept. And when she did, she had nightmares.

Dominique She hasn't been like that since the hurricane.

Kervens She is your shadow. She didn't understand why you had gone and why she couldn't see you. She thought she was being punished.

Dominique It would have scared her more to see me like that.

Kervens Maybe. Or she might have understood.

Dominique I will talk to her. I just don't want there to be secrets between us. We won't survive what we're about to face if we can't trust each other.

Kervens I didn't consider this a secret because I had intended to tell you about it. I didn't think they would make a decision this quickly.

Dominique I understand. What else does it say?

Kervens Nothing. The rest is just instructions about cleaning my office and where to return my keys.

Dominique *does not believe him.*

She reaches her hand out for his phone.

Reluctantly, he gives it to her.

Dominique "We think this is the best decision owing to your wife's recent conduct." What does my conduct have to do with you?

Kervens I am guilty by association.

Dominique Guilty of what?

Kervens Spreading anarchy, inciting a riot.

Dominique I did no such thing.

Kervens As good as.

Dominique Still. (*She hands him back his phone.*) You shouldn't be punished for it.

Kervens The university is funded by the government. The president heads that government. I was instructed to rein you in.

Dominique (*surprised and appalled*) Rein me in? Seriously?

Kervens They knew how futile it was to suggest it.

Dominique This is why it would have helped if we had talked.

Kervens Why? Are you saying you wouldn't have led the protest?

Dominique No, but I could have disguised myself.

Kervens The police have been tracking you for months. It wouldn't have done you any good.

Dominique I could have tried.

Kervens Listen, the work you're doing is too important to stop.

Dominique What if you tell them that I'm leaving?

Kervens The decision is final. There are no conditions. They want me to return my office keys.

Dominique You built that Economics department.

Kervens It will go on without me.

Dominique That's not the point.

Kervens They would've lost funding. Besides a handful of endowments, they rely solely on the government.

Dominique Fuck their funding. We can organize a protest. You should write an OpEd.

Kervens I'm not going to do that.

Dominique Fine. I'll do it. Forward me the email. I'll have them print the whole thing.

Kervens No, Dom, you're not going to do anything either. You have to focus right now.

Dominique This is an injustice, Kervens. It's a part of what we're fighting against. They want to punish anyone who speaks out. Anyone who demands equality and freedom. Anyone who holds them accountable for their crimes and neglect. And anyone associated with those of us who are fighting are at risk.

Kervens I would've had to resign when I left for America.

Dominique That could take months. You still have to make a living.

Kervens I have my consulting work. And it'll just be me. There won't be too many expenses.

Dominique Still, we may have to give up the apartment.

Kervens Probably. I'll speak with my brother about it when the time comes. But I don't want you to worry. You have to focus on getting to the US.

Dominique But I am worried. I'm worried about you, about Grace, and about our country.

Kervens The fight for our country will continue. And I will be fine. And Grace will be fine as long as she's with you.

Dominique But she's still so young.

Kervens It's good that she's young. It will be an adventure. Try not to worry. Let's finish packing.

Dominique *and* **Kervens** *pack the backpacks.*

Dominique, **Josie**, **Kazima**, **Sarita**, *and* **Kervens** *stomp their feet three times in unison.*

Dominique What to pack when you leave home forever.

Everyone stands.

Dominique *faces the audience.*

Dominique/Kervens Official documents.

Josie/Sarita/Kazima Passport—

Sarita Tax identification card, certificate of identity—

Kazima Birth certificate, marriage license, Grace's adoption papers.

Dominique/Kervens Toiletries.

Josie Tampons, toothbrush, toothpaste—

Sarita Deodorant, razor, toilet paper—

Kazima Lotion, chapstick, more tampons.

Dominique/Kervens Clothes.

Josie Two shirts, two pairs of jeans—

Sarita Underwear, bra, socks—

Kazima Gloves, hat, jacket, an extra pair of shoes.

Dominique/Kervens Miscellaneous.

Jose Bible, batteries, cellphone—

Sarita Charger, flashlight, pocket knife—

Kazima Medicines, a makeshift first aid kit.

All Water.

Josie/Sarita/Kazima Food.

Kazima No room for food. Pray you can eat along the way.

Josie/Sarita/Kazima What else? What else? You've got to hurry.

Dominique You remember she's a child and she'll be scared. You pack her favorite teddy bear.

Kervens And her favorite book.

Dominique And because you'll miss your husband—

Kervens The gold heart necklace that he bought you on your first anniversary.

Dominique The wedding ring was sold last week to pay for the journey.

Josie, **Kazima**, *and* **Sarita** *return to their seats.*

Dominique That's it.

Kervens Are you sure?

Dominique *looks at her backpack.*

Dominique Nothing else will fit.

Kervens I wish you didn't have to go through South America.

Dominique I don't have much of a choice. After Obama increased deportations, Miami stopped being an option. He gave us a slight reprieve after Hurricane Matthew, but with this new administration, I can't take that risk. No, the further distance I put between myself and Haiti the better.

Kervens I know you're right. I just wish this didn't have to be so challenging for you.

Dominique It will be challenging . . . and there are no guarantees, but if I stay here—

Kervens I know. Let's go. You've got to get as far as you can before sunrise.

Kervens *starts to exit.*

Dominique *remains still.*

Kervens *turns back to face* **Dominique**.

Dominique I love you.

Kervens *crosses back to* **Dominique**.

He kisses her.

Kervens I love you too.

Beat.

Josie, **Kazima**, *and* **Sarita** *stomp their feet three times in unison.*

There is a collective breath.

Scene Three

Josie Morning.

Kazima Morning. A courtroom.

Dominique Morning. A courtroom. One year and one month ago.

Kervens The same day as the protest in Port-au-Prince.

Josie The same day as the protest more than fifteen hundred miles away.

Dominique The same day, more than fifteen hundred miles away in Bushwick, Brooklyn.

Josie Sarita enters the courtroom.

Kazima She has exciting news to share.

Kervens Exciting, but rather inconvenient.

Sarita *addresses the audience.*

Sarita Good morning, your honor. (*She listens.*) No, I haven't taken on this case. I'm here to ask for a continuance on behalf of my colleague, Mrs. Josie Lamont-Patterson. (*She listens.*) Well, it's just that she's having her baby, who has come a week early. (*She listens.*) If we could have two to three weeks—(*She listens.*) Sure, I understand. The thing is, if I took on the case, it would take me that long to get caught up. I'm scheduled to be in court each morning. And two more lawyers left our firm this week. They couldn't take it anymore. First it was the "travel ban" then the "zero tolerance" policy and the suspension of visas, it's . . . it's all been too much. I've actually been sleeping on my sofa at my office, which I know isn't healthy. I mean, I've showered. There's a gym on the first floor of the building. But my husband thinks I'm having an affair. He actually said that to me today when he brought me breakfast, clean underwear, and this suit. It might have been a joke. I don't know. It's not something he's ever joked about— (*She listens.*) Yes, of course. My apologies. *She listens.*) Thank you, your honor. We really appreciate it.

She returns to her seat.

Dominique, **Josie**, **Kazima**, *and* **Kervens** *stomp their feet three times in unison.*

There is a collective breath.

Scene Four

The sound of a thunderstorm is heard.

Kervens Three days later.

Dominique Three days later. In the midst of a storm.

Sarita Three days later. In the midst of a storm. Josie and Kazima return home.

All Alone.

Dominique Alone, as in singular . . .

Sarita Alone, as in singular. As in without the child . . .

Kervens Alone, as in singular. As in without the child . . . the much-loved and longed-for child who was conceived after six IVF cycles.

Dominique They are without this child because the child was born dead.

There is a collective breath.

Dominique They return home alone.

Sarita To an empty home.

Kervens An empty home where a child should be is the loneliest house in the world.

Josie *and* **Kazima** *enter the home.*

Sarita They are bereft.

Dominique They have nothing left to give.

Kervens Absolutely nothing.

Josie *and* **Kazima** *bring chairs to the table.*

Josie *sits at the table.*

Kervens *hands* **Kazima** *an infant car seat.*

Kazima *sets the car seat on the table.*

Josie Why did you bring the car seat in?

Kazima I just . . . what should we do with it?

Josie Kazima, we agreed to leave it in the car.

Kazima I know—

Josie You asked me, what should we do with it. I said, let's leave it in the car and decide tomorrow.

Kazima Josie, I know.

Josie You agreed. You said it was a good idea.

Kazima I went back. I couldn't leave it. It was the first thing we bought for her.

Josie Aliese. (*Pause.*) You can say her name.

Pause.

Kazima I didn't want it to get stolen.

Josie Who is going to steal a car seat?

Kazima Anyone. Everyone. Car seats are expensive. I know this one was.

Josie Fine.

Kazima I just didn't want the first thing we bought for her—

Josie Aliese.

Kazima *takes a deep breath.*

Kazima Aliese. I didn't want it to get stolen.

Josie Got it.

Kazima So, where should we keep it?

Josie The coat closet. We can take it with her clothes to Goodwill.

Kazima Wait. When are you planning to do that?

Josie After the funeral service.

Kazima The funeral is this Friday.

Josie Okay, on Saturday or Sunday. Is Goodwill open on Sunday?

Kazima I'm not ready to do that. I'm not ready to erase her.

Josie I carried Aliese for thirty-nine weeks; I don't think it's possible to erase her.

Kazima You know what I mean.

Josie I do. But someone could use her clothes and toys and books and all of that equipment. God, that entire room is filled with her.

Kazima *sits next to* **Josie** *and holds her hand.*

Kazima *kisses* **Josie***'s hands and holds them to her heart.*

Kazima We could still use them.

Josie For what?

Kazima We can try again.

Josie *stands up and steps away from* **Kazima**.

Josie Everything we bought was for Aliese. Besides, there's no guarantee we'd have another girl.

Kazima We went gender neutral on most of the clothes.

Josie I don't think I could go through it again. The injections. The miscarriages. At least not right away.

Kazima I could try to carry the baby this time.

Josie *does not respond.*

Kazima I know what my gynecologist said, but it's worth a try.

Josie Can we give it some time?

Kazima Of course. (*Pause.*) But I still want a child.

Pause.

Kazima Do you need anything?

Josie No. Not right now.

Kazima I'm going to make you a cup of tea.

Josie I don't want any tea.

Kazima It will help.

Josie I'm not British.

Kazima All kinds of people drink tea, Josie. Do you want jasmine or chamomile?

Josie *doesn't respond.*

Kazima Chamomile. That always helps me calm my nerves.

Josie I don't want to feel calm.

Kazima Feel whatever you need to feel. I just think a cup of tea will help us both.

Josie How? How will it help?

Kazima It'll give us something to do. It'll be the first step to practicing self-care. It'll be warm.

Josie Your baby is dead. Have a cup of tea. There's got to be another option.

Kazima I asked you what you wanted.

Josie I want our baby. I want her home with us. I want to put her in the room that we painted and watch her sleep in the crib that we built. I want her to keep us up at night. I want us to be at our wits' end not knowing what she wants or what to do. I am so filled up with her and I don't know what to do with all of her now that she's gone.

Kazima *crosses to embrace* **Josie**.

Josie *steps away.*

The sound of a buzzer is heard.

Kazima Oh God, who could that be?

Josie Sarita. I let her know that I had been discharged.

Kazima Would it hurt for us to be on our own for five minutes?

Josie We have the rest of our lives to be on our own.

Sarita *crosses to the center.*

She has a large tote that is filled with prepared meals.

Sarita Hello, you two. I can't imagine what you are going through. Especially after everything you had to do to conceive. Please know that David and I are here anytime day or night; all you just have to call or text and we'll be here. I'm so completely heartbroken for you both. There just aren't any words.

Sarita *embraces* **Josie**.

Sarita How are you feeling?

Josie That's an impossible question to answer.

Sarita Of course. Do you need any help planning the funeral?

Josie Yes, if you could— **Kazima** No, that's fine—

Sarita Well, you just let me know after you've had time to think about it. I arranged my mother-in-law's funeral—that selfish woman didn't deserve half of what I did for her, but David was at such a loss and he did love her. Dearest, you should sit down. (**Sarita** *guides* **Josie** *to sit.*) Are you in any physical pain? Are you on painkillers?

Josie Yes, extra strength.

Sarita Any stitches?

Josie Just a few.

Sarita What are you doing about your breast milk?

Josie I took the med to stop it.

Kazima We did consider donating it—

Josie You considered it.

Kazima I know. I'm just saying—

Josie That was never something I wanted to do.

Kazima Yes, you made that very clear.

Josie Well, it's my breast milk. It's not up to you to decide what to do with it.

Kazima We're usually on the same page about things like that.

Josie We've never been in a situation like that.

Kazima Well, no—

Josie So, I just suggest in the future that you ask me what I'd like to do with my body fluids.

Kazima *is hurt by this.*

Sarita Listen, it's alright. There's no wrong choice here. You're both tired.

Kazima We are tired. I didn't realize we were having guests.

Josie Please! **Sarita** I'm hardly guests.

Sarita And I've brought you food. I've been cooking nonstop since yesterday.

Kazima You really didn't have to do this.

Sarita I'm my mother's daughter. I had no choice. (*She sets the containers on the table.*) Egg muffins; four different kinds. I know how much you love them, Kazima. For lunch or dinner, your choice of chicken curry, turkey pot pie, spinach lasagna, enchiladas, and three different types of soup. For dessert, brownies, cupcakes, and cookies. They're color coded. Breakfast is red; lunch is purple; and dinner is blue. Everything is gluten-free, nut-free, soy-free, and sugar-free. Plus lots of flax seed.

Kazima Can we freeze some of it?

Sarita Yes, everything can be frozen. I've written the date and heating instructions. This should last you three weeks. The last thing the two of you need to be worrying about is cooking.

Josie That must have taken you hours. Weren't you meant to be in court yesterday?

Sarita The day before. I got you the continuance.

Josie Thank you for doing that. Of course, we won't need it now.

Sarita You'll want to take some time off.

Josie No, I won't. I want to get back to work

Sartia Josie, you need time to grieve.

Josie The grief will come whether I work or not. I'd rather be working. And, Zima, you can go to that conference in Montreal to present your research.

Sarita What conference?

Kazima The World Congress on Human Genetics and Genetic Diseases. The world can wait for my findings.

Josie That's not what you said last week. You made it sound like groundbreaking, lifesaving conclusions.

Kazima She's deflecting. She was the same way after her mother died.

Sarita That's right. She attended the funeral in the morning and gave closing arguments at the Supreme Court that afternoon.

Josie She is standing right here.

Kazima Sorry, love.

She holds **Josie***'s hand.*

Kazima I'm going to put this food away.

She puts the containers back in the tote and returns to her seat.

Josie We won that case.

Sarita I know we did. You were magnificent.

Josie I'll call the judge in the morning.

Sarita I'll call her. Take the rest of the week off at least.

Josie I know how to take care of myself.

Sarita Then show me. Allow your body to heal. Our clients need you at your strongest.

Josie *thinks about this.*

She stands and winces in pain.

I'll see you on Monday.

Sarita And not a day sooner.

Dominique *and* **Kervens** *stomp their feet three times in unison.*

There is a collective breath.

Scene Five

Dominique *sits at the table.*

She carries a large piece of fabric with her.

Kervens *sets a sewing machine on the table.*

Dominique *threads the machine and begins to sew the fabric.*

She is making a designer shirt.

Josie Brazil.

Kazima Brazil. Two months later.

Sarita Brazil. Two months later. Dominique has taken a job working at a garment factory.

Josie She will earn $4 per day.

Kazima She will work a total of fifty-five days.

Sarita She will only be paid for forty.

Kazima/Sarita But she knows not to complain.

Josie She knows not to complain. She saw a woman beaten for complaining her first week there.

Josie She didn't know any Portuguese before arriving, but now—

Kazima Now, she can hold her own in most conversations.

Sarita Well, enough to get by.

Josie Enough not to get oversold at the market.

Kazima Enough to know when she's been cheated out of her salary.

Sarita Enough to ask her neighbor in the refugee camp to watch Grace while she's at work.

Josie Fed up, she will leave tomorrow.

Kazima Fed up, and having earned enough for the bus fare for two to Peru, she will leave tomorrow.

Sarita By leaving tomorrow, she will miss the fire that kills thirty of the women.

Kazima Women she worked with and lived side by side for fifty-five days.

Josie She won't learn of the fire for several months.

Kazima But she will carry the guilt of her survival for the rest of her life.

Sarita She will carry the guilt and mourn the loss of these extraordinary women.

Josie The extraordinary women who will not be named in any of the footage about the fire.

Kazima The extraordinary women whose families could not afford to bury what was left of their remains but pulled together enough money to buy stones to mark their graves and honor them.

Sarita The extraordinary women whose lives were rich, full, complex, and completely ordinary in every way.

Josie The extraordinary women who argued and laughed and drank and danced and made the very best of the little life had given them.

Dominique *stands and removes the sewing machine.*

Josie, **Kazima**, **Sarita**, *and* **Kervens** *stomp their feet three times in unison.*

There is a collective breath.

Scene Six

Dominique Two weeks later.

Kervens Two weeks later, Kazima decides to return to work.

Sarita Two weeks later, Kazima decides to return to work. But no one expected her back—

All Maternity leave.

Josie But now that there is no baby . . .

Sarita Now that there is no baby, being at home alone . . .

Josie Now that there is no baby, being at home alone, in such an empty home,

All Has become intolerable.

Kervens But returning to work means having to explain what happened.

Sarita And she doesn't want to explain what happened twenty different times.

Josie So, she volunteers to attend an International Conference on Genetics and Genetic Disorders.

Dominique/Sarita/Josie/Kervens In Milan.

Kazima *crosses the center.*

She addresses the audience.

Kazima We lost our daughter. (*She takes a deep breath.*) Lost isn't quite the right word. We didn't lose her. We knew exactly where she was the whole time. She was in Josie's womb. She was in the cab with us. We were in the cab on the way to the hospital. Our daughter died before she was born. It's called an intrapartum death. Such deaths are extremely rare and almost always inexplicable. What we know is that our child could not breathe. What we also know is that we did nothing wrong. Our OBGYN made sure we knew this above all else. Here's the thing though: I'm a geneticist, a community organizer, and a black woman living in America. So, I have some understanding of what could have led to the death of our child. If you are black and have lived in this country, you'll have some idea as well. Even though it won't be diagnosed, I blame racism and intergenerational trauma, which has been killing our people, our children for decades. We all know that racism impacts us in the most intimate and holistic of ways. It seeps into our dreams, our lungs, our blood, our cells. It becomes stress, cancer, asthma, high blood pressure, heart disease, diabetes, obesity, bipolar disorder, maternal mortality, preterm births, and intrapartum deaths. Racism, the trauma of racism, also alters our DNA. And intergenerational trauma means that we are not only dealing with the trauma of our own lives, but we are carrying the trauma of our parents, our grandparents, our great-grandparents, and our great-great grandparents. Some of us may not know their names, but the lives they lived impact every aspect of our being. So, is it any wonder that my child, when faced with the possibility of entering this world, found it impossible to breathe . . . and succumbed?

She looks expectedly for an answer.

Dominique, **Josie**, **Sarita**, *and* **Kervens** *start to stomp their feet.*

Kazima *turns to them and gestures with her hand to stop them.*

It is a single gesture; they do not stomp.

She faces the audience.

There is a collective breath.

Scene Seven

Sarita The next day.

Josie The next day. Haiti.

Kazima The next day. Haiti and Ecuador.

Kervens *and* **Dominique** *enter and cross to the center.*

Sarita Two lovers speak across a great distance.

Josie Kervens is just home from work.

Kazima Dominique is on a bus that had left Peru and is making its way through Ecuador en route to Colombia.

Josie Grace is fighting sleep beside her.

Kazima It has been some time since they spoke.

Josie But not for a lack of effort.

Sarita Not for lack of want.

Kazima Some would doubt their ability to hold on to each other.

Josie Some would question their faith.

Sarita Some would just be so damn tired of it all.

Kazima But not these two.

Josie No, not them.

Sarita Theirs is a love for the ages.

Josie Written in stone.

Kazima Tested too many times by hardships—

Sarita Too great to name—

Kazima And disappointments—

Josie Too many to count—

Kazima To begin to doubt now would be laughable.

Sarita If ever two people were meant to love each other forever—

Kazima/Sartia/Josie It would be the two of them.

Kervens *sets his takeaway food on the table.*

Dominique *sits and places her backpack on the floor.*

He sits . . . exhausted from his day.

Dominique *makes a call.*

Dominique Grace, go to sleep. (*She listens.*) Not right now. You can read when you wake up. Get some rest

Kervens *answers his phone.*

Kervens Hello, my love.

Dominique Hi. It is so good to hear your voice.

Kervens I was just thinking about you.

Dominique Were you?

Kervens Yes, I ordered dinner from the Arc-en-Ciel.

Dominique You were feeling nostalgic.

Kervens I was missing you.

Grace *says something to* **Dominique**.

Kervens I can hear Grace. What is she saying?

Dominique She wants to speak with you.

She holds the phone to **Grace***'s ear.*

Kervens Hello, sweetheart. (*He listens.*) Yes, the bus ride is long. Much longer than going to school. (*He listens.*) Well, you've traveled a great distance. You've gone the full width of South America. Where did you start? (*He listens.*) That's right, Brazil, then Peru, and now Ecuador. (*He listens.*) Why? Well, because of the rainforest. (*He listens and laughs.*) Too many trees, not enough roads. (*He listens.*) Alright, you should get some sleep, Sweetheart, you sound tired. (*He listens.*) Good night. I love you too.

Dominique *returns the phone to her ear.*

Dominique I'm back.

Kervens She sounds good.

Dominique She is holding up very well. Better than I thought she would.

Kervens I never doubted for a moment.

Dominique Tell me, Kervens, did you order the tablet cocoye?

Kervens No, my love, not tonight.

Dominique That's not like you.

Kervens They don't taste as sweet when you're not here with me to enjoy them.

Dominique I feel this way too. If you were with me now, I'd be able to see the beauty in all that surrounds me. I see it, of course, the landscape and the people, the food and the languages, the endless skies. But . . .

Kervens It's not the same

Dominique No, it isn't.

Kervens Where will you sleep tonight?

Dominique On the bus if I can. These roads are barely paved, so it might not be possible.

Kervens The road to Damascus was unpaved.

Dominique And there were no buses.

Kervens Paul had God on his side.

Dominique Who do we have?

Kernens You have me.

Dominique *smiles.*

Dominique You sound tired.

Kervens I am.

Dominique How is the new job?

Kervens Good. Rigorous. I like my colleagues. I respect them, but I have concerns.

Dominique What kind of concerns?

Kervens We don't have to talk about it now.

Dominique I want to know. Besides, I don't know when we'll speak again.

Kervens Fitting a lifetime in one phone call.

Dominique Yes. Now, what is troubling you.

Kervens The goal is to rebuild Haiti from an infrastructure standpoint. This will provide jobs, boost the economy, and strengthen the community by keeping families in place and together. But we do not have the funds to do any of it. The president is still refusing to release them.

Dominique Still? Nothing came of the protests?

Kervens He comes up with new guidelines and regulations, and he just moves the line each time they are met.

Dominique Forget the president, appeal to the people. You have to have them on your side.

Kervens The people are starving. They don't care about this fight.

Dominique They will care. You must show them how this will help them.

Kervens They are being fed lies by everyone.

Dominique You have to earn their trust. When you do, the people will fight with you. You must come up with a plan.

Kervens I wish you were here.

Dominique I know. I know people who will work with you. They will help you with this. I will contact them.

Kervens Thank you, but you must take care of yourself first.

Dominique I will. But if you succeed, then there will be a Haiti to come home to.

Kervens Is Grace asleep?

Dominique *looks down on her lap.*

Dominique Yes, I think so.

Kervens I envy her.

Dominique She is ready for this adventure to end.

Kervens It will soon.

Dominique Not soon enough. Do you think I did the right thing?

Kervens What other choice did you have?

Dominique For me, yes. But I'm worried about how to protect her.

Kervens That was always your worry. Only now, you're not a target. No one is hunting you.

Josie, **Kazima**, *and* **Sarita** *stomp their feet three times in unison.*

There is a collective breath.

Scene Eight

Dominique The same day.

Kazima The same day. New York.

Kervens The same day. New York. Some three thousand miles away.

Kazima Josie has been back at work.

Josie *enters with a laptop and an armful of files. She opens her laptop and sets the files down.*

Dominique To say it has been difficult is an understatement.

Kervens It's been a complete disaster.

Dominique Not complete.

Kervens Well, no, she's accomplished a great deal.

Kazima To be fair, the current administration isn't making her job easy.

Dominique, **Kervens**, *and* **Kazima** *stand and cross to center.*

They face the audience.

Dominique, **Kervens**, *and* **Kazima** *receive news alerts on their phone.*

As the headlines are read, **Josie** *removes an article from a folder and sets it down in front of her.*

Dominique/Kervens/Kazima Breaking news! Breaking news! Breaking news!

Dominique Parents fearing deportation pick guardians for US children.

Kervens Administration seeks border wall, crackdown on unaccompanied minors for 'Dreamer' deal.

Kazima Dozens of refugee resettlement offices to close as Administration downsizes program.

Dominique/Kervens/Kazima Breaking news! Breaking news!

Dominique New order indefinitely bars almost all travel from seven countries.

Kervens Travel ban fight heads toward Supreme Court showdown.

Kazima Immigrants in US seeking safe haven worry government may send them back.

Dominique/Kervens/Kazima Breaking news!

Dominique Six migrant children have died in US custody at Border Patrol Holding Centers.

As **Josie** *says each name, she removes and sets down an article in front of her.*

Josie Darlyn Cordova-Valle, ten, El Salvador. Jakelin Caal, seven, Guatemala. Felipe Alonzo, eight, Guatemala. Juan de Leon Gutierrez, sixteen, Guatemala. Wilmer Vásquez, two and a half, Guatemala. Carlos Hernandez, sixteen, Guatemala.

There is a collective breath.

Dominique/Kervens/Kazima Breaking news! Breaking news!

Kervens Administration says travel ban should be "larger, tougher and more specific."

Kazima Haitian asylum seekers, fearing US deportation, pour into Canada.

Dominique "Zero tolerance" separation policy separates more than 3,000 children from their parents.

Dominique/Kervens/Kazima Breaking news! Breaking news! Breaking news!

Dominique Still, some lives were saved.

Kervens Some. Not all of them.

Dominique No, not all.

Kazima It's the lives that are lost that she'll remember.

She starts to go through the files.

Distressed, **Sarita** *crosses to the center.*

Josie Finally.

Sarita I know. That took longer than I thought.

Josie Did we win our motion?

Sarita No, we didn't. José Ramirez will be deported sometime in the next two weeks.

Josie Can we file a motion to reconsider?

Sarita We can try, but the traffic violation on top of the drug possession charge is going against him.

Josie It was his nephew's car. José didn't even know the drugs were there.

Sarita It doesn't matter. It's on his record.

Josie I met with his nephew today. He still won't testify.

Sarita I don't blame him. He's got his future to consider. He's playing football for Princeton this fall.

Josie Fuck. So, that's it. There's nothing I can do.

Sarita As far as I can see, yes. But if you want to spend the rest of your afternoon in court, be my guest.

Josie I have to. He's got two small children. He's the only one working in his family. They will suffer.

Sarita That's fine, but wait.

Josie What is it?

Sarita I was actually on the phone with Judge Harris.

Josie We don't have a case in front of her for another two weeks.

Sarita She was just . . . you should sit down.

Josie Sit down for what?

Sarita Diego Garcia was killed.

Josie He was just deported last week.

Sarita I know. He was shot two blocks from his home.

Breathless, **Josie** *sits.*

Jose Jesus Christ. It was the gangs, wasn't it?

Sarita Yes. His wife and son are safe. They were at a cousin's house when it happened.

Josie We are sending them to their deaths.

Sarita You did everything you could.

Josie Obviously not.

Sarita Diego was the perfect client. He had no criminal record.

Josie Still, you never wanted me to take his case.

Sarita I didn't think we could win it.

Josie We've taken impossible cases before.

Sarita Yes, but you . . .

Josie What?

Sarita This was your first case back.

Josie You didn't think I was up for it.

Sarita No, I didn't.

Josie Thanks.

Sarita I also knew you needed a win.

Josie He needed the win more than I did. We should see if ICE can be held liable for his death.

Sarita Okay, who else? The NYPD for holding the drug possession charge against José?

Josie Yes, if it guarantees our client receive a fair trial.

Sarita It won't. It'll just take time away from clients who might stand a chance. If we were a larger firm, maybe. I'd do it just to prove a point. But in case you haven't noticed, our numbers are dwindling.

Josie We're five partners strong. Just like when we started. We know how to work at this capacity.

Sarita Ten years ago, we could work at this capacity. Hell, five years ago we could. But not now. Not with the number of clients we have and we're still trying to take on pro bono clients. And the laws are changing every single day.

Josie Morale is low, I get that, but we can do this. (*She crosses to* **Sarita**.) We can hire more attorneys. Universities are graduating them faster than we can count.

Sarita Yeah, but the burnout is quick. Cases are becoming harder and harder to win and government policies are changing every single day and becoming more draconian.

Josie That's why we have to keep fighting.

Sarita Yes, but, Josie, you're not functioning at full capacity. You haven't been since you got back. Hiring more attorneys won't make up for that.

Josie What is that supposed to mean?

Sarita You're scattered and unfocused. And now we have two huge losses on our books.

Josie When have I ever backed down from a fight?

Sarita Never, but you fumbled both of these cases from the beginning. Your presentation was sloppy. Your cross-exams were weak. Your arguments were based on emotions, not fact. Even though the facts in both cases were overwhelming. And you've been late to file motions and appeals.

Josie You're saying my performance is off?

Sarita I'm saying you should not have come back to work when you did. And starting right now, you need to take some time off.

Josie But I have cases.

Sarita Your remaining clients have been reassigned.

Josie On whose authority?

Sarita By their request.

Josie *is stunned by this.*

Josie Fuck. Sarita?

Sarita *crosses to* **Josie**.

Sarita Look, I hate this. You're my best friend and you're the best lawyer at this firm, but our clients deserve better than what you're giving them right now. And you deserve time to heal. Truly heal.

Josie *thinks about this.*

She doesn't want to admit that **Sarita** *is right.*

She clenches her fists in deep frustration and fights back tears.

Josie Fuck this. And seriously fuck you.

She gathers her laptop and exits.

She takes a seat in her chair.

Sarita *remains and exhales.*

After a moment, **Dominique**, **Kazima**, *and* **Kervens** *stomp their feet three times in unison.*

There is a collective breath.

Scene Nine

Sounds of a community meeting in progress: people talking, chairs being moved, etc.

Sarita The next day.

Dominique The next day. Haiti.

Kazima The next day. Haiti. A local community center.

Kervens *crosses to center.*

He has notes in his hand for a speech he's about to give.

He starts to cross out a sentence and then another.

After a moment, he tears the cards in half.

Dominique He has gathered fifty or so people.

Sarita He has gathered fifty or so people to plan a way forward.

Josie He has gathered fifty or so people to plan a way forward for the future of Haiti.

All The stakes are high.

Sarita It will be his first time leading a meeting like this.

Josie It may be his first time, but he's been to the ones led by Dominique.

Kazima He's been to the ones led by Dominique, but he wishes now that he had paid more attention.

All The stakes are high.

Dominique If the people don't trust him, he'll never get another chance.

Sarita If the people don't trust him, he'll be run out of town.

Dominique If the people don't trust him, he'll have no way to support his wife.

All The stakes are high.

Kazima But he has something going for him—

Dominique He has something going for him that most of the people don't—

Sarita He has something going for him that most of the people don't. He believes everything he's about to say.

There is a collective breath.

Kervens Thank you for coming, for taking time out of your day, especially in the middle of your week. We have food coming. Plenty of food. My wife told me that it's important to feed people, that if you're planning to overturn the government, you ought to break bread together first. I agree with her. I wish she were here tonight. I'm certainly no substitute. But what we have in common is our love for Haiti and our deep admiration for all of you. As leaders of your churches and youth groups, as teachers and organizers, you are the heart of your communities. If she were here, she would point out all the ways you're working to rebuild your neighborhoods. And that's why I've invited you here. I want to learn about the work you're doing and see how my firm might be able to assist you. The president refuses to collaborate on a national budget, but that doesn't mean the work can't get done. If we pool our resources together and fundraise, there's a future here in this country, a future that's worth investing in and fighting for. But it has to start with you, with each of you and your families and your neighbors. Otherwise, we'd be one more organization coming in and taking over without giving a thought to what the people need. And that's not what we're interested in doing. It looks like the food is here. Let's all get a plate and settle in.

Dominique, **Josie**, **Kazima**, *and* **Sarita** *stomp their feet three times in unison.*

There is a collective breath.

Scene Ten

Sounds of a busy border patrol station.

We hear families talking, children talking and crying, guards giving orders, etc.

Josie Two months later.

Kervens Two months, and more than 2,000 miles later.

Kazima Two months, more than 2,000 miles later. Now, in Laredo, Texas.

All A border patrol station.

Josie, **Kervens**, *and* **Kazima** *look to* **Sarita**.

Sarita I don't know what to say. (*Pause.*) This is going to be hard.

Dominique *and* **Grace** *cross to the center.*

Josie, **Sarita**, **Kazima**, *and* **Kervens** *stand and step forward.*

They speak as if speaking to children.

Josie No, Dearest, don't cry.

Sarita *Sé que estás cansado.* (I know you're tired.)

Kazima But we've made it.

Kervens We're here in the United States of America.

Josie/Kazima/Kervens We're safe now. **Sarita** *Estamos a salvo ahora.*

Josie I know this has been hard on you.

Sarita *Espero que no recuerdes esto.* (I hope you won't remember this.)

Kazima But I know that's not how it works.

Kervens I have to fill out this paperwork.

Josie/Kazima/Kervens Rest your head and sleep, my dear. **Sarita** *Descansa y duerme, querida.*

Dominique *sings the lullaby "Dodo ti pitit manman."*

Dominique (*singing*)

Dodo, ti titit manman (Sweet sleep, mommy's little one)
Dodo, ti titit papa (Sweet sleep, daddy's little one)

Si li pa dodo, krab la va manje (If you do not sleep, the crab will eat you)
Si li pa dodo, krab la va manje (If you do not sleep, the crab will eat you)

Papa ou pa la, l ale la rivyè, (Your daddy's away, he's at the river)
Manman ou pa la, l ale chache bwa (Your mommy's away, getting fire wood)
Si ou pa dodo, krab la va manje ou (If you do not sleep, the crab will eat you)
Si ou pa dodo, krab la va manje ou (If you do not sleep, the crab will eat you)

Dodo titit, Krab nan kalalou. (Sleep, little one, Crab's in the gumbo.)
Dodo titit! Krab nan kalalou! (Sleep, little one, Crab's in the gumbo!)

The song comes to an end.

Josie Under the zero tolerance immigration policy—

Invisible to the audience, a guard enters and wakes up **Grace***.*

Dominique *stands suddenly.*

Invisible to the audience, the guard guides **Grace** *to stand and starts to walk her out.*

Dominique No, she has to stay with me. What are doing? Where are you taking my daughter?

Kazima More than 5,000 children have been separated from their parents.

Invisible to the audience, the guard warns **Dominique** *to step back.*

Dominique *is startled by the gesture.*

Dominique Listen, please! I was told to wait here. I was told to fill out my asylum statement and wait here.

Kervens The majority of the children were ages twelve and under—

Josie Including more than 200 considered "tender age" because they were under five years old.

Invisible to the audience, the guard slams a baton down on the table.

The sound of a baton hitting a table hard is heard.

Dominique *takes a protective, but submissive stance in response.*

Dominique Listen, please! I was told to wait here. I was told to fill out my asylum statement and wait here.

Kazima Under the administration's policy, children can be removed from parents who are facing criminal prosecution for any charges.

Invisible to the audience, the guard guides **Grace** *to walk out.*

Dominique No, stop! Take your hands off of her. Where are you taking her? Grace! Please, please let her go.

Kervens What's more, the agency knew—

Josie/Sarita/Kazima The agency knew—

Kervens The agency knew that it lacked the technology to track and reunite children with their parents.

Dominique *collapses to the floor.*

She reaches out to **Grace**.

She pounds the floor with her fist.

Dominique Please! Grace!

A bright light shines on **Dominique** *still on the floor.*

Josie, **Kazima**, *and* **Sarita** *help* **Dominique** *to stand.*

They form a circle around her.

She releases a deep primal scream, but there is no sound.

She screams again and again; there is still no sound.

After a moment, **Dominique** *stands in line with the others.*

There is a collective breath.

Scene Eleven

Dominique The same day.

Sarita The same day. Bushwick, Brooklyn.

Kervens The same day. Bushwick, Brooklyn. Josie and Kazima's empty home.

Dominique What follows is an act of love and charity—

Sarita An act of love and charity that is filled with grief.

Kervens An act of love and charity that is filled with grief . . . and a way forward.

Josie *enters with a laundry basket overflowing with baby clothes.*

She places the basket on the table.

Kazima *enters with several boxes.*

Together, they fold the clothes and place them in the boxes.

They do this in silence, barely looking at each other.

The pain of this task is palpable.

They finish folding and packing the clothes.

This will take the time it takes.

Once done, they close and tape the boxes shut.

They look at each other.

Kazima *reaches out to* **Josie**.

Josie *kisses* **Kazima**, *but does not take her hand.*

Instead, **Josie** *picks up a box and returns to her seat.*

Kazima *picks up the remaining two boxes and returns to her seat.*

Dominique, **Sarita**, *and* **Kervens** *stomp their feet three times in unison.*

There is a collective breath.

Scene Twelve

Sarita One week later.

Josie One week later. Jamaica, Queens.

Kazima One week later. Jamaica, Queens. A detention center.

Kervens No, a federal prison that is being used to house asylum seekers.

Sarita A federal prison that is plagued with human rights abuses.

Kazima A federal prison that has seen suicide attempts and hunger strikes.

Sarita/Josie/Kazima It is a privately owned federal prison.

Josie *escorts* **Dominique** *to the center and hands her a prison uniform.*

Dominique *puts on the uniform.*

She hands her clothes to **Josie**.

Josie *returns to her seat.*

Kervens *and* **Sarita** *bring on the prison bed*

Exhausted and distressed, **Dominique** *lies down on the bed.*

All Lights on at six.

Dominique *stands at attention.*

All Line up.

Dominique *steps in line.*

All Head count.

Dominique *looks to her right and her left, then forward.*

All Breakfast at seven.

Dominique *holds her hands up as if holding a tray.*

All No phone calls.

Dominique *looks dejected.*

All Lunch at one.

Dominique *holds her hands up as if holding a tray.*

All Rec time; one hour.

Dominique *jogs in place.*

All Shower, fifteen minutes.

Dominique *washes her hair.*

All Dinner at five.

Dominique *holds her hands up as if holding a tray.*

All Head count.

Dominique *looks to her right and her left, then forward.*

All Line up.

Dominique *steps in line.*

All Lights out at eleven.

Judy Garland's "Have Yourself a Merry Little Christmas" plays.

Dominique *falls into bed.*

Dominique *stands at attention.*

Dominique *steps in line.*

Dominique *looks to her right and her left, then forward.*

Dominique *holds her hands up as if holding a tray.*

Dominique *looks dejected.*

Dominique *holds her hands up as if holding a tray.*

Dominique *jogs in place.*

Dominique *washes her hair.*

Dominique *holds her hands up as if holding a tray.*

Dominique *looks to her right and her left, then forward.*

Dominique *steps in line.*

Dominique *falls into bed.*

This repeats once more.

Dominique *stands at attention.*

The music scratches to silence.

Josie, **Kazima**, **Sarita**, *and* **Kervens** *stomp their feet three times in unison.*

There is a collective breath.

Scene Thirteen

Kervens *brings on a small, lighted, and decorated Christmas tree. He sets it atop the table.*

Dominique The next day.

Sarita The next day. Bushwick, Brooklyn.

Kervens The next day. Bushwick, Brooklyn. Josie and Kazima's still empty house—

Dominique But empty now for another reason.

Sarita Yes, another all too familiar reason . . .

Kervens It's what happens when two people live together side by side, but are very far apart from one another.

Dominique Well, given what they've gone through.

Sarita Sure. It's a wonder they've made it this far.

Josie *enters and crosses to the table.*

She opens her laptop and just stares at it.

After a moment, **Kazima** *enters.*

Kazima What are you doing?

Josie Checking work email.

Kazima It's Friday night.

Josie I know.

Kazima We're supposed to unplug.

Josie I have a deposition to write. I can't do that without the research. The research is in my email. I have to check my email.

Kazima Once a week, we're supposed to unplug, spend an intimate time together, and write an appreciation list.

Josie Can we do it tomorrow?

Kazima You picked Friday nights.

Josie *closes her laptop and stands to face* **Kazima**.

Josie I'm asking if we can move it to Saturday this week.

Kazima No. I could have made plans for tonight, but I didn't. I kept this night free like we promised.

Josie Zima, this is a really important case.

Kazima Nothing should be more important than our marriage and getting back on track.

Josie Oh, we're on track. We've done wine and painting, couple's yoga, trust falls, flea market Saturdays, brunch on Sundays. We even hiked the fucking Brooklyn Bridge. There and back. We couldn't be more on track. All I'm asking for is one day. I have to be in court on Monday morning.

Kazima No.

Josie Why not?

Kazima Because . . . I want to have a baby with you and you won't even talk about it.

Josie All we do is talk about it. Every second of every minute of every hour of every day. At breakfast. I want a baby. Do you want pancakes? At lunch. I want a baby. Don't burn the toast. At dinner. I want a baby. Pour me another glass of wine please.

Kazima Josie, I want to have a child.

Josie I know that. I just need more time.

Kazima Okay, it's been four months. How much more time?

Josie I don't know.

Kazima A month? Six months? A year?

Josie That's not really a fair question.

Kazima It's a practical question given everything it involves for us to conceive.

Josie I don't know. I don't honestly know what to tell you.

Kazima I'm really trying to be patient with you.

Josie This is what patience looks like?

Kazima Yes, it is.

Josie You're constantly on at me about it. I can't even think straight right now, Zima. This was supposed to be her first Christmas. And I've lost my job.

Kazima You didn't lose your job. You're on a break.

Josie I got someone killed.

Kazima No, you didn't. Barrio 18 did.

Josie He was deported because I didn't do my job well enough. A man lost his life because of me. My failure. Another man is probably going to be killed right now. We lost our child because my body—

Kazima Oh, for God's sake, stop this! You are so selfish. None of that is true. And you know it. You can't even step outside of your own grief long enough to remember there is someone else here.

Josie What?

Kazima I lost her too.

Josie Aliese.

Kazima Aliese! Aliese! Aliese. It's like you don't remember that I was a part of this pregnancy too.

Josie That's not it at all.

Kazima It sure as hell feels like it.

Josie I'm sorry if that's the impression I've given you. I just . . . I can't move on as quickly as you have.

Kazima I haven't moved on. I'm in as much pain as you are.

Josie Then how can you think about having another child?

Kazima Because I don't want to stop my life. I don't want her death to be the end of what we do as a family. I want our family's legacy to be more than the blood and the sweat of the formerly enslaved people is buried in this soil.

Josie Zima, you're thirty-five years old. Your eggs are viable for at least seven more years.

Kazima When can we talk about it being a reality?

Josie When it stops hurting so damn much. When she stops filling every minute, every second of my day.

Kazima That's not good enough.

Josie Sorry. That's the best I've got right now.

Pause.

Kazima I'm going to go.

Josie Go where?

Pause.

Kazima Caroline's.

Josie You're going to your ex's apartment?

Kazima She's not home. She's in Kuala Lumpur doing research.

Josie How do you even know that?

Kazima We still talk. She knew you were pregnant. She asks about everything. You haven't really been available.

Josie Wait. You still have a key?

Kazima It's just an apartment.

Josie It's not just an apartment.

Kazima Josie, you need time. And I need to clear my head. It's probably best we do that on our own right now.

She exits and takes her chair.

Josie *remains.*

She sits at the table.

In a fit of rage, she knocks the Christmas tree off the table.

She covers her mouth with her hand to stifle a cry.

Dominique, **Sarita**, *and* **Kervens** *stomp their feet three times in unison.*

There is a collective breath.

Scene Fourteen

Sarita Two weeks later.

Josie Two weeks later. Haiti.

Kazima Two weeks later. Haiti. Kervens' family home.

Sarita Kervens has sold their apartment.

Josie He awaits word from his wife—

Kazima He awaits word from his wife about when he may come.

Josie He awaits word from his wife about when he may come. But reaching her has proved rather difficult.

Kazima/Sarita/Josie Reaching her has proved impossible.

Josie, **Sarita**, *and* **Kazima** *carry packed boxes onto the stage.*

The boxes are marked: bathroom, kitchen, bedroom, living room.

They line up at the foot of the stage.

Kervens *crosses to center.*

He carries a box marked: office.

He sets the box on the table and makes a phone call.

Kazima/Sarita/Josie Breaking news! Breaking news! Breaking news!

Each time he calls her, a spotlight rises on **Dominique**.

She stands away from the others.

She is at the detention center.

There is a prison bed.

She stands at attention.

She runs through the pantomimed routine of her day at the detention center.

Kervens Hello. (*He listens.*) Yes, I'm trying to speak with my wife. (*He listens.*) Dominique Jean-Baptiste. (*He listens.*) Yes, I know she is there. Her lawyer told me. You're not letting her make calls.	**Dominique** *steps in line.* *She looks to her right and her left, then forward.* *She holds her hands up as if holding a tray.* *She looks dejected.* *She holds her hands up as if holding a tray.* *She jogs in place.*

As **Dominique** *steps in line, the lights go out.*

Kervens *looks at the phone with frustration.*

The call is disconnected.

He redials the number.

Kazima/Sarita/Josie Breaking news! Breaking news!

Josie Lawyers and advocates say detainees remain cut off from family and friends.

As he speaks, **Dominique** *stands at attention.*

Kervens Hello. (*He listens.*) Yes, please. Don't hang up. I'm trying to speak with Dominique Jean-Baptiste. (*He listens.*) Yes, I just called. The phone was cut off. This is her husband.

Dominique *holds her hands up as if holding a tray.*

She looks dejected.

She holds her hands up as if holding a tray.

She jogs in place

She washes her hair.

She holds her hands up as if holding a tray.

As **Dominique** *looks to her right and left, the lights go out.*

Kervens *looks at the phone with frustration.*

The call is disconnected.

He redials the number.

Kazima/Sarita/Josie Breaking news!

Kazima Making calls prove impossible. Long wait times, confusing instructions, dropped calls, and the cost.

As he speaks, **Dominique** *stands at attention.*

Kervens Hello. I must speak with Dominique Jean-Baptiste. (*He listens.*) Jean-Baptiste, yes, that is her last name. First name Dominique. This is an emergency. (*He listens.*) I have to make sure she is okay.

Dominique *stands at attention.*
She steps in line.
She looks to her right and her left, then forward.
She holds her hands up as if holding a tray.
She looks dejected.
She holds her hands up as if holding a tray.
She jogs in place.

As **Dominique** *washes her hair, the lights go out.*

Kervens *looks at the phone with frustration.*

The call is disconnected.

He redials the number.

Josie/Dominique/Kazima/Sarita Breaking news!

Kazima We have had reports of parents having a hard time getting through to their children in detention centers.

As he speaks, **Dominique** *lies in bed.*

She does not move.

She only cries silently.

Kervens Hello. Please don't hang up. Please. I'm trying to reach my wife. (*He listens.*) Yes, she is there. Her name is Dominique Jean-Baptiste. She's been there for two months. Please. Yes, I'll hold.

The call is disconnected.

He redials the number.

Josie/Dominique/Kazima/Sarita Breaking news!

Kazima Family members are only allowed to talk to their loved ones for a few minutes.

Kervens Hello. Yes, I'm trying to speak with my wife. Dominique Jean-Baptiste. (*He listens.*) Yes, I'll hold. I'll wait forever. Please just let me speak with her.

As he speaks, there is a spotlight on **Dominique**.

Finally, they talk.

Dominique Kervens, is that you?

Kervens Yes, it's me. I've been trying to reach you.

Dominique They won't let me make any calls.

Kervens What's going on with your lawyer?

Dominique I'm meeting with a new one tomorrow. I have to appeal—

Lights go out on **Josie**.

The call is disconnected.

Dominique *returns to her seat.*

Kervens *slams his fist on the table.*

He sits and redials the number.

He returns to his seat.

Josie, **Kazima**, *and* **Sarita** *stomp their feet three times in unison.*

There is a collective breath.

Scene Fifteen.

Josie Six months later.

Kervens Six months later. Jamaica, Queens.

Kazima Six months later. Jamaica, Queens. A detention center

Josie A great deal has happened.

Dominique *and* **Sarita** *are seated at the table.*

Sarita *has a notepad and pen.*

Dominique *has a folder of documents and photos.*

Sarita Where were you living when you were in Brazil?

Dominique A refugee camp. I was there for nearly two months.

Sarita Why did you stay there so long?

Dominique I had been robbed.

Pause.

Sarita Is that all that happened?

Dominique Well, no, I was beaten up.

Sarita Were you raped?

Dominique No, my daughter scared him off. She wouldn't stop screaming.

Sarita Thank goodness

Dominique When can I see her?

Sarita I'm still trying to locate her.

Dominique What do you mean?

Sarita She wasn't brought to a detention center in New York.

Dominique Why not?

Sarita Overcrowding, but my team is looking. I promise you. Given your entry point—

Dominique I went to the port of entry in Laredo. This was in December of 2018. A week before Christmas.

Sarita Right, you did exactly what you're supposed to do.

Dominique Then why am I here? Why isn't Grace with me?

Sarita Politics. You're here because of a racial prejudice, a campaign promise, and an inept system.

Dominique Yes, I tried to keep up with the news.

Sarita It's a disaster. There's not much I can do about any of it, but everything is going through the courts.

Dominique What does that mean for my asylum?

Sarita Here's what it should mean: If we can prove that you and your family will be persecuted in your country for your political beliefs, then we will grant you political asylum. We need more than just your word for it.

Dominique I can get you my medical records and the police report.

Sarita Good. You're going to need that.

Dominique What about Grace?

Sartia Right, since you came through Laredo, there are only eight or nine places where Grace can be. It may take some time, but we will find her.

Dominique Have you found other children?

Sarita Yes. Now, let's continue. You were in Brazil for two months. This would have been—

Dominique September and October of 2018. I had to stay because I had to earn money.

Sarita I understand. Where did you go from there?

Dominique Peru then Ecuador then Colombia. I was robbed again in Bogota. I stayed there for one month working.

Sarita Right, November. And were you . . .?

Dominique No, it was just the robbery. At gunpoint. I earned what I could plus what Kervens sent me.

Sarita You went to Panama next?

Dominique That's right.

Sarita Were you and your daughter traveling on your own?

Dominique For the most part, but once we got to Costa Rica, we joined a group of migrants, mostly women.

Sarita Were they all from Haiti?

Dominique No, only about twenty or so. The rest were from Cuba, Benin, Nepal, Senegal, the Congo, and Sudan.

Saratia How did you manage to get through Guatemala?

Dominique It wasn't easy.

Sarita That's what I've been hearing, which is why I'm surprised you got through.

Dominique We had to bribe the police. We all pulled our money together and they let us continue heading north. A week later, I arrived at the Texas border. I made a request for asylum and was transferred to this facility.

Sarita Why did ICE deny your first parole request?

Dominique They said I was a flight risk. I have no family here. No community ties. But I want to appeal. I want to ask the judge to reconsider.

Sarita You have a right to.

Dominique I can't find anyone to take my case.

Sarita You had an attorney assigned to your case from the Keep Families Together Project.

Dominique Yeah, but this is as far as he's willing to take it. He's overloaded.

Sarita We're all overloaded right now. Unfortunately, I can't take your case either—

Dominique Why did you meet with me then?

Sarita Let me finish. I can't take it, but I know someone who can. She used to work with me.

Dominique Is she good?

Sarita She's the best there is. She's just lost her way a bit. Needs to find her confidence again.

Dominique I don't want to be someone's charity case.

Sarita It's either her or someone else who is just as slammed as me.

Dominique Some choice you're giving me.

Sarita I can guarantee you that thirty lawyers will meet with you, all of them overloaded—all of them with something to prove, but none of them will fight for you as hard as she will.

Dominique *thinks.*

Dominique Will she find Grace?

Sarita Yes, she will. It may take some time, but she won't stop looking until she finds her.

Dominique Alright.

Sarita *gathers her things and returns to her seat.*

Dominique *remains.*

Josie, **Kazima**, *and* **Kervens** *stomp their feet three times in unison.*

There is a collective breath.

Scene Sixteen

Kervens The next day, early.

Kazima The next day, very early.

Dominique The next day, very early. Bushwick, Brooklyn.

Kervens Josie and Kazima's empty house—

Dominique Empty now, but filled with memories.

Kazima Every inch of the apartment has a story—

Kervens Stories that scream themselves to be remembered.

Kazima Stories that scream and ache and do not subside when asked.

Dominique Stories so loud and wanting that you fill your life with noise to keep going.

Josie *crosses to center.*

She has a cup of coffee and her laptop.

She is on the phone.

Josie Good morning, Miguel! (*She listens.*) No, I've been up for hours. I'll be at the coffee shop at eight thirty. (*She listens.*) No, it's fine. I'm the Brand Ambassador. I should be there to greet everyone. (*She listens.*) Listen, the *Times*, *Vogue*, and *Vanity Fair* won't be there until next Thursday, but there are a handful of bloggers and influencers coming today. I want them to see how Ida B's Books and Tea will be a central hub for artists and activists in the city. Otherwise, they'll just focus the article on the vibe, specialty drinks, and renovations. (*She listens.*) Kazima . . . no, I don't think so. She didn't RSVP. (*She listens.*) Of course, Miguel, I'm honored to do this and I'm so proud of you, of everything you've accomplished since coming to this country. (*She listens.*) That's right. I'll open the law clinic in a few months. Let's give the place a little to settle first.

The sound of a buzzer is heard.

Josie There's someone at the door. (*She listens.*) Alright, I'll see you in a few hours.

Sarita *enters.*

She carries a folder and a smoothie.

Josie It's five o'clock in the morning.

Sarita *hands* **Josie** *the smoothie.*

Sarita I brought you breakfast.

Josie What's wrong?

She sets the smoothie down.

Sarita Nothing.

Josie Sarita.

Sarita Wait, did I wake you?

Josie No, I haven't slept. We're opening open the bookstore and coffee shop today.

Sarita I thought I invested in a boho chic restaurant.

Josie You did. It's a boho chic, cultural hub, consciousness-raising bookstore and coffee shop with a full-service restaurant, bar, and event spaces.

Sarita It can't possibly be all of those things at once.

Josie It is, and it's exactly what the community needs.

Sarita What precisely is happening today?

Josie The soft opening of the coffee shop and bookstore. We're doing it in stages.

Sarita You'll have to. It's the only way anyone will make sense of it.

Josie Are you planning to come in with me this morning? Is that why you're here?

Sarita No, I'm in court all day, but I'll drop by this evening. I've got a case that I want you to look at.

Josie I'm not taking any cases.

Sarita You'll want to take this one.

Josie No, that life is behind me.

Sarita You don't just stop being a lawyer.

Josie You do when your best friend fires you.

Sarita I didn't fire you. I told you to take a break.

Josie Well, I did and then my wife left me.

Pause.

Sarita I'm sorry about that. I thought the two of you were still talking.

Josie We are talking. Every other week or so. When she answers. Her ex returned from Malaysia and they're getting comfortable.

Sarita What does that mean?

Josie I don't know.

Sarita What do you think it means?

Josie Caroline wants children. But that's just a guess. I haven't asked because I'm not yet ready to face what that means for us.

Sarita Did you see this coming?

Josie No, but that's part of the problem. According to my therapist and Zima, I was so mired in my own grief that I couldn't see how I was pulling away from her.

Sarita They've got a point.

Josie Yeah.

Sarita But I was wrong. You never should have left. You didn't need a break, you needed my support.

Josie No, I needed the break. I was having a nervous breakdown.

Sarita You were heartbroken and exhausted.

Josie I know. You probably saved my life.

Sarita I'll accept that.

Josie (*laughing*) I figured you would.

Sarita But tell me, how is running a bookstore/coffeeshop/restaurant/bar/event space taking a break?

Josie I don't know. It just is. It's a different level of stress. This, I can do this in my sleep.

Sarita Josie, this feels like a side project to me.

Josie How can you say that?

Sarita You're not the CEO or the manager or the Executive Chef, you're the Brand Ambassador.

Josie It takes a lot of work to be the face of the company.

Sarita You're bored.

Josie I'm even thinking about opening a law clinic.

Sarita Come on, Josie, this isn't going to feed your soul or even begin to satisfy you.

Josie It won't destroy me either. I can't be responsible for someone's life. I can't hold the weight of that.

Sarita You're afraid to fail again. I get that. But you can help this woman.

Josie Why can't you take it?

Sarita I'm good, but I'm nowhere near as good as you are.

Josie What are you not telling me?

Sarita There's a young child involved.

This stops **Josie** *breathless.*

She takes the file and opens it.

She removes a photo.

Josie What is her name?

Sarita Grace. She's five years old. They were separated when she entered the US.

Josie Jesus. Have you located her?

Sarita Not yet, but we've narrowed it down to six facilities.

Josie *removes another photo.*

Sarita Her name is Dominique.

Josie She's seeking political asylum?

Sarita Yeah, she's an activist. She started a powerful movement that got the attention of their government. A police officer was killed at one of the rallies. She cannot go back.

Josie She could be me. That's what gets me about all of these cases. If you or I were born anywhere else in the world and we felt compelled to speak out against a corrupt government or that we wanted more out of our lives—something better, and we decided to leave and take our chances in the big promise that is America, this is what we would face.

Sarita An invisible line determines someone's fate—

Josie And their value. She's a human being, a mother. That should mean something. It's horrible enough to lose a child, but at a least I get to mourn her. I can't imagine having a child torn from my arms. Knowing that she's . . . that she's out there somewhere, but there's nothing I can do to find her.

Sarita I know. And it's inconceivable this is happening. But the shock of it will wear off. People stop will caring. They'll go back to their lives. And if that happens, we can't stop it. And if we can't stop it, there's no way we come back from this.

Josie *takes this in.*

She looks at **Sarita**.

She takes a deep breath.

Josie *sits and looks through the file.*

Josie Does Dominique have any family here?

Sarita No.

Josie This is going to be a fight.

Sarita I know. That's why she needs you.

She sits down with **Josie**.

They review the file together.

Dominique, **Kazima**, *and* **Kervens** *stomp their feet three times in unison.*

There is a collective breath.

Scene Seventeen

Sarita One week later.

Kervens One week later. Jamaica, Queens.

Kazima One week later. Jamaica, Queens. A detention center

Sarita So many questions!

Dominique *sits.*

She has a folder filled with documents and photos.

Josie Have you ever been in immigration removal proceedings?

Dominique Yes, I already went through all of this. My asylum was denied, but it was appealed.

Josie By ICE. I know. Listen, you're going to have to answer these questions. Again and again. So, we just have to get through them.

Dominique Fine. Yes, I've been through the proceedings.

Josie Are you married?

Dominique Yes, I am. My husband's name is Kervens Jean-Baptiste.

Josie Where is your spouse now?

Dominique He is still in Haiti.

Josie Is he applying with you?

Dominique Yes.

Josie Where did you live before coming to the United States?

Dominique Port-au-Prince, Haiti. I've lived there all my life.

Josie Where did you work for the last five years?

Dominique Well, I worked at the university until I was fired. I'm an ethics professor. But I also worked at a garment factory in Brazil and I taught English as a foreign language in Colombia.

Josie That's fine. Are there records of you working at either of these places?

Dominique No, they were cash in hand.

Josie Okay. How did you arrive in the United States? Did you travel by boat or swim? Did you walk or drive?

Dominique We did everything, but swim. But Grace, my daughter, she has trouble with her lungs.

Josie Okay. Now, tell me, why are you fleeing your country?

Dominique I am seeking political asylum for fear of persecution.

Josie Why can't you return to Haiti?

Dominique I will be killed and so will my family.

Josie Why do you believe this? Were you harmed?

Dominique Yes. I was beaten. The government wanted the names of the people working with me.

Josie Imprisoned?

Dominique Yes.

Josie Detained?

Dominique Yes.

Josie Alright. Now, what was the extent of your injuries?

Dominique I had a concussion, two broken ribs, and a fractured pelvis.

Josie *removes a police report from her folder.*

Josie It's good that you reported what happened to you.

Dominique Not that it made much of a difference.

Josie It may not have helped you then, but it can go a long way here.

Dominique Did you also get my medical records?

Josie *removes a medical report from a folder.*

Josie Yes. Your husband sent them to my office. How did he get them so quickly?

Dominique His sister works at the hospital.

Josie He sent these photos as well.

Josie *removes photos from the folder and shows them to* **Dominique**.

Dominique These were taken right after they dumped me in my front yard.

Josie You're lucky to have these.

Dominique You think they will make a difference?

Josie Yes, these photos along with the medical and police reports show definitive proof. It's in my notes, but I'd like you to tell me what led to all of this.

Dominique I spoke out against the president, against the corruption. I led a rally that got out of hand. It wouldn't have if the guards hadn't thrown tear gas at us, but it did.

Josie Were you present when the police officer was killed?

Dominique No, I wasn't there. I had already been arrested.

Josie How do you know that you were harmed for that reason?

Dominique The guards who beat me told me so.

Josie What exactly did they say to you?

Dominique They said they had been sent by the president to shut me up. It was meant to be a warning.

Josie Have any of your friends or family members experienced harm? Mistreatment? Threats?

Dominique My husband was fired from his job at the university because of me.

Josie Would you be safe if you lived somewhere else in your country?

Dominique No, I wouldn't. The island isn't large enough.

Josie Are you still in danger now?

Dominique Yes. I'm only alive because I left.

Josie Thank you.

Dominique Is that it?

Josie For now, yes.

Dominique What happens next?

Josie We fight. I'll ask the appeal board to reconsider their decision in light of new information. They will make a determination and send an order to the judge. The judge could uphold her ruling to grant asylum, but the Department of Homeland Security can appeal again.

Domiinique But you're going to help me?

Josie I am. It's not going to easy.

Dominique None of it has been.

Josie *stands.*

Josie I do have good news.

Dominique About Grace?

Josie Yes. I was going to wait to tell you, but—

Dominique You found her?

Josie Yes.

Dominique Praise God. Is she alright?

Josie She's far from alright after everything she's been through—

Dominique But she's alive.

Josie Yes, she's alive. She is healthy. I'm having here transferred here. You won't be together, but you will be able to see each other.

Dominique That is a blessing. What happens if she is deported?

Josie We will be in touch with your husband. But it's possible she could be placed in a foster home.

Dominique No, you can't let that happen.

Josie I'll do all I can to keep you together.

Dominique No, you must. She's all that I have left of my sister.

Josie I will try. I just wanted you to be aware of that possibility. And I will always keep you informed.

Dominique Thank you.

Josie I'll see you tomorrow at the hearing.

They shake hands.

Josie *stands and crosses back to her seat.*

Dominique *remains.*

Kazima, **Sarita**, *and* **Kervens** *stomp their feet three times in unison.*

There is a collective breath.

Epilogue

Dominique *and* **Josie** *remain seated.*

Kazima, **Sarita**, *and* **Kervens** *cross to center.*

They look at each other.

Kazima Today, in detention centers—

Sarita Today, in detention centers across the country—

Kervens Today, in detention centers across the country conversations like this play out over and over.

Kervens/Sarita/Kazima Very little progress has been made.

Kazima Because if you're an immigrant—

Josie *and* **Dominique** *stand and face the audience.*

All You are guilty until proven innocent.

Josie Myth #1: Immigrants are overrunning our country, and most are here illegally.

Dominique Myth #2: Immigrants bring crime and violence to our cities and towns.

Sarita Myth #3: Immigrants take our jobs and use our services. And they don't pay taxes.

Kazaima Myth #4: Immigrants are coming to the US to obtain welfare and other benefits.

Kervens Myth #5: Immigrants are coming to the US with the express purpose of having babies here.

Josie Myth #6: Immigrants are bringing diseases into the US.

Dominique Myth #7: Terrorists are infiltrating the US by coming across the border of Mexico.

Sarita Myth #8: All undocumented immigrants sneak across the Mexican border.

Kazima Myth #9: We can stop undocumented immigrants coming to the US by building a wall along the border of Mexico.

Josie, **Dominique**, **Kervens**, **Sarita**, *and* **Kazima** *walk in a circle at first and then cross each other.*

They repeat their lines, overlapping with each other, three times.

There is a cacophony of their voices.

Josie So it goes.

Sarita So it goes.

Kazima So it goes.

Dominique So it goes.

Kervens So it goes.

All So goes we

Sarita, **Kazima**, *and* **Josie** *surround* **Dominique**.

They help her to undress.

The women sit cross-legged and stretch out their arms to each other.

They become the pool of water.

Dominique *steps into the water.*

She bristles at the coolness of the water, but then settles in.

She cleans her face and body.

She steps out of the water and dresses.

She takes a deep breath and looks out to the audience.

Dominique Grace . . .

Josie/Sarita/Kazima/Kervens When we get to America—

Dominique We'll be safe. We'll have a better life.

Josie/Sarita/Kazima/Kervens When we get to America—

Dominique We'll be able to fight for what we believe.

Josie/Sarita/Kazima/Kervens When we get to America—

Dominique It will be strange and beautiful, different and new. It will be difficult too. I cannot pretend that it won't be.

Josie/Sarita/Kazima/Kervens When we get to America—

Dominique You'll have the best education possible. You'll be able to accomplish your dreams. You'll have a long life and live to your fullest potential.

All When we get to America—

Dominique We will know what it means to be free.

Dominique, **Josie**, **Kazima**, **Sarita**, *and* **Kervens** *stomp their feet three times in unison.*

There is a collective breath.

End of play.

Timeline

Key Events
A magnitude 7.0 earthquake—January 12, 2010
Hurricane Matthew—October 4, 2016
Trump announces end of Temporary Protected Status (TPS) for Haitians—November 20, 2017
Zero tolerance immigration policy—April 8, 2018

Timeline of Play
At Rise: Start of the play. **Now.**

Prologue: Dominique in Haiti. **October 2018.**

Scene One: Haiti. Dominique leads protest. **End of July 2018.**

Scene Two: One month later. Haiti. Dominique prepares to leave. **Mid-August 2018.**

Scene Three: One month ago. Same day as protest. Manhattan . Sarita asks for a continuance. **End of July 2018.**

Scene Four: Three days later. Brooklyn. Josie and Kazima return home from hospital. **Mid-August 2018.**

Scene Five: Two months later. Brazil. **Early October 2018.**

Scene Six: Two weeks later. Brooklyn. Kazima goes to therapy. **Mid-October 2018.**

Scene Seven: The next day. Haiti. Kervens in Haiti and Dominique and Grace in Ecuador. **Mid-October 2018.**

Scene Eight: The same day. Manhattan. Josie at work. **Mid-October 2018.**

Scene Nine: The next day. Haiti. Kervens gives a speech to the community. **Mid-October 2018.**

Scene Ten: Two months later. Dominique and Grace arrive in Texas. Grace is taken away. **Mid-December 2018.**

Scene Eleven: The same day. Brooklyn. Josie and Kazima pack Aliese's clothes. **Mid-December 2018.**

Scene Twelve: One week later (Christmas Day). Queens. Dominique at the Detention Center. **December 2018.**

Scene Thirteen: The next day (Day after Christmas). Brooklyn. Kazima leaves Josie. **December 2018.**

Scene Fourteen: Two weeks later. Haiti. Kervens tries to reach Dominique. **January 2019.**

Scene Fifteen: Six months later. Queens. Sarita and Dominique meet. **June 2019.**

Scene Sixteen: The next day, early. Brooklyn. Sarita convinces Josie to take Dominique's case. **June 2019.**

Scene Seventeen: One week later. Queens. Josie and Dominique meet. **June 2019.**

Epilogue: Chorus on stage. **Now**, then Dominique in Brazil. **October 2018.**

Those Who Live Here, Those Who Live There

Geeta P. Siddi and Girija P. Siddi

Translated by Channakeshava G. and Nagaraj Pattar

Geeta P. Siddi belongs to the Siddi tribal community of Karnataka and lives in the North Kannada district of Karnataka state, India. She is a member of the Siddi Trust, Manchikeri, an organization devoted to working with children. She sings, dances the Siddi tribal dance called *Dhamami*, and has performed and directed numerous plays. She trained at the Ninasam Theatre Institute in Karnataka, a cultural institution known for fusing culture and activism with art. Geeta received her master's in performing arts in theatre from Bangalore University in India and completed her PhD at the same university where she conducted research on women in theatre in Karnataka. She participated in Telling Our Stories of Home: Exploring and Celebrating Changing African and African American Diaspora Communities, a conference/festival held at the University of North Carolina at Chapel Hill in 2016. With her sister, Girija, she performed their original dance drama *NIMILITA: Story of a Girl with Half Closed Eyes*. Geeta and Girija made their film debut as singers and dancers in *Salaga* in 2021. Geeta is an assistant professor at Folklore University of Karnataka where she teaches performing arts for master's students. She is the first known Siddi woman to receive a PhD as well as to become a professor in Karnataka State.

Girija P. Siddi was born and raised in the North Kannada district of Karnataka state in India where she belongs to the Siddi tribal community. She trained at Ninasam Theatre Institute in Karnataka, a cultural institution known for fusing culture and activism with art. She is an actress, dances the Siddi tribal dance called *Dhamami*, and is the first Siddi woman to perform classical Indian Hindustani vocal music. She also teaches Hindustani classical music in Bengaluru, where she resides. She has traveled throughout the state of Karnataka performing in numerous plays, and in 2016 she participated in Telling Our Stories of Home: Exploring and Celebrating Changing African and African American Diaspora Communities, a conference/festival held at the University of North Carolina at Chapel Hill. She and her sister, Geeta, performed their original dance drama *NIMILITA: Story of a Girl with Half Closed Eyes*. Girija is an active trustee of the Siddi Trust in Manchikeri that works mainly with Siddi community children's theatre. She is also an active trustee of Bengaluru's Lokacharita Trust, which is a theatre group comprising professional artists, students, and different communities. Geeta and Girija made their film debut as singers and dancers in *Salaga* in 2021.

Setting

Two sisters share personal stories about their lives as Siddis in India. Their African ancestors, enslaved by Europeans, were brought to India during the 16th century. India is the only home the Siddis know, but the country and government still view them as outsiders.

"Yonth Majo Gaov . . . Ingath Rehta Haov . . ."

This is my village . . . I will stay here only . . .

Our Appa (father), he has built a house for us in the middle of thick forests, Lake Valley. If you stand in our house yard, you can see the entire lake. Appa himself, along with our Avva (mother), he had split and flattened the bamboo then made them to stand as wall. We all kids were pasting ant hill mud on it to make it firm. Always we were building house and Appa was frequently moving and building house. He was constantly developing it. Later he made mud bricks along with our Avva. He built a huge window with wooden railings where we kids can sit and see the lake. We were used to seeing tigers, elephants, deer, foxes, and many varieties of birds. Later our Appa built a wood beam and red-tiled roofing house. He carved designs on windows. We felt that we were so secure there! Appa used to work every day to build our home. For the main wooden door of the house, he carved a design himself. After that we had a feeling that we were not dependent on anyone. That became our permanent home. We felt so safe there with our family!

But we never get that security in any metro cities. We look like foreign bodies in cities, because of our hair and color.

* * *

We started living in the pockets of western forests of Karnataka, with courage and without fear as we remember. Scholars called us Siddis. Our curled hairs and dark skin color differentiate us from other communities. Animals are far better than some human beings. We don't have our own particular design of house, god, land, farm, or customs. Everything is borrowed from other communities, but we used to practice them in our own way: we dance differently, sing our own songs, and prepare our own food and medicine.

We heard stories that our ancestors were gigantic in their physique. They were used for working on others' farms. They worked just for food. Later, instead of eating food available in natural forest, we also started eating *Gote* (rice) with *Sambar* (a gravy)—like other communities. We started imitating them. We changed our dress. We trained to work in others' farms. We started to earn money. We became useful to others. They started using us, but we accepted that for our daily food. We stopped hunting because government banned hunting. We lost our native food, which our ancestors used to eat and passed down to us that practice.

* * *

We don't have our ancestors' memories with us, we never heard them in person. Because they heard their ancestors' stories from their parents and grandparents. Their real struggling experiences was passed down and became folk stories for us now. We are merging with other communities. Our recognition in this world is through our curly hair, thick lips, and dark skin color. Yes! Of course, we look different and we are different. It is a proud thing for us. But at the same time, it is the saddest thing for us in our society.

Why are we like this? Why not like others? That is the question, which always follows us like dark shadow. This makes us scared to go out from our nest. But we have to travel, right? If we cannot, we lose ourselves! So, we have to travel to reach out, prove ourselves.

Yes, we look like Africans. But we are Indians. Maybe we belong to the whole world. Everyone is our ancestors and belong to our family. No matter how much we wear Indian attire, we are called Siddi here.

* * *

For many years, our Appa and Avva were migrating from place to place, to overcome their own economic, cultural, and social conditions. The main crisis is they wanted to build their own house in a permanent place to stay at one place. We used torn gunny sacks as blankets, in our tiny bamboo hut while sleeping. At dawn sunlight used to enter into it from all sides through many holes. Though the sun's rays were tickling us, we sisters were not in a state of wakefulness, but the sun rays tickled us until we woke up. After that, our day started with washing our face in a big vessel!

Besides, our morning started with many birds' calls like bee-eater, wood pecker, bulbul, hornbill, and others.

One instance we remember: a waterhen bird was sitting on the tip of a tree branch and it was calling our home chicken to fight. Answering to that our chicken was also scrubbing the ground and offering to fight them. Both are born and formed to live in their own places. It is difficult for our chicken to climb the tree. But it doesn't stop trying to climb the tree. We learnt from our chicken too.

* * *

All our vessels are used for cooking and also toys for us. And our parents used these same vessels to fight each other. Tiger's roar, deer's fighting sound is reminding us that we are there in their peaceful world.

We used to wear one cloth as top; for bottom Ajji (Granny) stitched a *Chaddi*[1] which looks like *Kound*.[2] Avva was wearing colorful old *Kound* as a sari. Appa used to wear a shirt stolen from a scarecrow, which was found on another's farm.

We feel like it's our land, but actually it belongs to rich people. They could have evicted us from that place, anytime.

During that time our main food was *Ponas* (jackfruit). We did not know much about the outer world. If the landlord of that place did not give us work, then we used to move to another place in search of work.

Sometimes we were fearful and angry, when others called us "thieves" and "dirty people." Avva used to tie our short hair with her old sari ribbon. We were angry about

1 Shorts stitched by hand, with different cloths

2 *Kound* is a quilt, stitched by elder women of the community by hand. It is also called *Kaundi, Kawdi.*

others who insulted us by pulling our short hair and for our torn *Kound* skirt. We used to feel that we were surrounded by a world attacking us! Question always arises . . . Why are we like this? How can we pull our curly hair to make it become straight? How to wash our body color to make it white?

When we are back home, we get hungry, but the sound of *Dhamami*[3] used to make us happy. How did this magical instrument *Dhamami* come to be with us? We are surprised. Are we Hindu, Muslims, or Christian? We could not compare ourselves with anyone. The Bhats and Hegdes,[4] mullahs[5] and bishops gave us a religion and caste which is not ours! We are still living with lot of confusion. We don't know from where we came, where we are belonging to. Appa says always: "We don't belong to any other religion; we belong to Siddi religion. Be proud about it." It is difficult to understand and digest. But same time it is also true.

* * *

Once, when we two sisters were in our thatch-roof house, by chance we saw fire around our home. The dry grass and dried leaves were burning! It was spreading towards our home. It is our home! We both were simply crying. We were helpless. We were not aware of how to save our home. Suddenly Appa approached us and he insisted that we quickly clear all dried leaves around our home. As he told us, we did it as quickly as possible. After that the fire perished a few yards before our home. We are happy! We saved our home. We and our house escaped a terrible mishap. Appa's time sense saved all of us. He taught us. He was our hero for always.

* * *

In our childhood, the forest was so thick around our house! During the night time we lit fire for fear of wild animals. Sometimes wild animals used to come to the lake next to the house. We used to see them in the moonlight. We were watching them with curiosity and fear. During that time Appa used to explain about wild animals' behavior. Also, he used to build stories of his forest and hunting experiences. He was teaching us how to escape from wild animals, in case we meet them on the way to school. We used to walk around four kilometers from our house to school. Appa used to train us in different skills to escape from wild boars, bears, foxes, snakes, wild honeybees, and so on.

* * *

Usually, Appa was coming to school to take us back home. Once we three were on the way home. In the woods, we saw a tiger was walking our way. We were behind the tiger. Appa whispered that we should copy the tiger's step then it won't know that we are behind him. That means, if the tiger turns back, we also look like a tiger to

3 Dhamami is an instrument of the Siddi community. It is a singing and dancing tradition with the Dhamami drum.

4 Bhat and Hegde are the major community of our region. They are also the upper-caste Brahmins. Most of the Siddi people work on their farms. In olden days, most of the Siddis used to live on their farms, for many a lifetime.

5 Muslim priests

tiger. Finally, we stepped like the tiger and reached our home. Now if we recall that memory, we are not sure that we have seen a tiger. That might have been a dog, fox, or something else. But we feel our Appa's lesson is true.

* * *

Our "thick mustache Appa" was always an angry person. We used to wait quietly for his anger to decrease. He played the role of Okonkwo in Chinua Achebe's *Things Fall Apart*[6] directed by Chidambar Rao Jambe in 1985. After playing that character, our Appa's personality completely changed. He started to behave like a leader. Till today we are proud of him. He is one of the major leaders of our community. Whenever meetings happen in our community and family, he does not speak for a long time. He waits for his right time and context. He speaks at the right point. That is how he still remains for us as *Point Parashuram*.[7]

We feel that Appa did not have any inferiority about his hair and skin color. He used to walk like a leader, a lion. He is a Christian. His surname is Girgoli (which may be derived from Gregory). Bishops and fathers who converted us used to give their names as our surnames, like D'soza, Fernadis, John, etc. People from other communities used to call Appa *GuriGoli* (good at aiming a gun), because he is a good hunter. Avva is from the Hindu religion. Her name is Lakshmi Siddi. We used to follow both Christian and Hindu customs. We children faced discrimination about our skin color and our hair because we used to sit with other community students with long hair and white skin color in school.

* * *

We used to pray always to God for long hair! "Oh! God somehow give me long hair." God did not respond. We cried, cursed and scolded him a lot. Sometimes other community kids used to *kindle* (tease) calling to us, "Hey! Siddi!" We used to fight with them always for that and beaten marks on our body were quite common. Later we understood that we should be proud about Africa and say to them, "Yes we are from Africa. "But the question remains, "Where are we from?" In the same land "we live here . . . they live there . . ." What a small distance! "Oh! God! Are you still alive?"

* * *

We are proud of Nelson Mandela, Chinua Achebe, Michael Jackson, Kofi Annan, Nina Simone, and many more elders; because we feel they also belong to our community. This is how we console ourselves. We also wanted to be like them, instead of roaming in the forest. But still the forest accepted us with love and affection. We belong to nature. We cannot forget pond fish, crabs, red ant chutney which our Avva prepared with *Sengolli* (rice roti). It has rejoiced us and it is never ever forgettable.

6 *Things Fall Apart* was adapted to Kannada, as a play. The Kannada name is *Kappu Jana, Kempu Neralu*. That means *Black people with red shadow*.

7 This is a nickname we used to call beside him. His full name is Parashuram Girgoli Siddi.

* * *

Dhamami, the instrument, is our god, which made us forget all our sorrows. It is there forever with us. God has given us melodious voices and beautiful bodies. We know farming but it's not for us, it is for others.

We want to write. But sometimes we feel that we don't have our own voice. We want to be singers, writers, actors, dancers, officers, and politicians; but looking for the chance. Our expressions are waiting with hope. We started dreaming to move towards light from this darkness.

Many people visit us and ask weird questions like, "What do you all eat? What kind of dress do you wear? What job you all do? Does long hair come?" And so on . . . They made us stand like models and clicked photos of our untied hair, and disappeared. This did not help our community much anyway. They promised us that we will be introduced to the civilized society. Question again arises: What are we then? Are we not civilized? Are we not part of this society? Question continues . . .

Our grandfather was saying that, as many hairs as we have, many organizations have been built by others to stabilize the Siddi community. Most of the people are outsiders who made NGOs in the name of us. But most of the people brought bitterness into our community.

Our world is different from all of them. Maybe it is difficult for them to understand us, or maybe for us to understand them.

* * *

In childhood we were walking slowly from home to the school barefoot, but we are fast runners in stadium grounds. It was only a few times that we reached school in time for morning prayers, because we were interested in the search for wild *Jambala* (jamunfruit),[8] *Avoale* (gooseberry), *Ponas* (jackfruit), *Amboo* (mango), etc. on the way. Sometimes we used to steal fruits from other farms. Unless we eat those fruits we never get to sleep properly. During the night we were jumping from one tree branch to another tree branch like flying cats. We used to cross streams and canals to steal those fruits from Bhats' and Hegdes' farms. Those are mainly mango, coconut, betel nuts. That is the real prayer for us rather than school prayer. When our Avva got to know about this, our cheeks used to become red from her slap, because the whole day she will be working in Bhats' or Hegdes' houses for our livelihood.

* * *

Once we came home drenched in heavy rain. We used teak wood tree leaves as an umbrella, but our shirts were fully wet. We placed them on the fire stove to get them dry. Next day the color became dark and they smelled smoky. All our friends were laughing at us in school. The mathematics teacher was calling us buffalo. His subject was so boring, it never entered into our brain. He used to watch us through his spectacles, which sit on his nose. Whoever made mistakes, he used to beat. Our sports

[8] Jamunfruit resembles a plum, which grows in trees.

teacher cared for us during the school sports day. He was giving us glucose powder, as he ran the 100 meters himself. One of our loved teachers who was persistent saying that "I will work for Siddis" was simply transferred to another place.

* * *

As Nelson Mandela said: "It is music and dance that makes me at peace with the world and at peace with myself." We construct our own songs. Those are related to our nature and about our lifestyle. We speak and sing in mixed Konkani and Kannada languages. We want to learn more languages and culture. We want to be in our home. This is our home. We live here, only. We belong here. Not there.

* * * *